THE MYSTICISM OF WILLIAM BLAKE

THE MYSTICISM OF WILLIAM BLAKE

BY
HELEN C. WHITE

NEW YORK
RUSSELL & RUSSELL · INC
1964

UNIVERSITY OF WISCONSIN STUDIES
IN LANGUAGE AND LITERATURE
NUMBER 23

CONTENTS

ACKNOWLEDGMENTS

It is obviously impossible to acknowledge all the sources of help and criticism and interest to which a first book such as this is indebted. There are, of course, to begin with, the works of other students in the same field. Unfortunately, Mr. Damon's interpretation and Dr. Keynes' text of Blake's works appeared too late to be used for the main body of this study, but their work has proved helpful in the revision.

More particularly, I am heavily indebted to a number of my friends and colleagues. I should never have undertaken so prolonged and arduous a study without the always kind interest and prodigally generous help of Mr. Frederick A. Manchester, who brought the generel subject to my attention when I was a student in one of his classes at the University of Wisconsin, and who has encouraged and helped the progress of the book ever since. It is with great pleasure that I acknowledge my indebtedness to a friend and teacher whose power of stimulating and aiding struggling thought it is impossible to describe adequately.

My teachers, Mr. William Ellery Leonard and Mr. E. B. McGilvary, have been especially helpful in criticisms and suggestions. Mr. Karl Young, my former chief, gave much-appreciated interest and advice, while Mr. H. B. Lathrop, the present chairman of the English department, has given tireless interest and criticism and counsel.

Miss Esther A. Tiffany and Miss Ruth C. Wallerstein have come in on the making of this book at various stages of its development, always to encourage and to stimulate. To Miss F. Louise Nardin I am heavily indebted for many fruitful suggestions and for unflagging interest and help. For the verification of citations and the arduous work of the first proofreading I have to thank my sister, Miss Olive B. White, and my mother who has given her usual interest and help to this undertaking.

Two libraries have been especially gracious: the Widener

Library of Harvard University with its customary hospitality in sharing its magnificent resources with the visitor, and the Library of the University of Wisconsin, which has generously obtained expensive and unusual books for my use.

Finally, I am very grateful for those provisions of the University of Wisconsin which have made possible the publication of the book.

H. C. W.

MADISON, WISCONSIN
April 20, 1926

INTRODUCTION

Time was when a book on William Blake had to open with a very explicit account of the remarkable poet-painter-mystic who wrote some of the most fascinating of romantic verse some twenty years before the *Lyrical Ballads* were published, and whose long life of seventy years saw the complete triumph of the movement so inaugurated without any share in its fame. For the great question that confronted the writer on Blake until very recently was "Who is Blake?" But the amazing series of brilliant and learned books that the last two years, in particular, have seen has brought Blake so completely before the attention of the literary world that that is scarcely necessary any longer. As the recent letter to the *Times* of the distinguished memorial committee points out, Blake's verses at the present time "even appear in advertisements in our streets and are sung at national gatherings." And now, on the eve of the centenary of his death, it is proposed to raise a memorial to Blake, one of the most anti-ecclesiastical even of mystics, in St. Paul's, which, whether it is the artists' Pantheon or not, is after all a cathedral. The wheel of time has come full circle. And the volume of comment and exegesis and reprint and appreciation continues to swell almost daily, so that today the question which the Blake student must answer is no longer "Who is Blake?" but "Why another book on Blake?"

The present book offers as the justification of its existence the fact that it attempts what so far has not been done—an extended *critical* study of Blake's mysticism. And it relies on its subject for two reasons. The first is its importance at the present time. While it may be reasonably questioned if this is the most important element in his significance for literary or artistic history, there is no question that it is the aspect of his genius which most warmly engages the interest of the present day, and that it is the ground at present most commonly advanced for ranking him among the ignificant figures of the last century and a half. Moreover, it is the

7

most distinctive element in all he does, and since it was what Blake himself regarded as the end and the substance of all his work, it is quite the most fundamental for any consideration of his work as a whole, especially from the literary point of view to which the present study is devoted.

The second reason for this reliance upon the subject is the lack of any thoroughgoing criticism of Blake's mysticism. It is true that much has been written on the subject in the last few years. But in most of the discussions no effort has been made to arrive at any very definite conclusion as to what is meant when Blake is called a great mystic. And even in those few cases where the various aspects of Blake's mysticism have been expounded in detail, the general approach has been uncritical. Blake's opinions and tendencies and methods have been accepted as significant in a very unusual degree, without any scrutiny of the relation of these things to the corresponding elements in other mystics, or their relation to mankind's experience in general. And what is, in many ways, of much greater consequence, these critics have neglected the problems involved in the nature of mysticism itself, problems such as those arising out of the facts that not all mystics are equally significant, and that mysticism is not equally valid from all points of view. In other words, the great bulk of what has been written on Blake, especially in the last ten years, has been devoted to explanation and to eulogy rather than to real criticism. The result is that while Blake's fame is no longer in any danger of suffering from neglect, there is a very real danger that the enthusiasm of his admirers will on the one hand overweigh his very just claims to distinction with a stifling burden of extravagant and ill-suited praise, and on the other, cloud the whole field of mysticism with the suspicion and repugnance that is inevitably born of the reaction to prolonged uncritical eulogy.

The present criticism attempts to study Blake's mysticism, not only in itself, but in relation to the whole field. Since it takes its rise from the existing body of criticism, it opens with a history of the recognition and appreciation of Blake, "The Blake Criticism." Then, as a preliminary and a background to the explicit study of Blake as a mystic, it attacks the problem of understanding what a mystic is, with all the difficulties that the definition of a word used with such all-but-universal vagueness entails. It attempts to answer the question in the two chapters following, the third and the fourth, the third presenting a careful study of the mysticism of the typical mystics, and the fourth, a sketch of the rest of the mystical field.

The fifth chapter approaches Blake's mysticism from the angle of his life and personality in a sketch that assumes no responsibility for biographical completeness. While it has grown out of a painstaking perusal of every available source of information, from the investigation of Blake's ancestry to the results of the effort to determine the precise location of his grave, it presents only those elements of general circumstance and tendency and influence that are indispensable to a consideration of his mysticism.

The next chapter, the sixth, carries on the description of Blake's mysticism to what may be called his message, what Blake as a mystic has to say about man's life and destiny. While fundamentally indebted to the work of men like Ellis and Yeats, this summary view of the essentials of Blake's mystical teachings has been arrived at from a careful study of all Blake's works, including his letters (fortunately Dr. Keynes' new edition came to hand in time to be useful in the revision), and all of his drawings and paintings (in the majority of cases reproductions) to which the present writer had access. Its claims to originality of interpretation are slight. All that it tries to do is to present as simply and clearly as possible the main features of Blake's system, and the dominant tendencies of the philosophy back of that system that must be taken into account when we try to understand Blake as a mystic.

The seventh and last chapter brings the findings of the preceding chapters together, and, viewing Blake's mysticism against the background presented in chapters iii and iv, attempts to determine its value. In so doing it tries to define briefly the spirit and direction of his achievement in this field, and to appraise its power of satisfying those fundamental spiritual needs that in this as in all ages have led men to hearken to the voice of the mystic.

CHAPTER I

THE BLAKE CRITICISM

It is not quite a hundred years since William Blake was laid in an unmarked common grave in Bunhill Fields, with no pomp of funeral or homage of press, but only the mourning of a few friends whose chief claim upon remembrance today is their appreciation of their obscure friend. And now it is safe to predict that the full centenary of his death will call forth from the entire world a burst of enthusiastic eulogy to be equaled only by the volume of the praise already heaped high above his works in the last quarter-century. The history of Blake's fame for the intervening century is one of the most dramatic chapters in modern literature. Indeed, the critical history of the last one hundred years with regard to many of its most important issues of thought and spirit could be very adequately written from a chronicle of the vicissitudes of Blake's reputation. For no man's hold upon critical attention is a thing apart and of itself. It stands and falls according to the set of the current of general artistic interest and purpose; consequently the reaction to any personality of unusual distinctiveness becomes a gauge of the general level of artistic sympathy with regard not only to that particular man's work, but to all the tendencies which it represents.

It was partly a matter of accident that William Blake was neglected so profoundly in an age that, whatever the direction of general public interest, saw in the work of a series of great geniuses the full maturity of the literary revolution which he had been one of the earliest to herald. In the first place, the men with whom he was thrown by his professional work were, until practically the end of his life, men without the slightest understanding or capacity for the understanding of his fundamental interests. Secondly, the way in which he chose or was forced to bring out his work made any general interest impossible, even if Blake had been the man to make the most of whatever opportunities for general fame came his way.

11

After the abortive production of the *Poetical Sketches* of 1783, a production in which he seems to have taken as little interest as the rest of the world, he published all the rest of his work in a form that was by its very nature more likely to minister to the delight of the connoisseur and the profit of the dealer in rarities of a century later than to any wide currency in his own day. For even the most universally accessible and popular, as it proved, of his works, the *Songs of Innocence and of Experience*, were laboriously engraved on copper plates and then printed and colored and bound by hand. The result is today one of the greatest treasures of the collector, but such a method of reproduction is so costly of time and labor, and consequently so expensive, that it is not surprising that their sale was practically negligible and that their very existence remained practically unknown even to the enlightened reading public.

Moreover, when the Blake of the early lyrics, enriched by a normal poetic development and maturity, might have commanded the interest of men who had come to understand and value the success of Wordsworth and Coleridge in directions which Blake himself had marked out in 1783, that Blake was lost in the wildernesses of the "Prophetic Books." Probably the most revealing of the few contemporary comments on Blake's poetry which we have is Charles Lamb's, for it goes pretty much to the heart of the matter so far as even the most sympathetic and intelligent of his contemporaries who came in contact with him are concerned. It was in 1824, when Blake was still living, an old man of sixty-seven, that Lamb wrote to his friend, the Quaker, Bernard Barton:

> Blake is a real name, I assure you, and a most extraordinary man, if he be still living. He is the Robert [William] Blake, whose wild designs accompany a splendid folio edition of the "Night Thoughts," which you may have seen. . . . . He paints in water colours marvellous strange pictures, visions of his brain, which he asserts that he has seen. They have great merit. . . . . His poems have been sold hitherto only in Manuscript. I never read them, but a friend at my desire procured the "Sweep Song." There is one to a tiger, which I have heard recited, beginning—
>
> > Tiger, Tiger, burning bright,
> > Thro' the desarts of the night

which is glorious, but, alas! I have not the book; for the man is flown, whither I know not—to Hades or a Mad House. But I must look on him as one of the most extraordinary persons of the age.[1]

In other words, so little was known about Blake the poet in his own lifetime that even the curious would not know where to turn for his work, and the sympathetic would regard him as a most extraordinary person, not untouched with madness.

Nothing shows better the consequences of Blake's estrangement from the common ways of men in literary matters than a comparison of his poetic reputation with his reputation as an artist. For Blake, the artist, made a very real, even though modest, impression upon his contemporaries. When, for instance, he did make a normal bid for fame in the ill-fated exhibition of 1809, for which he seems to have selected his most astounding, rather than his most successful or most accessible, work, he attracted the attention of some very notable people. True, the exhibition was a heartbreaking failure, and the one journalist we can be sure visited the exhibition condemned it roundly in the *Examiner;* still, even Robert Southey saw that, for all what he thought his insanity, Blake was a great painter, and Seymour Kirkup invoked the word "noble" for one of the stiffer of Blake's masterpieces, while that delightful amateur of genius, Crabb Robinson, bought four copies of the catalogue and apparently set to the pursuit of Blake's acquaintance at once. For we find in the illuminating chatter of his diary under date of 1810 his conclusion that Blake was probably artist, genius, mystic, and madman all in one. And he adds, with the touch of patronage of the great man of society, "A good creature & of his poetical & pictorial genius there is no doubt I believe in the minds of judges. Wordsworth & Lamb like his poems, & the Aders, his paintings."[2]

And the publication in 1825 of Blake's masterpiece of design, the illustrations to the *Book of Job,* evoked, according to J. T. Smith, "the highest congratulations from some eight Royal Academicians headed by Sir Thomas Lawrence." And when the German painter, Gotzenberger, returned home from a visit to England in

---

[1] "Letters," *The Works of Charles and Mary Lamb,* edited by E. V. Lucas (New York and London, 1905), VII, 642.

[2] *Blake, Coleridge, Wordsworth, Lamb, etc., Being Selections from the Remains of Henry Crabb Robinson,* edited by Edith G. Morley (Manchester, 1922), p. 6.

1827 he is reported to have said: "I saw in England many men of talents, but only three men of genius, Coleridge, Flaxman, and Blake, and of these Blake was the greatest." This does not mean that even Blake's art was in any sense of the word generally or fully appreciated in his own day. It was "the eccentric little artist, by name Blake" that the elegant Lady Charlotte Bury patronized one night at dinner, with a feminine pleasure in the fancied sneer on the face of Sir Thomas Lawrence at her attention to the humble artist. What all this means is that Blake's art did receive notice, slight as it was in proportion to his deserts, in his own day, and that whatever notice the man himself received was in general on account of his work as an artist. This conclusion is strikingly confirmed by the evidence of the three obituary notices of 1827. The *Literary Gazette* addressed its notice on "The Illustrator of the Grave, etc." to "those few who have sympathies for the ideal and (comparatively speaking) the intellectual in art," and went on to speak appreciatively of its subject as a "very singular and very able man," while the *Gentleman's Magazine* paid tribute to the engravings and designs of an "excellent but eccentric artist." "Singular," "able," "excellent," "eccentric artist"—so we may sum up the very slight reputation Blake enjoyed in his lifetime.

After his death Blake was remembered in two biographical sketches, in both cases primarily as an artist. The first, the fullest practically contemporary account, was written in 1828 by John Thomas Smith, keeper of the prints and drawings in the British Museum, as the last of his "Biographical Sketches and Anecdotes of Several Artists and Others Contemporary with Nollekens." It is a perfectly simple, straightforward account of the main facts of Blake's artistic development by a man who had known him and who had been impressed by the predictions of Flaxman and Fuseli that "a time will come when Blake's finest works will be as much sought after and treasured up in the portfolios of men of mind, as those of Michel Angelo are at present."[3] Two years later, and three years after Blake's death, Allan Cunningham included in his *Lives of the Most Eminent British Painters, Sculptors, and Architects* an account of Blake's life that, while obviously based to a very con-

[3] Reprinted by Arthur Symons, *William Blake* (New York, 1907), p. 373.

siderable extent on Smith's account, undertook a measur/
scription and criticism of Blake's work which the original ..
had not attempted. He evidently knew a good deal of Blake's literary work as well as of his painting, but his judgment was much
less favorable to the former, as the following conclusions show:

> If we look at the man through his best and most intelligible works, we
> shall find that he who could produce the *Songs of Innocence and Experience*,
> the *Gates of Paradise*, and the *Inventions for Job*, was the possessor of very
> lofty faculties, with no common skill in art, and moreover that, both in
> thought and mode of treatment, he was a decided original. But should we,
> shutting our eyes to the merits of those works, determine to weigh his worth
> by his *Urizen*, his "Prophecies of Europe and America," and his *Jerusalem*,
> our conclusion would be very unfavourable; we would say that, with much
> freedom of composition and boldness of posture, he was unmeaning, mystical,
> and extravagant, and that his original mode of working out his conceptions
> was little better than a brilliant way of animating absurdity.[4]

It was as an artist, then, that Blake received the very scant
measure of recognition that his contemporaries gave him. When
they thought of his literary work they usually confined their understanding and approval to the early works, like the *Songs*, and recognized the mystical elements only for wonder or disparagement.

It is not surprising, therefore, that the first effort made to bring
Blake's literary work before the world was the printing for the first
time of the *Songs of Innocence and of Experience* from the original
engraved plates, in 1831. This was the first real publication of what
is now recognized as one of the great masterpieces of the early Romantic Movement. Eight years later, in 1839, an edition of the
Songs appeared with an introduction that forecasts interestingly
some conspicuous developments of the interest in Blake of seventy-
five years later. The editor, Garth Wilkinson, had been conducting
some curious experiments in what we may call automatic composition, a method probably very similar to the writing from ouija-
board dictation that we sometimes hear of nowadays. He discovered that by merely slipping the rein on his imagination and aban-
doning his pen to the involuntary impulse of fancy he obtained
poems that were original and by no means devoid of meaning. As a
result, what he had heard of Blake's writing at the dictation of

4 Reprinted, *ibid.*, pp. 430 f.

heavenly agencies aroused his interest, and he paid Blake's memory the tribute of a fresh edition. Although Crabb Robinson has left a note on this edition, it seems to have attracted little attention, if we may judge from the dearth of periodical notices for the years that followed.

The Blake revival really dates from Alexander Gilchrist's *Life of William Blake, "Pictor Ignotus,"* completed by his widow and published by her in 1863. The title indicates what Gilchrist tried to do—to bring Blake before the general literary and artistic public by a full and sympathetic presentation of his life and personality, and by as full a survey of his work as he could come at. He not only caught all the legend and rumor he could discover, but attempted to reconstruct, physically and spiritually, the world in which Blake lived. It is easy to laugh at Gilchrist. He was sentimental, alternately blind and sixth-sensed, very often muddled and irrelevant. But he succeeded in what was a bold piece of pioneer work, and his book is still current among Blake students.

In general, Gilchrist was most interested in the painter and designer, but he was far from insensitive to the imaginative quality revealed in the illustrated poems. And he was half-understandingly enthusiastic about what he deemed strange and "mystic" in both Blake's poems and his illustrations, as in what he says of the illustrations to *Jerusalem:*

> The subjects are vague and mystic as the poem itself. Female figures lie among waves full of reflected stars: a strange human image, with a swan's head and wings, floats on water in a kneeling attitude, and drinks: lovers embrace in an open water lily: an eagle-headed creature sits and contemplates the sun.[5]

Gilchrist was also very much impressed by the bits of philosophy which he discovered in Blake's works, but even his general sympathy with his subject did not prevent his expressing his enthusiasm with certain reservations typical of the general attitude of his time:

> We need hardly observe that Blake does not set up as an instructor of youth, or of age either, but rather as one who loves to rouse, perplex, provoke, to shun safe roads and stand on dizzy brinks; to dare anything and

[5] Alexander Gilchrist, *Life of William Blake, "Pictor Ignotus,"* edited by Anne Gilchrist (London and Cambridge, 1863), I, 194.

everything, in short, if peradventure he might grasp a truth beyond the common reach, or catch a glimpse "behind the veil."[6]

Five years later, however, there appeared a critical essay on the revived Blake that is quite free from any such dampening caution, a glowing appreciation by Swinburne. This time, forty years after his death, Blake comes into his own as a thinker and a mystic. For already in 1868 Swinburne brings to his subject that sympathy for the antinomian tendencies of Blake's thinking and that joy in the energy of his expression, the *élan vital* in his poetry and his designs, that are to be the distinguishing motives of a large part of twentieth-century criticism. The result is a brilliant panegyric, the glow of which it is impossible to communicate in a brief space, but the fervent quality of whose thought may be suggestively represented by a sentence on the "Proverbs of Hell": "Each, whether earnest or satirical, slight or great in manner, is full of that passionate wisdom and bright rapid strength proper to the step and speech of gods."[7]

The success of these two efforts to arouse interest in Blake may be gauged by the fact that whereas we find recorded under Blake's name in *Poole's Index* only three magazine articles for the years between 1849[8] and 1863, we find for the decade following 1863 nearly a score. In view of later developments it is interesting to notice the tone of these early reviews. Even when friendly and interested most of them are fairly reserved. Even the reviewer who goes so far as to call Blake "the most spiritual, intense, and imaginative of English mystics" makes certain very important qualifications when he proceeds in his eulogy to say:

Blake had imagination and spirituality of vision; and even when he, to his own bewilderment, and to the lowering of his genius, abjured command over his thoughts, and yielded himself to the wayward impulses of unchecked fancy, even then he could not divest himself of the qualities of genius; and his mystic utterances, when most remote from intelligibility, are swollen with a vague grandeur, and are now and then interrupted by passages of genuine spiritual discernment, and illuminated by clear flashes of redeeming imagination.[9]

---

[6] *Ibid.*, I, 78.

[7] Algernon Charles Swinburne, *William Blake: A Critical Essay* (London, 1868), p. 213.

[8] The date of the first article recorded under the heading of Blake in the edition of 1881.

[9] *North American Review*, CVIII (April, 1869), 641–46.

All in all, a sentence from one of the reviews of 1864 may be taken as a fair summary of the state of unbiased critical opinion in the early years of the Blake revival—"After carefully weighing the matter, it is impossible to doubt that William Blake was the maddest of authors and artists, and an extraordinary genius among madmen"[10]—an opinion by no means rare today in non-literary circles.

But by 1876 Rossetti and Swinburne and a small host of enthusiasts of lesser fame and consequence had acclaimed the revolutionary and visionary Blake to such good purpose that they had provoked the inevitable reaction from a world by no means abreast of them. One evidence of this reaction is especially interesting because it indicates that the ethical import of much of the Blake criticism was beginning to be recognized. It is the conclusion to an article in the *Contemporary Review* of 1877, whose general point of view may be gauged by the title "Imperfect Genius: William Blake." The author says: "The impression forced upon us by the tone of Blake's most zealous advocates, that he has chiefly been commended to their acceptance by his serviceableness as a stalking-horse for revolutionary propaganda, is so distinct that it would be uncandid to conceal it."[11] In other words, by 1877 we find that certain tendencies which are not going to reach their full maturity until about thirty years later are for the first time manifesting themselves strongly enough to provoke the inevitable reaction.

Although the next decade saw a falling-off in volume of magazine articles, the number was still sufficient to indicate a sustained attention to Blake, while it revealed a marked interest in his work from another point of view. The rapid succession of Muir's facsimile reproductions of the major portion of Blake's writings, which appeared from 1884 to 1890, made accessible portions of Blake's work not hitherto widely available.

It must have been a consciousness of a considerable spread of interest in the obscurer portions of Blake's writings that led Edwin John Ellis and William Butler Yeats to attempt their monumental

[10] W. F. Rae, "The Life and Works of William Blake," *Fine Arts Quarterly Review*, III (October, 1864), 56–79.

[11] Henry G. Hewlett, "Imperfect Genius: William Blake," *Contemporary Review*, XXIX (January, 1877), 207–28.

edition of *The Works of William Blake: Poetic, Symbolic, and Critical,* which appeared in 1893. But the outstanding feature of their edition was not so much the reproduction of the text as the accompanying *Memoir and Interpretation* which established once for all the fact that back of the obscurity and complexity of the so-called "Prophetical Writings" lay a coherent and relatively organic body of symbol and meaning that may be termed a system. Beside the painstaking and critical exegesis of Mr. S. Foster Damon's interpretation of 1924 or the scholarship of Dr. Geoffrey Keynes' three-volume edition of 1925, this work seems often fantastic and naïve. But it must not be forgotten that to these men belongs the credit of pioneering in a very laborious and confused field, and that all the brilliant writing on Blake of the next thirty years is more or less heavily indebted to them.

In spite of the new editions and the fresh criticisms and appreciations with which the stormy nineties celebrated Blake's growing vogue, it was not until the first decade of the twentieth century that Blake really came into his own among the minor prophets and the young poets. In a superficial, but nevertheless significant, fashion we may gauge the magnitude of Blake's vogue at this time by the fact that *Poole's Index* and the *Reader's Guide* list almost half a hundred magazine articles on Blake for this period, and that the very valuable bibliography that the American translator added to Berger's distinguished work on Blake records over a score of editions of Blake's works in whole or in part for that period, and more than a dozen books on Blake. The editions include the most critical edition of the better-known poems so far published, Mr. Sampson's *Poetical Works,* and Maclagan and Russell's useful editions of *Milton* and *Jerusalem,* which afforded until this last year the easiest access to the "Prophetical Writings." The criticisms include the ecstatic character sketch of Edwin J. Ellis, the interesting general volume of Arthur Symons, and the most discriminating of English criticisms, the *William Blake* of Mr. Basil de Sélincourt. And what is perhaps even more interesting, in this decade foreign criticism begins to play a very conspicuous part in the appreciation of Blake, Germany producing three very substantial contributions, and France, what is still in many ways the best general book on the subject, M. Berger's *William Blake: Poet and Mystic*. Indeed, if we may judge from some of the accounts of the time, the interest in Blake, particularly in the Blake of the more obscure mystical writings, had come to assume the proportions and the characteristics of a cult. There is some caricature, but a suggestive modicum of truth in the description by one reviewer of a then conservative journal: "There is to-day a class of hungry souls who, having graduated from Dante, Shelley, Whitman, and a succession of other gospels, have at last fixed their intellectual teeth on Blake. You will meet little circles of them here and there in the country, sad-eyed women and feline-looking men, who find in the Prophetic Books the last word of spiritual truth."[12] By the end of the decade this Blake cult had attained to such proportions that obviously a reviewer no longer dared to dispose of Blake as a madman without reading him. And few but real Blake enthusiasts would go very far toward doing that.

It must have seemed very unlikely that the enthusiasm for Blake would do anything but wane after the pitch of lyric intensity which it had reached in the first decade of the present century. Nevertheless, the ten years that followed were even more prolific of editions of Blake's *Songs*, while the stream of criticism both in magazines and in books survived even the impact of the war. It is to the second half of this decade that we owe what are quite the most exuberant of all panegyrics of Blake, Mr. Charles Gardner's *Vision and Vesture: A Study of William Blake in Modern Thought*, of 1916, and his *William Blake the Man*, of 1919. These two books may be taken in a certain sense as the final flowering of that glorification of the antinomian and vitalistic Blake which Swinburne had begun about a half-century before.

But the enthusiasm for Blake does not stop at the threshold of the third decade, but continues unabated, in many ways with increased certainty and power. M. Saurat's *Blake and Milton* of 1920 is scholarly in a more technical sense than any of the foregoing criticisms, being, as it is, a fairly concentrated study in a special line of influence upon Blake's ideas, and indirectly a keen, though not always thoroughly aware, study of Blake's personality. The more general interest in Blake is ministered to in Mr. Allardyce Nicoll's

[12] *Nation*, XXCV (September 26, 1907), 286–87.

contribution to the "Poetry and Life Series," his *William Blake and His Poetry,* of 1922.

At the present moment Blake and his mysticism are very live issues, for the last two years have seen a notable series of books of considerable variety of purpose but of fundamentally pretty much the same point of view. The first in point of time is Mr. S. Foster Damon's *William Blake: His Philosophy and Symbols,* which appeared in 1924. Mr. Damon's is a brilliant solution of the problem which Ellis and Yeats were the first to attack some thirty years ago. It is easy to impugn any exegesis of Blake's meaning on various details, but Mr. Damon has done his work so thoroughly and so resourcefully that it is very unlikely that anyone else will feel any need of doing it for some years to come. Last year Mr. Harold Bruce gathered up the old material on Blake's life and, to a very limited extent, brought the point of view of modern psychology to bear upon Blake's letters in a sketch of his life, called *William Blake in this World,* that is convenient for reference and eminently readable. A little later appeared Dr. Geoffrey Keynes' three-volume *The Writings of William Blake,* a "complete" and scholarly edition of the text, attempting to complete what Dr. John Sampson had already done for the text of the lyrics (1905) and for the text of the minor prophecies (1913). While it is by no means unlikely that fresh material may be discovered, this beautiful edition of the text may be taken as definitive for what we now know of Blake's work. The distinctive feature of Dr. Keynes' edition, the careful reproduction of the hitherto badly corrupted texts of the longer "Prophetical Writings," is very much in line with the present trend of Blake criticism and makes possible to a degree hitherto unknown the critical pursuit of its great interest in the prophetic Blake.

The last year has also brought the first comprehensive study and presentation of the paintings of Blake. The word comprehensive is here used advisedly, for the one hundred plates of the late Mr. Darrell Figgis' *The Paintings of William Blake* reproduce of necessity, even for its generous limits, only a small proportion of Blake's known work; but it is a comprehensive view in the sense that both the highly representative selection of plates and the very fresh and in some ways original study of Blake's life as an artist aim to give a sense of Blake's pictorial art as a whole. Again, this book is a landmark in the history of the Blake criticism, for while at various times efforts have been made to study and reproduce part of Blake's etchings and paintings—notably Mr. Lawrence Binyon's memorable reproduction of the illustrations of the *Book of Job* in 1906, and Mr. H. J. C. Grierson's reproduction of Blake's designs for Gray's *Poems* in 1922—this is the largest and most thoroughgoing presentation of Blake's art yet attempted.

All in all, the last three years have been without any question the most fruitful years, for so short a period, in the history of the Blake criticism, especially as regards the appreciation of Blake's mysticism. For all of these men have been profoundly interested in Blake's mysticism and enthusiastically sympathetic with it. It is true that Mr. Darrell Figgis has in general considered the manifestations of Blake's prophetic power in literature very much less complete and adequate than the corresponding expression in painting. But the very insistence upon the fact that Blake was "as a true visionary," "a prophet of greater moment in his paintings and drawings than in the complicated mythology of his Prophetic Books" indicates the point of view from which the introduction is written and the selection is made. In the words of the very intelligent prospectus which announced the book, "Blake's own point of view is taken as the only true basis of understanding what he himself meant to do as a painter." And as Mr. Figgis says, "What Blake meant to do as a painter followed as a natural consequence from what Blake meant to be as a man in a world of baffled meanings."[13]

Mr. S. Foster Damon, who is expressly interested in the writings and who, not surprisingly, values them much higher than Mr. Figgis, who is only incidentally concerned with them, best expresses the attitude of the Blake cult today with regard to that aspect of his work in which we are most interested. First of all, "The key to everything Blake ever wrote or painted," according to Mr. Damon, "lies in his mysticism."[14] Mr. Damon confesses that when he began

[13] Darrell Figgis, *The Paintings of William Blake* (New York, 1925), p. 77.

[14] S. Foster Damon, *William Blake: His Philosophy and Symbols* (Boston and New York, 1924), p. 1.

collecting comments on Blake he "thought him mad and the *Jerusalem* trash. But as the work went on, and plane after plane of sanity was opened, my conversion began. Now I firmly believe that the last of Blake's works are his greatest; that the *Jerusalem* ranks with its contemporary, the *Inventions to Job*." As a result of that conversion, Mr. Damon declares that the attitude of the public which "has been baffled so long with hints of mysteries and madnesses, that it has come to regard Blake's work as too eccentric and remote to repay personal investigation . . . . is completely wrong." For, he goes on to say, "Blake's thought was of the clearest and deepest; his poetry of the subtlest and strongest; his painting of the highest and most luminous. He tried to solve problems which concern us all, and his answers to them are such as to place him among the greatest thinkers of several centuries."[15] It is on this note of Blake's importance as a thinker that Mr. Damon ends his very interesting and valuable discussion of Blake's ideas:

> This swift and wide-spread cult of Blake is significant in that, for all his obscurity, and for all his reputed madness, his doctrines are slowly being found valuable by the entire world. The evils which he attacked are even stronger now than when he wrote; and at last the world, beholding the errors, searches for solutions. Whether or not Blake's solutions are the only ones may well be doubted; but, at the very least, he has opened the way to fearless discussion, without which these errors will be triumphant everlastingly.[16]

The Blake criticism of the last twenty-five years has been, then, not only a constantly increasing appreciation of Blake's powers as artist and writer, but much more an ever growing enthusiasm for his significance as a mystic. Where the early Blake critics, with a few notable exceptions, looked upon his mysticism as an offense and a stumbling-block, recent critics on the whole have regarded it as the heart of his mystery and have sought in it a fuller understanding, not only of Blake, but of the modern world for which he so amazingly speaks out of his century before. There are many reasons for this change in estimate. Probably the most obvious is the inevitable reaction against the time that neglected him. Less obvious is the subtler undercurrent of sympathy and understanding which has brought a large section of the literary world into a much more pro-

[15] *Ibid.*, p. ix.
[16] *Ibid.*, p. 250.

found sympathy for the point of view that Blake expressed than ever existed before. Then, too, there are certain trends of fad and interest in our day to which what had before seemed grave impediments to interest have now come to be the surest claims to attention. The joy of understanding the misunderstood and appreciating the neglected is one which makes an unusual appeal to the connoisseur in ideas. And then there is probably the most important reason of all: the marked increase in the fascination of the mysterious and the mystical which appears on every side in the increasing roster of treatises on the subject of mysticism, in the growing interest in the mystical aspects of religion, and in the effort to bring the resources of modern psychology and the science of comparative religion to bear upon this field, a series of developments by no means unparalleled in the history of preceding ages of rationalism and scepticism.

This interest in mysticism, whether Blake's or anybody else's, does not mean, as people sometimes think, any one special thing. It means with different men very different things. And yet if we are to understand either the significance of the Blake criticism or the issues of its present-day estimates, we must attempt to find out what all these men have meant by the word "mysticism," and just what they have meant when they have called Blake a great mystic. That is not an easy thing to determine, for two reasons: first, few people, even critics, take pains, in the course of more or less unscientific appreciations, to define even key terms in any very systematic fashion, and secondly, the task of definition, even when most rigorously attacked, is a very complex one, involving in any realm like this a number of highly important questions, such as: What manner of man was Blake? What did he say? How did he say it? Any one of these questions in itself is sufficient enterprise, but to answer all three at once, as one must in defining a term like "mystic," is a problem to appal the hardiest. Consequently it will be possible to suggest only in a general way the various senses in which this vaguest of terms has been used by the critics of Blake.

It is true that a few of the Blake critics have essayed fairly systematic definitions of mysticism in general or of Blake's mysticism in particular. Of these, one of the most discriminating, at least in degree, if not in kind, is M. Berger, in his brilliant *William Blake:*

Poet and Mystic. Although M. Berger approaches Blake's mysticism from what he terms the literary point of view, leaving the full discussion of his theories to the philosopher, he takes his departure from a philosophically explicit definition of mysticism: "Mysticism is, in its essence, a concentration of all the soul's energies upon some supernatural object, conceived of and loved as a living personality."[17] And he invokes, at least cursorily, the great body of mystical tradition, of which most of Blake's critics are practically unaware, when he points out in his general discussion of Blake's mystical writings that:

> They present certain very striking features . . . . which clearly distinguish Blake's mysticism from the mysticism familiar to us in the lives of the saints. . . . . Blake was no saint. He had never renounced the world, its passions or its pleasures. He had never mortified his body by ascetic practices . . . . had never experienced that intense longing to behold their God which had filled the souls of the saints. . . . . He never prepared himself, by prayers and meditations, for his celestial visitors. . . . . Finally, he lacked what the theologians have always regarded as the most essential mark of the Christian visionary—humility. . . . . He would not humble himself even before God. . . . .
>
> He cannot therefore be called a religious mystic, in the ordinary sense of the term. He himself would have classed himself rather among the old Hebrew prophets, or the great poets of all time, compelled to proclaim to all men the way of escape from eternal death, and to open their eyes to the divine light, which, at the appointed hour, will reveal itself and shine forth in full splendor upon all.[18]

M. Berger is quite aware of the difficulties in the way of a whole-hearted acceptance of the "Prophetical Writings," but, unlike most critics who blame the mystic for the wreck of the poet, he blames the poet for the marring of the prophet: "In Blake, the poet has spoiled the prophet, causing him to rank as a mystical writer of secondary importance, when he might have been one of the first."[19] But he believes this difficulty can be got over, for he says of the "Prophetic Books,"

> Read them simply as collections of isolated but richly suggestive fragments, united only by a common bond of thought and inspiration. Regarding them thus, we shall find their faults of composition diminish till they all but

[17] Paul Berger, *William Blake: Poet and Mystic,* translated by Daniel H. Conner (London, 1914), p. 68.

[18] *Ibid.,* pp. 59 f.

[19] *Ibid.,* p. 211.

disappear, while the genius of the poet and the splendour of the artist's visions are shown in a light which will enable us to appreciate them more completely.[20]

Viewed from this angle, Blake's work may be said to make its own place in a second *genre*, that of poetic mysticism, which he defines as an "intellectual vision, which leaves a profound impression upon the mind, and at times even produces an actual image of the thing perceived,"[21] and in this sense, though every great poet is a mystic, M. Berger believes that Blake is "in England, at any rate, the only real mystic among the poets."[22]

In general then, M. Berger sees what is in Blake very clearly (within the accepted limits of his undertaking). In many ways his exposition of Blake's ideas and his criticism of Blake's style can hardly be bettered. But his own critical predilections inevitably predispose him to take much of Blake for granted where critical scrutiny is demanded by his premises, and his acquaintance with the typical mystics is apparently too limited for him to realize the significance of the differences which he so well points out between Blake's mysticism and religious mysticism. Consequently, penetrating and even illuminating as his treatment of Blake's mysticism very often is, the reader misses in it thoroughgoing critical activity, for all too often he gets to the threshold of a judgment only to surrender his case. And at some very critical points his logic is swept away by his enthusiasm into a vague use of key words for which his careful approach has not warned us. A very good example of this general use of words is to be found in a characteristically charming passage on the *Songs of Innocence:*

What the book does reveal to us is Heaven: the Heaven that we see reflected in the eyes of our own little ones. By an extraordinary effort of imagination, or rather by the spiritual power that his mysticism naturally gave him, Blake carried himself back into the days of childhood, when all was joy and innocence, and when the new-born soul felt no other emotions but life and the joy of living.[23]

One is, however, profoundly grateful to M. Berger for his awareness of his own mind and for his effort to set forth explicitly both his definitions and his conclusions. And this appreciation is

[20] Berger, *op. cit.*, p. 220.   [22] *Ibid.*, p. 211.

[21] *Ibid.*, p. 73.   [23] *Ibid.*, p. 286.

deepened when the student turns to those of his fellow-critics who have been neither so conscious of their meanings nor so explicit in their definitions. For here the lack of precise investigation or definition of terms creates a very serious problem for the student who is endeavoring to find out what a critic means when he calls Blake a mystic. First of all, in such an undertaking one faces the fundamental difficulty of doing two things at once: of laying hold of the critic's interpretation of Blake's mystical experience and teaching, and at the same time of divining the general understanding of mysticism that has colored, if not directed, the investigator's findings. Then one faces the difficulty of drawing conclusions from suggestions, implications, casual generalizations, things left vague or half-said. Here one is grateful for even the sketchiest analysis or the most meager definition, because either represents at least an effort to grasp intellectually what all too often has been left to foggy intuition or vague assumption.

In gathering up these implications one is confronted at the outset by a certain amount of obscurantism that seems almost inevitably to beset even the wisest handling of subjects such as these. Some of it is unabashedly animistic, as in one brilliant passage in which Swinburne tries to convey some sense of the way in which Blake saw the world:

About his path and about his bed, around his ears and under his eyes, an infinite play of spiritual life seethed and swarmed or shone and sang. Spirits imprisoned in the husk and shell of earth consoled or menaced him. Every leaf bore a growth of angels; the pulse of every minute sounded as the falling foot of God; under the rank raiment of weeds, in the dripping down of thistles, strange faces frowned and white hair fluttered.[24]

The same state of mind and feeling is apparent again and again in some of Mr. Yeats's discussions of the general subject of mysticism which are later brought to bear upon Blake. But here the animism gives way to a tinge of Nietzschean idealism, as in the following passage:

Opposed to this [the philosophy of all who, because of the absorption in active life, have been persuaded to judge and to punish] was another philosophy, not made by men of action, drudges of time and space, but by Christ when wrapped in the divine essence, and by artists and poets, who are taught

[24] Swinburne, op. cit., p. 41.

by the nature of their craft to sympathize with all living things, and who, the more pure and fragrant is their lamp, pass the further from all limitations, to come at last to forget good and evil in an absorbing vision of the happy and the unhappy.[25]

Sometimes this obscurantist state of mind makes use of more specifically intellectual concepts and even invokes theology, as in the following Rousseauistic application of the classical theory of regeneration to the *Songs:*

The adult cannot sing like a child; but Blake in these songs does so: he did not *act* the infantine, for he *was* infantine, by a regeneration as real while as mysterious as ever purest saint experienced in the religious life. And this regeneration, so far as we can learn, was effected without the throes of agony and doubt and despair, which the saints all pass through in being born again.[26]

But in general the most characteristic manifestation of this large obscurantist element in the Blake criticism is to be found in a passage which, more nearly than any other definition of mysticism appearing in this group, gives not only the intellectual but the emotional state which has inspired the greater number of these interpretations of Blake's mysticism. Like the preceding passages it has an imaginative as well as an emotional glow that makes the author's impression seem peculiarly vivid:

Visionary and mystic though he was, he did not differ from ordinary men so much in the quality of his mental state as in the consistency with which he preserved a mental state that is for most men a very fleeting one. To the dullest of us come rare keen moments when in the glow of some sunrise the material phenomena of earth and sun are obliterated by the overwhelming spirit of flaming joy and new creation that cries out of that dawn; and for every man who has ever lived, the physical vesture of some woman has in a magic hour dissolved to nothing and left him staring into the spiritual Eden of a world beyond.[27]

To practically the same general region emotionally and imaginatively, though not intellectually, belongs the conception of mysticism which lays its main stress upon the seeing of visions. This is, indeed, by definition or by implication one of the commonest understandings of this much-vexed term. It plays a very large part in

[25] William Butler Yeats, *Ideas of Good and Evil* (New York, 1903), p. 198 f.

[26] James Thomson, "The Poems of William Blake," *Biographical and Critical Studies* (London, 1896), pp. 240–69.

[27] Arthur Davison Ficke, "A Divine Visionary," *The Dial*, LIX (October 14, 1915), 323–25.

even the more fully developed conceptions of mysticism, as in the case of M. Berger, who, when he tries to find the center of Blake's mystical power with greater precision than his preliminary definitions admitted, says: "It is in this, then, that Blake's strength lies: in the faculty that enabled him to create a world wholly different from ours, freed from the laws of time and space, existing only in his dreams, and as far removed from reality as the wildest ideal can be."[28]

This is, of course, an obviously rationalistic approach to the subject, but in this field the Blake criticism affords enough literal interpretations of Blake's claims to vision to belie any undue faith that ours is a highly rationalistic age. The critic who explains Blake's "system of symbolical myths" as a device "partly to clothe therewith the too startling nakedness of his philosophy, and partly to serve as an instrument of research in supersensuous regions,"[29] is in the second element hovering on the edge of spiritualism. But Ellis and Yeats, in some very interesting portions of their explanation of Blake's system, plunge boldly into that fascinating realm, as in the following:

While this work is going through the press some curious experiments have been commenced with persons who, on receiving a symbol, have the power of seeing and conversing with visionary forms raised by that symbol. Some of these seers have beheld personages that are recognizably identical with those of Blake's myth, though differing a little, as Blake himself said visions differ with the eye of the visionary. Orc, for instance, was viewed by one seer as black, instead of glowing, and by another as a wolf in armour. Urthona and Los, and Ololon, have also been seen, and independently described in terms almost identical with Blake's.[30]

This aspect of the discussion of Blake's visions is probably most justly recognized by M. François Bénoit, who tempers the Gallic edge of his analysis with a glowing enthusiasm for Blake when he writes:

Des singularités que nous a révélée l'analyse, il n'en est guère dont les sciences psychiques, la neurologie, et la médecine mentale n'aient connaissance

<hr/>

[28] Berger, *op. cit.*, p. 265.

[29] Francis Griffin Stokes, Introduction to the "Marriage of Heaven and Hell" and "A Song of Liberty" (London and New York, 1911), p. 32.

[30] Ellis and Yeats, *The Works of William Blake: Poetic, Symbolic, and Critical* (London, 1893), I, 96.

et n'essayent de rendre compte. Sans hésiter, elles classeraient Blake dans la catégorie des grands mystiques et aussi des médiums de la famille de l'extraordinaire exploratrice de la planète Mars dont M. Flournoy a consigné les "découvertes."[31]

In other words, it is very difficult for a conception of mysticism which lays very much stress upon what we may call the geographical aspects of vision to keep clear of spiritualism, and some of the critics interested especially in this point of view have not been troubled by any anxiety to do so.

The group of those who believe that the fact that a man sees visions makes him a mystic is not inconsiderable. In some way or other this enters as one element into almost all estimates of Blake. But while perhaps more universal than any other, it does not play the major part that the fact that Blake was a man who looked at the whole world from a certain point of view and tried to penetrate its mystery from that point of view does. But perhaps because this is a matter of such importance it is the most difficult point of all at which to arrive at any composite picture of the Blake criticism.

This is not at all surprising, for it is very difficult to discover precisely what Blake himself believed or intended to say on that subject. It is therefore possible for one scholar of distinction to say: "An interesting point, and one wherein Blake differs from other mystics, is that, in spite of his feeling for symbolism, he did not look upon the natural world as a ladder by which he could arrive at the real,"[32] and for another to say quite to the contrary: "In nature he always saw God, and through time, he could perceive eternity,"[33] or, as Mr. Gardner puts it with the characteristic heightening of enthusiasm:

Nature is the mirror of man's inner life. Hence Blake feels the ecstasy of the Hindoo mystic and

". . . . looks out in tree and herb, and fish, and bird, and beast,
Collecting up the scattered portions of his immortal body
Into the elemental forms of everything that grows."[34]

[31] François Bénoit, Un Maître de l'Art, Blake, le Visionnaire (Lille et Paris, 1907), pp. 43 f.

[32] Caroline F. Spurgeon, "Mysticism in English Poetry," Quarterly Review, CCVII (October, 1907), 427–59.

[33] Berger, op. cit., p. 97.

[34] Gardner, Vision and Vesture: A Study of William Blake in Modern Thought (London, 1916), p. 24.

While the comparison of Blake and the Hindu mystics is scarcely accurate (the passage quoted is much closer to Mr. Yeats than to Yagnavalkya), it expresses succinctly the point of view of a very considerable group of critics. Many of the others, who would not regard this as an adequate statement of their position, would subscribe to the interpretation that one of the writers on "The Visionary Art of William Blake" gives:

> Everything, in his eyes, has conscious spiritual existence:
>
>> Each grain of sand,
>> Every stone on the land,
>> Each rock and each hill,
>> Each fountain and rill,
>> Each herb and each tree,
>> Mountain, hill, earth and sea,
>> Cloud, meteor and star,
>> Are men seen afar. . . . .
>
> It is the creed which made Eckhart and Joachim of Flora tell the people to seek God as much in the green fields as in the church. It is the mystical creed of every age.[35]

For that aspect of the universe which is of more immediate importance to the practical mystic, the relation of God and man, the critics have in general stressed two striking phases of Blake's views: first, the highly anthropomorphic character of his conception of God, and second, his tendency to carry the identity of God and man beyond the lines of orthodox Christianity into pantheism. Of the first, the critics have almost unanimously ratified Mr. Gardner's statement: "His conception of God is in terms of Man. He has a horror of a God who is abstract, vague, or indefinite, for though God is infinite and all-present, yet he is terrible to the imagination unless he has outline. Man is God's outline."[36] And although M. Saurat, in his interesting comparison of Blake and Milton, insists that Blake accentuated Milton's tendency "to make God unknowable and inconceivable," still in his recognition of the fact that it is not God who acts in Blake's poems, but the Eternals and the Zoas, or secondary powers (beings conceived of in very physical, even if often abstract, terms), he really confirms the gen-

[35] *Edinburgh Review*, CCIII (January, 1906), 161–79.
[36] Gardner, *Vision and Vesture*, p. 60.

eral impression that the source of active power in Blake's universe is distinctly and characteristically anthropomorphic.[37] In general the emotional reaction to Blake's God is probably best summed up in Bénoit's " 'God is nothing more than man.' "[38]

When it comes to the relation between God and man, the import of such a position depends entirely upon the terms in which it is defined. With some interpretations it may mean little more than a vigorous assertion of the biblical statement that man is made in the image of God. On the other hand, it may be so understood as to mean something far different, and in general it has been so understood, as, for instance, in the following: "Blake believed that the real self was made in the image of God, and therefore it must be loved, reverenced, and obeyed. The recognition of the same divine principle in others enables one to love one's neighbor as oneself. All German mystical talk of hatred to self and death to self was repudiated by Blake as artificial and unreal."[39]

The likeness between Blake's point of view and that of Meister Eckhart and Joachim de Flore in this identification of the nature of man and God has already been noticed. It raises the question whether or not Blake had drawn the ethical conclusions that the two medieval antinomians had reached from those premises. At least one student of Blake has felt that he did: "The perfect man has no conscience. He has knowledge of God as his Self; knowledge of himself as God's. Even between himself and God the distinction is due to his own incomplete development only, to his partial realization as yet of God. . . . . Blake, in a word, is a Mystic"; and further of the ideal man this same critic writes: "He is inspired. God looks, gesticulates, speaks, acts through him. He is not 'moral'; he has no standard of good, no choice to make. The choice was made long ago."[40]

In other words, man is justified by faith rather than works. As Swinburne was the first to point out:

[37] Denis Saurat, *Blake and Milton* (Bordeaux, 1920), p. 65.

[38] Bénoit, *op. cit.*, p. 33.

[39] Charles Gardner, *William Blake the Man* (London, 1919), p. 72.

[40] William N. Guthrie, "William Blake, Poet and Artist," *Sewanee Review*, V (October, 1897), 438–39.

Translated into crude practical language, his creed was about this: as long as a man believes all things he may do anything; scepticism (not sin) is alone damnable, being the one thing purely barren and negative; do what you will with your body, as long as you refuse it leave to disprove or deny the life eternally inherent in your soul. That we believe is what people call or have called by some such name as "antinomian mysticism": do anything but doubt, and you shall not in the end be utterly lost. Clearly enough it was Blake's faith.[41]

Now this stress on believing the right thing, coupled with the faith in vision which plays so large a part in the critic's definition of Blake's mysticism, is probably responsible for what is one of the most important grounds which Blake's critics have taken for calling him a mystic. It is that through his visions, wherever they came from and whatever they signified, he had received important revelations of truth, he had discovered sources of insight and understanding that made what he had to say of peculiar importance and value to all of us. As Mr. Chesterton long ago observed, the young Blake "came out into the world a mystic in this very practical sense, that he came out to teach rather than to learn."[42] And while M. Berger thinks that Blake's ideas and his message to the age in which he lived can scarcely be called a doctrine, he, too, admits that "it is indisputable . . . . that he had a doctrine to preach."[43] That is also, as has been suggested in certain passages already quoted from Mr. Damon's book, the position of Mr. Damon: "Blake . . . . was trying to rationalize the Divine ('to justify the ways of God to men'), and to apotheosize the Human. He was trying to lay bare the fundamental errors which are the cause of misery. These errors he sought, not in codes of ethic nor in the construction of society, but in the human soul itself."[44]

Two notes are adduced by many of the critics as guaranties of the authenticity of these revelations. The first is a very old one, the esoteric quality of Blake's revelation of truth. As one sympathetic critic has pointed out: "It needs the insight of the mystic—of those belonging to the 'world inside'—to understand the mystic soul of

[41] Swinburne, *op. cit.*, p. 96.

[42] G. K. Chesterton, *William Blake* (London, 1910), p. 13.

[43] Berger, *op. cit.*, p. 63.

[44] Damon, *op. cit.*, p. ix.

William Blake."[45] And the other is the newness of what Blake reported from his sojourns in the world of vision. While it might be
hard to prove Swinburne's assertion that "There is no case on record of a man's being quite so far in advance of his time,"[46] it would
be very difficult to contradict M. Berger's opinion on the relation of
Blake's ideas to those of his age when he says: "He seems, almost
purposely, to have formed his system of religion and philosophy out
of everything that was regarded by the eighteenth century as con-
temptible or ridiculous."[47] And the force of the appeal which this
newness makes is well suggested in its emotional intensity by the
apocalyptic fervor of a brilliant passage in Mr. Yeats' discussion of
the revolutionary Blake:

> We write of great writers, even of writers whose beauty would once have
> seemed an unholy beauty, with rapt sentences like those our fathers kept for
> the beatitudes and mysteries of the Church; and no matter what we believe
> with our lips, we believe with our hearts that beautiful things, as Browning
> said . . . . have "lain burningly on the Divine hand," and that when time
> has begun to wither, the Divine hand will fall heavily on bad taste and vul-
> garity. When no man believed these things William Blake believed them, and
> began that preaching against the Philistine, which is as the preaching of the
> Middle Ages against the Saracen.[48]

This is a very common state of mind among Blake's critics, not
a few of whom have gone on from this delight in the revolutionary
impact of Blake's ideas to Story's conclusion: "The fact that . . . .
it [Blake's work] is so full of novel and startling thought is almost
enough in itself to indicate that he had struck some new vein or
source of truth."[49]

Probably the first of Blake's teachings to appeal to the sympathetic interest of his critics is his insistence, through all the lyrics
especially, upon the fact and the necessity of universal sympathy.
Of "the primitive feeling of fellowship with all living beings" which
pervades Blake's work one critic says: "We must go back to the old

[45] Adeline Butterworth, *William Blake, Mystic*, etc. (Liverpool and London, 1911),
p. 2.

[46] Swinburne, *op. cit.*, p. 14.

[47] Berger, *op. cit.*, p. 76.

[48] Yeats, *Ideas of Good and Evil*, pp. 169 f.

[49] Alfred T. Story, *William Blake, His Life, Character, and Genius* (London, 1893),
p. 158.

Indian philosophers, or to medieval mystics like St. Francis of Assisi, to find this sentiment of brotherhood with animals, plants, and inanimate things, this immense feeling of tenderness toward them, in which there is neither condescending pity nor any sense of man's superiority."[50] "The true life," writes another, "is that which in all its reactions makes for human brotherhood. That man has found himself who has learnt to bind his brother man to his heart in healing, forgiving, long-suffering life. Blake saw with his swift insight that this was the real distinction of the Christian principle of conduct."[51]

The corollary to this love of all things even to the lowest orders of creation is Blake's doctrine of forgiveness which has elicited almost equal enthusiasm. For the relative importance of this tenet seen in the general perspective of Blake's teachings as a whole, we may rely on an amazingly complete sentence of Swinburne's: "As to matter and argument, the enormous *Jerusalem* is simply a fervent apocalyptic discourse on the old subjects—love without law and against law, virtue that stagnates into poisonous dead matter by moral isolation, sin that must exist for the sake of being forgiven, forgiveness that must always keep up with sin—must even maintain sin that it may have something to keep up with and to live for."[52] And the effect of this teaching upon the minds of Blake's critics is to be gauged by Sir Walter Raleigh's interpretation: "The only true forgiveness is a movement of love and pity called forth by the offense as inevitably as a grain of sand in the eye will cause the tears to flow. And this is the beginning and the end of religion."[53]

This stress upon the necessity of spontaneity and impulsiveness for complete forgiveness is only one example, among many that have attracted the critics, of Blake's insistence upon the spontaneous, impulsive action. It is not only Mr. Gardner, of recent years, who has been much attracted by this element, as in the following:

[50] Berger, *op. cit.*, p. 246.

[51] Richard Roberts, "The Ethics of William Blake," *Hibbert Journal*, XVII (April, 1919), 660–71.

[52] Swinburne, *op. cit.*, p. 277.

[53] Walter Raleigh, Introduction to the *Lyrical Poems of William Blake*, editor, John Sampson (Oxford, 1905), p. xlii.

"Strained action was an abhorrence to Blake. Only those acts are beautiful that are impulsive, and they are they that reveal the man."[54] M. Berger discovers in the injunction "To follow impulse and not rules" what he calls the great principle of Blake's Christianity. Indeed, Blake's emphasis on impulse approaches that faith in the natural life which in Blake's own day and since has attracted much attention. Almost thirty years ago a reviewer well summed up the reaction of the nineties and of kindred spirits since in what he said from this point of view about Blake's Christ:

> His Christ is the great vindicator of a natural life who preaches to men to be as lily, as sparrow, as little child, as fruitful tree. Faith in the ideal, and hope of manifesting it in one's final perfection—not self-schooling by a set of laws, forgiveness of sins—not the endless legal or illegal vendetta, which were futile: spontaneous virtue—not artificial righteousness; a life from within outward, seeing that the beginnings be right—not from without inward; the setting of desire on things above—not the dangerous starving and impossible killing of desire; indifference to the letter, when sure of the spirit, to the deed, when sure of the will; the essential unity of man and God—not their everlasting antithesis; the radical goodness therefore (not depravity) of human nature, needing only to draw its sap from its true root to become lovely in appearance; as teacher and demonstrator of such doctrines, as preacher of the Sermon on the Mount and utterer of the great prayer of atonement in the Garden of Gethsemane, the Christ was to him the Saviour, and in a peculiar sense "the very God."[55]

Of course, this faith in impulse presupposes an unusual degree of confidence in the nature of impulse, and involves an equally hearty criticism of anything that tends to interfere with, or restrict the expression of, impulse. As usual, Mr. De Sélincourt has defined a very common point of view with marked precision: "He [Blake] saw one truth only—that to restrict an impulse is to change its nature. He refused to believe in the existence of an unholy impulse. Man's whole desire is for the good. It is only by being thwarted and fettered that he becomes base. Sin is the child of the law."[56]

Probably no aspect of Blake's message has aroused more en-

[54] Gardner, *op. cit.*, p. 52.
[55] Guthrie, *op. cit.*, p. 447.
[56] Basil De Sélincourt, *William Blake* (London and New York, 1911), p. 48.

thusiastic interest in those critics who believe he is a great mystic than his sweeping and constantly sustained attack upon the conventional moral law. From Blake's point of view, the old morality —and here he has found many disciples—was a narrowing, stultifying, repressive code of negations. In this repudiation of the conventional morality, according to one of the most enthusiastic interpreters of this point of view:

> Blake's vigorous genius struck deeper into the soil of ethics; it was the active emanation of a soul which, as far as social and intellectual conventions were concerned, was in open revolt. He perceived that the life of man must be affirmative and aggressive rather than negative and passive. . . . . He perceived in Nature restless activity, endless progression; in man, on the other hand, he beheld only the apathy of content and retrogression. . . . . He called, and called loudly, for the removal of the restraint [conventional restraint upon natural desire], and was all for a plunge into the whirlpool with only his tutelary spirit as guide.[57]

But no attack of Blake upon the moral law in the abstract has been so picturesque or so challenging as his attack upon the problem in the concrete as represented in his picture of Christ. One of the earliest reviewers of Swinburne's book had called attention to that aspect of Blake's discovery: "Blake ardently vindicates Christ from having been virtuous in the theological sense; he is a rebel, an outlaw, a defender of the unchaste, an agitator for the freedom of the instincts and of the mind, and his sure triumph is to be the downfall of Jehovah, and his law the victory of divine man."[58] "Before all else," writes Mr. Gardner in our own day, "Blake saw in Jesus the lawbreaker,"[59a] who "lived, not by laws and rules, but by an all-compelling instinct and impulse."[59b] The moral for man's life is obvious, and again it is Mr. Gardner who points it out most eloquently: "As man's knowledge of God's will grows with the ages, the Saint with the fullest insight obeys God's will and breaks the law. Thus Jesus gave Himself in love to God. God's will was the inner law of His Spirit. By obeying impulsively and instinctively this will, He obeyed the eternal law of good, and broke every con-

---

[57] *The Fortnightly Review*, XCIII (March, 1910), 570–72.
[58] M. D. Conway, *Fortnightly Review*, IX (February, 1868), 219.
[59a] Gardner, *Vision and Vesture*, p. 205.
[59b] *William Blake The Man*, p. 167.

ceivable code of morals, ran counter to the traditions and conventions of man, and set aside all authority."[60]

In one region this scorn of morality has attracted particular attention, and that is in the field of sex, where the departure of this antinomian Christ from orthodox tradition is most conspicuous. Like Mr. Ellis, Mr. Gardner romances not a little about how Blake came to attack the problem of the place of sex in man's life. Whatever the facts about Blake's life, his analysis of Blake's position represents the generally accepted interpretation of his critics: "The sex question had never been dragged out into the light. The subject was unclean. Sexual morality consisted in repression. Nowhere as here does repression breed such poisonous fruits. Was not sex a part of that vital fire and passion in which Blake believed with his whole heart? Was it not true that whatsoever lives is holy? Must not there be liberty for the sexual instinct if it was to be kept clean?"[61]

But sex is more than this to Blake, and herein lies one of his peculiar claims upon the interest of Mr. Gardner and many other critics of the last twenty years, for:

> Sex passion when it sweeps in with irresistible force has its rhythm, its beauty and its ecstasy. It transfigures all it touches, and beautifies the human body. For it nothing connected with the body is common or unclean. Raised to its highest power it sees in the human form a direct revelation of the divine; and when trusted leads a man as it led Michael Angelo to the Fountain source of Beauty whence all forms are but partial manifestations. Here it is inseparable from religion.[62]

And what is true of sex passion holds true of pretty much all passion. "He cried again and again," says Mr. Yeats, "that everything that lives is holy, and that nothing is unholy except things that do not live—lethargies, and cruelties, and timidities, and that denial of imagination which is the root they grew from in old times. Passions, because most living, are most holy—and this was a scandalous paradox in his time—and man shall enter eternity borne upon their wings."[63] In spite of what these passages, unqualified, may suggest, passion, sex or otherwise, is not to be valued just for itself, but for its dynamic, for the sources of power which it affords

[60] Gardner, *Vision and Vesture*, pp. 202 f.
[61] Gardner, *William Blake The Man*, pp. 88 f.
[62] Gardner, *Vision and Vesture*, p. 35.   [63] Yeats, *op. cit.*, p. 171.

for all human effort. As Mr. Gardner again says, personifying passion: "His havoc in unregenerate man may be terrible; but once a servant of the regenerate man, he becomes the best of all servants, serving in all man's mental pursuits, quickening all man's joyous perception of beauty, beautifying all man's social dealings with his brother."[64]

In other words, the secret of this glorification of passion and the secret of Blake's great popularity with those whom Professor Saintsbury has very appropriately dubbed "the high-flyers of the army of Romanticism," lies in Blake's doctrine of energy. "He trusted the passions," says Symons, "because they were alive; and, like Nietzsche, hated asceticism, because

> Abstinence sows sand all over
> The ruddy limbs and flaming hair,
> But desire gratified
> Plants fruits of life and beauty there."[65]

In this comparison with Nietzsche, Symons pays tribute to Blake in a region where he is sure to find much appreciation today. There are many who will agree with Symons when he says, in his introduction to the book just quoted:

> Thought today, wherever it is most individual, owes either force or direction to Nietzsche, and thus we see, on our topmost towers, the Philistine armed and winged, and without the love or fear of God or man in his heart, doing battle in Nietzsche's name against the ideas of Nietzsche. No one can think, and escape Nietzsche; but Nietzsche has come after Blake, and will pass before Blake passes.

Mr. Gardner draws the same parallel, and in a very eloquent discussion of the Nietzschean superman makes clear the conception of energy that animates both his and Symons' handling of the subject:

> He [the superman] realizes early in his development that strength, growth, power, and beauty are effects of the Spirit of Life, and therefore he must, before all things, fan and nourish the flame of life in himself, and welcome whatever forms it shall throw out. His surest method is to trust his instincts, which are life's antennae, and as he does so he finds that he is being transformed by a mighty power within which brings him into sharp collision with dead virtues, dead moralities, and dead conventions.[66]

---

[64] Gardner, *Vision and Vesture*, p. 90.

[65] Symons, *op. cit.*, pp. 3 f.   [66] Gardner, *Vision and Vesture*, p. 195.

These critics find fresh light on Blake's theories of life, particularly his valuation of energy, in the fruit they bore in his work as artist. Sir Walter Raleigh expresses the verdict of the group when he says: "In poetry, as in the other arts, Blake cared only for impulse, spontaneity, primal energy."[67] But the most characteristic and explicit account of Blake's work from this side is a newspaper review of a recent edition of Blake's poems, the heart of which may be found in the following:

> The impulse in Blake's poetry does not come from particular events, which are the mere pretexts for the expression of it; it is rather a vast and continuous élan vital which we feel in the rhythm even when the sense is unintelligible or absurd. This élan vital, this dogmatic and spiritual appetite, always beating rhythmically, does not always achieve expression. Often it seems to function blindly in phrases, lines, verses even, repeated again and again, which find their proper context only in one poem. . . . .
> The greatest example of this élan vital is "The Everlasting Gospel," . . . . [which] is, with all its loose ends and ribaldries and obscurities, the most spontaneous piece of thinking in verse, the most naked poetry that exists; but the first five sections are all a preliminary, often wayward and intermixed with doggerel to the great sixth section in which his doctrine of love and forgiveness is uttered as if it were sounded on all the voices and instruments of Heaven :—
> > "Thou angel of the Presence Divine,
> > That didst create this Body of Mine,
> > Wherefore hast thou writ these Laws
> > And created Hell's dark jaws?
> > My Presence I will take from thee;
> > A cold Leper thou shalt be.
> > Tho' thou wast so pure and bright
> > That Heaven was impure in thy sight,
> > Tho' thy Oath turned Heaven pale,
> > Tho' thy Covenant built Hell's jail,
> > Tho' thou didst all to chaos roll
> > With the Serpent for its soul,
> > Still the breath Divine does move,
> > And the breath Divine is Love."

Here the élan vital in the words is like a great wind bearing a flight of rejoicing birds; all the language has come to life so that the words are what they signify.[68]

    [67] Raleigh, op. cit., p. xi.
    [68] The Times Literary Supplement, No. 1037 (London, December 1, 1921), "The Poetry of Blake," leading article.

Here again for Blake art and religion are one, and his practice and his teaching meet in a synthesis of the two that is very different from the conventional point of view on either art or religion. As one critic has very ably pointed out in a passage that compresses into a few sentences the whole history of the evolution of Blake's philosophy and art: "The starting-point of Blake's thought is the sovereignty of the creative impulse. The end of life is Art—creative imagination expressed in any medium, whether of sound or of substance, by which the human spirit may make itself articulate. Blake's God is the supreme Artist; Jesus was the incarnation of the Poetic Genius."[69] From this, of course, it was but a scarcely perceptible step to that identification of Christ with the imagination itself, probably the constituent of Blake's mysticism that has most impressed his critics. And if "Jesus is not only God, Saviour, Redeemer, Wisdom, Power, High Priest, Prophet, King, but also and pre-eminently Imagination," it is not surprising that at least one somewhat impressionistic logician has drawn the not entirely unreasonable conclusion that imagination is likewise all of these.[70] That is the essence of what is often called Blake's artistic mysticism.

Obviously, these men are not using imagination in the sense to which readers of Coleridge, for instance, are accustomed. Usually they do not stop to define what they mean by this important word, but most of them clearly assume some such general conception as that which Mr. De Sélincourt expounds in his paper on the "Parallelism of Religion and Art":

Art and Religion are a motion of the soul, ... a movement from within outwards: the life of both, their secret, is e-motion. Thus it was that Blake devoted all his strength to passionate preaching of a single doctrine—that this spontaneous "emanation," by which man rises into communion with the Divine, this power, which, according to the sphere in which it operates, he calls sometimes Imagination, sometimes Love, is the one thing needful, and that whatever in government or in society tends to check it and throw man back upon himself defeats the true end of living and robs man of his one pos-

[69] Richard Roberts, "The Ethics of William Blake," *Hibbert Journal*, XVII (April, 1919), 660–71.

[70] Gardner, *Vision and Vesture*, p. 47.

session of priceless worth. In short, Art and Religion are the same to him, because both give, what there is nothing else that can give, a complete expression to the spirit of life itself.[71]

With such an identification of art and religion it is clear that the mystic way, the method by which Blake strives to achieve his goal, will at many points be very different from the mystic way of orthodox Christianity. The expansion of the imagination will play a much larger part in it than the discipline of the will. In contrast to the rigorous discipline of the will and the mind and the feeling outlined in the *Imitation of Christ* of Thomas à Kempis, Blake's method "seeks Christ-likeness by a new life process. Starting with the new birth of the Spirit, it seeks to develop the Spirit of Life, by yielding to it and allowing it to transform it into the Christ-image. This is the real method for training Saints, the Saint produced being essentially a life product."[72] Practically the same process is outlined by Mr. William Butler Yeats when he says:

Instead of seeking God in the deserts of time and space, in exterior immensities, in what he called "the abstract void," he believed that the further he dropped behind him memory of time and space, reason builded upon sensation, morality founded for the ordering of the world; and the more he was absorbed in emotion; and above all, in emotion escaped from the impulse of bodily longing and the restraints of bodily reason, in artistic emotion; the nearer did he come to Eden's "breathing garden," to use his beautiful phrase, and to the unveiled face of God.[73]

Such, in brief, is the revelation that has led a small but distinguished group of critics of considerable potency of literary expression to acclaim Blake one of the major prophets of modern times and one of the great mystics of all time.

[71] Basil De Sélincourt, "The Parallelism of Religion and Art: A Comment on William Blake," *Hibbert Journal*, V (January, 1907), 397–406.

[72] Gardner, *Vision and Vesture*, p. 209. Most writers in this field stress the fact that "Blake maintained that true Christianity is only understood and enjoyed by the imagination and heart, and that therefore only the imaginative man could be a real Christian," as S. E. Keeble points out in "Imagination and William Blake," *London Quarterly Review*, CXXVII (April, 1917), 215–26.

[73] Yeats, *op. cit.*, p. 206.

CHAPTER II

WHAT IS MYSTICISM?

If one thing stands out more clearly than another from this sketch of what sympathetic critics have made of Blake's mysticism, it is the lack of any common or clear understanding of what we mean when we say that a man is a mystic, great or small. As we have seen, very few of these writers have had any very precise sense of what the word itself means, even when applied to Blake. And still fewer have had any background of acquaintance with other mystics who might afford opportunity for illuminating comparisons with the subject of their study. Where a few critics have had for this purpose a more or less extensive acquaintance among the mystics of history, their findings have been amazingly discrepant. On the one hand M. Berger, while very sure that Blake is a genuine mystic, has not hesitated to point out how entirely different from the mystics of the orthodox Christian tradition this heretic is. The English poet's writings, says M. Berger,

present certain very striking features . . . . which clearly distinguish Blake's mysticism from the mysticism familiar to us in the lives of the saints. . . . . Blake was no saint. He had never renounced the world, its passions or its pleasures. He had never mortified his body by ascetic practices . . . . had never experienced that intense longing to behold their God which had filled the souls of the saints. ... . . He never prepared himself, by prayers and meditations, for his celestial visitors. . . . . Finally, he lacked what the theologians have always regarded as the most essential mark of the Christian visionary—humility. . . . . He would not humble himself even before God. . . . . He cannot therefore be called a religious mystic, in the ordinary sense of the term.[1]

On the other hand, Mr. S. Foster Damon, who is quite as well informed in general about the saints as M. Berger, not only believes that Blake is a great mystic, to be counted among the great mystics of the world, but that he is a great mystic in the traditional sense, recapitulating in the history of his inner life as well as in the teachings of his books the conventional stages of orthodox mystical de-

[1] Berger, *op. cit.*, pp. 59 f.

velopment. Here Mr. Damon accepts Miss Evelyn Underhill's five divisions of the mystic way—the Awakening, the Purgation, the "enhanced return of the sense of the divine order, after the Self has achieved its detachment from the world," the "Dark Night of the Soul," and "the complete union with Truth"—as a literal description of Blake's experience.[2] Indeed, Miss Underhill herself, whose definition of mysticism is largely derived from an unusually wide study of the lives and writings of the saints, had already anticipated Mr. Damon's position when she closed her monumental *An Introduction to Mysticism* with a brief but enthusiastic note on Blake as "one of the greatest mystics of all time."[3]

But as has been said before, the majority of Blake students have used the term so vaguely, with so little sense of historic implications, that in most of them a definite issue like this above is hardly to be found. Consequently the average discussion of Blake's mysticism seldom comes to grips with any discrimination of real importance, or effects any analysis of sufficient precision to be even fully descriptive.

The Blake critics, however, are scarcely to be blamed for this vagueness of use, since it reflects quite fairly the general state of public opinion about mysticism today. Probably never before has there been so much or such sympathetic interest in mysticism as there is at the present time; never, certainly, since the latter days of the Roman Empire has there been so much curiosity as now when materialism and rationalism and pseudo-paganism are bringing about the inevitable reaction. And yet—and here one is reminded of the latter days of the Roman Empire again—it is hard to imagine a state of greater confusion or looseness of usage than that which exists today. Verily, mysticism has come to mean so many things that it has ceased to mean much of anything. Nine-tenths of the people who use the word today mean little more than a vague emotional reaction in which awe and the sense of strangeness play almost equal parts.

With a tool so blunted as this popular notion of mysticism it is

[2] Damon, *op. cit.*, p. 2.

[3] Evelyn Underhill, *Mysticism: A Study in the Nature and Development of Man's Spiritual Consciousness* (London, 1912), p. 562.

impossible to think, to say nothing of criticizing. Some sort of definition is needed, logically exclusive and discriminating enough to mean something, flexible and broad enough to be descriptive, and, for want of a better word, pragmatic enough to meet the contingencies of life fully and realistically. Ordinarily, such a definition is arrived at by one of three ways: by authority, by a sifting and a criticism of common use, or by a fresh study of the field under discussion with all the helps which authority and common use can afford.

There have been times, and there still are fields even now, in which the appeal to authority has been fruitful. But if there ever was a time when anybody felt competent to determine once for all what was meant when a man was called a mystic, that time is passed. If the world was ever agreed on matters so fundamental to man's spiritual life, it was at a time less devoted to variety of opinion than the present. Nowhere have toleration and equalitarianism triumphed more completely than in this field.

Common use is still in many cases a fruitful source of definition. Of course, most definitions derived from a sifting of what we mean, say, when we praise a man for his common sense, are more or less determined by the maker's own predilections, but if one takes a great many definitions, even though they are arrived at from very different points of view, he can usually find certain common elements which may be taken as suggestive for the class, if not final for the individual. But in the case of mysticism it is hard to arrive at even that modicum of agreement.

One may, for instance, hear a very discriminating logician of a naturalistic persuasion dismiss a discussion of literary values by the most thoroughly rationalistic humanist of his acquaintance as mystic because the humanist has discussed human conduct in terms of something besides purely physiological determinism. In certain' groups the possession of any sort of general idea is apt to expose one to the reproach of mystic. It is not difficult to see how this arose out of a common epistemological use of the term "mystic" for anyone who attempts to arrive at knowledge of truth by intuitive, as opposed to ordinary rational, processes of thought. But when such an extension of meaning takes place that the most ground-keeping of rationalists is lumped with the airiest of transcendentalists, clearly the term has ceased not only to be definitive, but even to be descriptive.

In contexts where thought counts for less than feeling, the same confusion prevails, with similar results. Not only are the medium and the holder of hands at the séance called mystics, but any poet or artist who can blur natural objects in such a fashion as to release them from the bounds of their normal appearance and normal meanings is given the same name as the masters of the spiritual life. Indeed, for half the human race obscurity is perhaps the readiest password to mysticism in any field. The formless, the vague, the nerveless, the will-less, the meaningless, are given the same name as the most heroic, the most dynamic, the most meaningful of spiritual activities. Phantasy and hallucination, dream and myth, take their places side by side with the most profoundly matured and richly invested thought and feeling and imagination of the race. Consequently no definition of mysticism arrived at from common use can be anything but a paradox.

The difficulty, after all, is in the field itself quite as much as in the lazy habits of the human mind in an age that is rich in substitutes and short-cuts for thinking. For mysticism, being a field of human experience that involves all the elements of man's nature, physiological and psychological, intellectual, and emotional, and aesthetic, as well as what is vaguely called spiritual, labors under the complexity and uncertainty of human life itself. That is what makes it so perennially interesting. Even while it defies definition, it challenges it.

First of all, mysticism, as the term is used with a thousand different varieties and shades of meaning, does include so many different elements: the rigorous self-discipline of a St. Paul, the joyous play of a St. Francis, the scarlet woman and the wondrous beasts of the Apocalypse, the voiceless and imageless openings of George Fox, the Nirvana of the Buddha, the ecstasy of fire of Pascal, the transfiguration of the everyday world for the successful lover, the fading away of all things of sense for the victorious ascetic, the transcendent intellectual vision of Spinoza, the drunken sense of power in the aboriginal who has eaten of the sacred weed—

all these things have their part in mysticism. It is broad as life itself.

And as mixed, for when man enters with all his being into any enterprise, what is base of him goes in with what is high; what is immature and childish, with what is of fullest stature. Nowhere is this more true than in religion. Where religion forgets the savage and the child in man, she loses her chance to reach the man. And where man steadfastly sets himself to pluck out the tares, he roots up the wheat. A vigorous onslaught upon superstition and idolatry usually casts out beauty, and a thoroughgoing endeavor to live by the light of reason starves feeling and imagination so that what was denied its right in the hall takes its revenge in the cellar.

Some of the men and women who have been honored as mystics by history have been as strangely mixed as most of us. Hysteria and eroticism and steadfast piety in a Catherine of Genoa or a Mme Guyon, heroic self-discipline and passion for love and for power in a St. Teresa, love of God and love of knowledge in an Eckartshausen, desire for the vision of God and craving for the philosopher's stone in a Paracelsus, heroic self-devotion and tragic self-deception in the pantheism of a Joachim de Flore—these tell on a heroic scale what is much more pitifully evident in a thousand lesser souls, what is, by any definition and any criterion, mysticism of a high type muddled sometimes indissociably with what can by no stretch of the imagination be called mystical, or at best, mystical only in a very elementary or debased form.

And finally, there is the difficulty that always confronts the student of art, of religion, or of any activity where humanity is engaged in the most human of activities, trying to transcend itself: the infinite differences and degrees of human interest and desire and power. The gulf between the rhymer who makes up jingles for billboards and for rallies and the great poet who frees the heart of humanity in a phrase of immortal beauty is no wider than the gulf between the adept who tries with magic words to raise a spirit and the great master of the inner life who rises into union with God. Sensitiveness and intensity of desire may go in company with great powers of mind or with none. An easily enkindled imagination may dwell with a will of singular energy and tenacity, or with the feeble purpose of a hysteric. Nowhere does the memorable law of life, that power shall be strong and weakness shall be weak, operate more cruelly than here. In other words, mysticism is as great or as little as the mystic and the spiritual world out of which he comes.

One mystic is therefore not as good as another, nor as much of a mystic. And in the spiritual world more even than in the material does it hold true that to prefer the inferior is to surrender the better. How then shall we draw distinctions in a field where better and worse are mingled inextricably with difference of kind and degree of relevance?

The present inquiry proposes a plan that does not claim either logical or parliamentary exactness, but that does afford a rough way of getting at the central meanings and issues of mysticism. It is this: In all discussions of mysticism, from whatever point of view they are written, certain names occur over and over again. Plotinus, St. Paul, St. Augustine, Bernard of Clairvaux, John of Ruysbroeck almost always are mentioned. The Buddha, the philosophers of the Hindu Upanishads, the *Bhagavad-Gita* come into these treatises almost as frequently. Jacob Boehme, Swedenborg, George Fox are not so often mentioned, but they come in very frequently. Cornelius Agrippa, Paracelsus, Eckartshausen, Saint-Martin belong to another group who are sometimes listed, although not so often discussed, as of the center. And then each writer has his own additions. A student of mysticism who happens to be a student of philosophy, like Mr. Leuba, will speak at least in passing of Bradley, or Hocking, or Bergson, while a student of literature, like Miss Spurgeon, will be pretty certain to bring in Wordsworth and Browning, and Miss Underhill will not include either group.

But, however large the number of mystics which a particular writer draws upon, and however special the group he may include, there will always be a certain group whom everybody will sooner or later mention. And this group will be found to be fairly homogeneous with certain well-marked characteristics. That is, Bernard of Clairvaux, George Fox, and the Buddha are homogeneous in a sense in which George Fox and Browning and Paracelsus are not, homogeneous in purpose and accomplishment rather than in interest and temperament. These people are usually called the typical mystics. If they are compared for personality, for point of view, for purpose, for interest and experience with the other mystics who are mentioned less universally, it will be discovered that the typical mystics represent a more developed form of certain characteristics than do the others; that sometimes where only particular aspects are very fully developed in some of the lesser men, the great mystics are more complete, presenting more of the essential characteristics. For instance, a mystic philosopher and a mystic may have much the same philosophy, or intellectual body of conceptions, about God and man and the universe, but where the philosopher rests with theory, the mystic goes on into a practical realization. Again, the typical mystic and the alchemist may have much the same definition of God and much the same theory of God's relation to the world, but the alchemist may divide his attention between an interest in God for his own sake and an interest in God as the central factor in an understanding of the universe. In other words, the chief difference between the great mystic and one of his fellows not so distinguished may be one of concentration. And, finally, the difference may be one of sheer human quality. No one can read the work of Dr. Pordage and William Law and question the sifting of time that has left the former all but forgotten and the latter, for the student, at least, still living. And a comparison of the writings of William Law and Bernard of Clairvaux or Pascal again leaves no doubt of the part that a large imagination or a great mind or very real powers of leadership may play in the making of a great mystic.

In other words, a study of the typical mystics presents the field of mysticism at its highest level, at its most fully developed and most fully expressed level; one is tempted to say, at its most mystical. The value of such a definition of mysticism as is derived from this study of the great mystics is further enhanced by the fact that its main lines, so far as they lie within the field of ethics (and that is where they belong, for the most part), are the lines of the great ethical recensions of the world, both religious, like those of the Jewish and Christian traditions, and philosophical, like those of Aristotle and Confucius.

But to rest our whole understanding of the field of mystical experience upon our knowledge of the great mystics would be like defining poetry on the basis of Homer, Dante, and Shakespeare. There would still be Pope, and Morris, and Swinburne, and Mr. William Butler Yeats. And there would still be people to whom Shelley would mean more than all the immortals put together. The intensive study of the highly developed, specialized, classical forms, if you will, must be accompanied by at least a survey of the rest of the field and a recognition, however generalized, of its diversities. That will mean that the chapter on the typical mystics must be followed by a chapter, even though shorter, on the rest of the field.

The definition so arrived at will not be above cavil at any point. It will not be epigrammatic; it will give no magic phrase or rule of thumb; seldom will it be positively or universally definitive. Above all, it will be open at almost every point to the challenge of a different point of view. For it is very hard to write a scientific treatise on mysticism, and the present enterprise makes no such pretense. The psychologist who studies mysticism dispassionately as a psychological phenomenon is open to challenge from the mystic, for whom there is nothing phenomenal about it. The devotee is hardly to be trusted for a discriminating analysis, and the epistemologist cannot deny that his definitions leave the heart of the mystery untouched. The student of literature, who must avail himself of the contributions of all of these, establishes a still different relation to his subject. He is not equipped for the scrutiny of the scientist, and he is not a mystic. He is bound not to accept without question, and he is bound to understand even where he depreciates. The question of scientific reality is not so important for him as the question of human experience. The question of whether or not Bernard of Clairvaux entered into God is not so important for him as the question of what happened to Bernard of Clairvaux when he thought he did, and to what in terms of human feeling and purpose and achievement—of experience, in short—that adventure amounted. It is the humanist's approach. He is laying himself open to the challenge of the scientist and the philosopher, perhaps of the theologian, and certainly of the mystic. His defense will be that he does not pretend to be any of these, that he pleads guilty to the charge of encroaching upon fields other than his own, or more serious still of getting into waters too deep for his cunning, and that he will gladly accept any correction that is couched in terms he can under-- stand and use. Finally, he who undertakes such a definition must face the fact that at a hundred points his interpretation and his criticism rest upon premises that are by no means universally acceptable. His only defense here is that his premises will be challenged on the basis of other premises quite as unacceptable to him as his are to his critics, and so on, ad infinitum. But this does not relieve him of the responsibility of being as clear-headed and straightforward as he can be with the processes by which he reaches his conclusions.

The definition so reached, with all its imperfections on its head, ought to be a useful working definition. Even where least complete and secure, it will describe the reality in terms of feeling and of power as well as in terms of image and of concept. And even where challenged, it will open up issues of importance and suggest discriminations that will be stimulating to other points of view. And finally, it should, especially in vexed questions of value, put the problem and define issues in such a fashion that critics approaching the question from a different point of view will find the ground cleared for their greater acumen or wider experience to confirm or correct its conclusions.

CHAPTER III

THE TYPICAL MYSTICS

"The Soul is created eternal, and therefore she cannot rest but in God."
—St. Augustine

The tradition of the typical mystics covers almost three thousand years of human experience. Some of the most beautiful mystical writing in the world may be found in the Upanishads, the records of those lovers of "religion pure and undefiled," who, unsatisfied by the increasing complexity and formalism of Vedic ritual, retired to the forests of northern India almost a thousand years before Christ was born. About the same time one of the unknown authors of the *Mahabharata* paused in the story of the fight between the Kurus and the Pandus for that dialogue between the philosophic young Arjuna and the Master, Krishna, that for all its typical oriental repetition and prolixity makes the *Bhagavad-Gita* one of the spiritual landmarks of the Aryan world. These are the high points of the great mystical tradition of the Brahmans that in its early power produced some undoubted masters of the spiritual life, such as the sage, Yagnavalkya. When its first vigor had been spent, and the waters that had risen so high in the dialogue between Nakiketas and Death in the House of Yama[1] had run into the sands of the Brahman caste, Gotama Buddha started a movement that in the simplicity of its early days not only strikingly anticipated many features of the later Christian revelation, but in a curious fashion that has been generally misunderstood afforded a most impressive example of mystic discipline and achievement. About the same time in China, a little before Confucius gathered together the "wisdom of the ancients" into one of the classical recensions of ethics, the philosopher, Lao Tzu, set down in the *Tao Teh King* the first surviving exposition of a certainly much older mystical teaching, the Tao.

[1] "Sacred Books of the East," XV. *Upanishads, Kath.*, edited by F. Max Müller (Oxford, 1879).

52

About two hundred years later Plato reported, or put into the mouth of his master, Socrates, a series of very informal teachings that, while they are not mystical in the central sense we are examining, have nevertheless proved a perennially fruitful and stimulating source of inspiration to succeeding generations of mystics. More definitely mystical, but not quite so stimulating ethically or imaginatively, was the philosophy of Plotinus, in the third century of our era. Plotinus seems to have believed that he carried the philosophy of Plato to its logical mystical heights. That is true, but the process seriously unsettled that robust emotional and imaginative balance which is perhaps the most remarkable aspect of Socrates' genius.

"The Jews require a sign, and the Greeks seek after wisdom,"[2] observed one whose writings would suggest that to a rare degree he combined the virtues of both races. Between Plato and Plotinus had come a new revelation that was destined in an extraordinary degree to minister to the needs of both types of mind. Moreover, it was destined to produce a long succession of mystics. In the first century of its history St. Paul and the author of the Fourth Gospel are the most distinguished. The fourth century brought St. Augustine, and the fifth, that unknown writer, probably an Alexandrian, who, as Dionysius the Areopagite, influenced more than any other the mystical thought of the Middle Ages. In spite of signs of undoubted mystical tendencies in the lives of various saints, the Dark Ages produced no mystic of distinction except the somewhat ambiguous John Scotus Erigena, who translated the writings of Dionysius. But in the Near East the extraordinarily rapid development of Mohammedanism had already, in less than two centuries after the flight of Mahomet to Medina (A.D. 622), led to mysticism in the appearance in Persia, toward the end of the eighth century, of the white-robed Sufis. From about the eleventh to the fourteenth centuries of our era they were to achieve the expression of various degrees of mystical experience in the works of a very interesting and gifted succession of poets. From the saintly Al-Ghazzali (1058–1111) to the bibulous and erotic Hafiz (d. 1388) we run a gamut of mystical experience and expression that in itself might furnish forth

[2] I Cor. 1:22.

a complete exposition of the weakness and strength of mysticism. Meanwhile the development of Western civilization and religion had again made possible the expression of Christian mysticism. The result is a period of remarkable mystical activity finding its apogee in the twelfth, thirteenth, and fourteenth centuries, but carrying on with diminished volume and different emphasis into the fifteenth, sixteenth, and seventeenth centuries. Every one of the great countries of Europe contributed of its finest in genius, in spiritual power, often in literary gifts, to this great drive of the human spirit "beyond the utmost bound of human thought."

The spectacle of these twenty-seven centuries is impressive not only for the picturesque variety of time and nation, circumstance and personality, but much more so for the extraordinary agreement on essentials to be found in teachings and testimonies that have arisen from such diverse sources. Gotama Buddha was the eldest son of a king before he left all to become the Buddha, and Catherine of Sienna was the youngest daughter of a poor wool-dyer; in John Tauler we breathe the air of criticism, of restlessness, that two centuries later was to precipitate the German Reformation, while in St. John of the Cross we find much of the doctrinal self-consciousness, the fear of the spurious and the heretical, that characterized the Spain of the Counter Reformation; to Julian of Norwich, God was pre-eminently Love (the simplicity and intimacy of her experience is shown by the fact that she uses the word "homely" in describing God's way with her), while to Ignatius Loyola he was above all a just God, and the difference may be measured by a comparison of the joyous pages of the *Revelations of Divine Love* with the somber pages of the *Spiritual Exercises* that dwell so terribly on the darker possibilities of another world. The Master of the Upanishads had been student, citizen, husband, father, priest, had performed all the social duties of his community before he divided his property among his heirs and went forth into the forest, and John of Ruysbroeck, from the time his uncle the priest and a priest friend took in the clever little runaway of eleven to live with them in the shadow of the great Cathedral of St. Gudule until he died in the wood of Groenendael, lived the life of a monk. But in the essentials of their undertaking and of their achievement, Brahman and

Buddhist, Catholic and Protestant, Mohammedan and Greek, of two centuries ago or of thirty centuries ago meet and agree.

In general, however widely divergent the circumstances under which great mystics have appeared, in certain fundamental respects they have been very much alike. First of all, the mystic is usually the product of a definite and well-developed tradition. The roots of even the very untheological Upanishads lie deep in the Vedas of the primitive Aryans; the Buddha was a heretic, if you will, but the basis of his teaching, with all its originality, was the wisdom of many centuries; Al-Ghazzali was one of the greatest of Persian scholars, with some three centuries of Sufiistic lore at his finger tips; Plotinus gathered up the fruits of some five centuries of Platonism, to say nothing of the occult odds and ends of all antiquity that made the fascination of the Rome and the Alexandria of his day; Bonaventura is an encyclopedia of the twelve hundred years of Christian thinkers who had preceded him; Jacob Boehme, whom, of all men, one would most expect to be innocent of any undue influence of the past, is clearly the product of a mingling of medieval chemistry, if not alchemy, and popular German Protestantism, to say nothing of the great tradition of the Old Testament upon which he drew so heavily. Curiously enough, it would seem that the more firmly fixed, the more authoritative the religious tradition, the simpler, the more direct, the more profound the teaching of the mystic. For all its scholastic subtlety of analysis, the writing of a Bonaventura is simpler than that of a Jacob Boehme or a William Law. The difference is probably due to the fact that an authoritative religious tradition tends, particularly in the region of metaphysics, to limit the field of speculation, partly also to the fact that it disciplines the logical while it restrains the myth-making faculties. Be that as it may, there can be no doubt that mysticism of a distinguished order is a flower that blooms only on long and carefully cultivated stems.

But the mystic is no blind follower of his tradition. Usually he appears at a critical moment of its history when the first fine power of its revelation is being lost sight of in the inevitable conventionality and inertia of everyday human practice. The main injunctions of an epistle can be repeated from generation to generation, but the ethical strenuousness of a St. Paul is a rare quality that with the ages must run the gauntlet of all the weakness and blindness of human nature. Again, very few religions have been able long to do without some form of ritual and ceremonial that may satisfy one of the noblest of human ambitions, that of making its offering and saying its prayer as beautifully as possible; yet even at their simplest, when the first ardor of religious passion informs the most elaborate of its external symbols with the constant sense of its purpose, they afford the temptation to formalism and superstition. Again, few religions have been able to develop institutions or assimilate a large number of proselytes without recourse to formulation and apologetics; yet there is the source of the aridities of scholasticism. Indifference, formalism, and rationalism—these are the three great foes of the continued life of the religious spirit. Against these the mystic invokes the reality which his contemporaries have lost sight of in their preoccupation with the machinery of its conquest. Whether it be the Master of the Upanishads retiring from the complexity of Vedic rite to meditate on the realities behind the elaborate show, or St. Paul appealing from the legalism of the Pharisees to the spirit of the law in Christ, or the retreat of the fourteenth-century Richard Rolle from the increasing rationalism of the University of Oxford—again and again we discover the same phenomenon.

Always it is from his tradition that the typical mystic draws the power by which he criticizes that tradition. It is his own personal vision of the truth that sends him forward, but the truth is not his fancy or his construction. It is the light that his fellows have let grow dim in their weakness and blindness that he beholds again and strives to rekindle for the others. The sources of his power, the initial impulsion, and the goal toward which he strives in his revolt— all these he derives from his tradition.

Most critics of lukewarmness, formalism, and rationalism do not, however, become mystics. More is needed: the special temper, the genius of the mystic. This does not mean the ability to see the world of the spirit in visions. Much has been said about the mystic's power over the supernatural, but most of it is to little purpose. For to him who believes, the objections of the non-believer will seem sceptical and perverse. To the sceptic the asseveration of the believer will merely savor of superstition and weak-minded credulity. One thing is certain, however: most of those who see visions and dream dreams are in no sense of the word mystics. If we grant all that the most literal believer could demand, we need not say that such phenomena go beyond the elementary stages of the mystic way. The greatest mystics either place relatively little emphasis upon such manifestations, or are frankly critical of them. The eastern mystics deal very little in such matters. Most of the Catholic mystics, of course, esteem visions highly as favors of God, but the greatest hold with St. John of the Cross, that the soul should not lean upon imaginary visions, forms, and figures, but should reject them that it may go on to things of greater profit.[3]

But three qualities we may note in all the typical mystics: first, an intense and immediate consciousness of spiritual reality; second, an extraordinary faculty of spiritual concentration; and third, great ethical strenuousness. From the point of view of the mystic, the last is a by-product; from the point of view of the student of human nature, it is his most significant and winning quality. Mystics are lovers of the reality that lies behind the shows of things, lovers of goodness, lovers of God. Most of us are well described by the words of the Indian sage: "Though they have been told that there is a grove before them, they cling to a small shrub." But the mystics are more fastidious, for where their fellow-men are content to muddle about in perpetual compromise and uncertainty, the mystics cannot rest. They are more exacting, for where most of us beguile ourselves with pleasure and business even while we acknowledge the transitoriness and the emptiness thereof, they will have nothing short of perfect felicity. And where most of us scatter and dissipate, they concentrate. Divers rare and beautiful gifts of mind and spirit do they possess, but the heart of their genius is to be found in these three things: a deep and immediate consciousness of the reality of the spirit, a rare ability to concentrate all upon one end, and an ethical strenuousness that is the inevitable and logical outcome in such spirits of their way of looking at the world.

[3] St. John of the Cross, *Complete Works*, translated by David Lewis (London, 1864), I, 118.

Whatever haziness popular belief may attribute to mysticism, there is nothing hazy about the way of looking at the world that has characterized the typical mystic. First of all, he affirms the existence of a reality beyond the ken of the senses, essentially and eternally different from the order of things which the senses can report to him. And, secondly, he declares that it is that reality which the senses can never touch, and not the seeming reality about which they so distractingly busy themselves, that is his sole concern. Other things there are, many, and interesting, and delightful, but they are not his affair. The first of these two affirmations is the basis of his faith; the second, of his conduct.

The first essential of the mystic's view of the world is, therefore, a sharp discrimination between what the senses cannot perceive and what the senses can perceive, between being and non-being, the self and the illusion of the Brahmans, the form and the matter of Plotinus, the God and the creatures, the spirit and the body of the Christians. Not all mystics have agreed as to the reality of the sceond member of each of these pairs, but all have agreed as to its immeasurable inferiority to the first. Where does man stand with regard to this dualism? All the great mystics agree that this dualism finds its consummation in man. All agree that his body belongs to the inferior and less real order, and that what we call his soul belongs to the superior. Bernard of Clairvaux, for instance, likens the relation of the soul to the body to the sojourn of a great lord in the cottage of a peasant.[4] Not all mystics are ascetics in the rather extreme sense in which that word is usually understood, but all mystics recognize the essential dualism of man's nature, the law of the body warring against the law of the soul, and the necessity of man's spirit, enlightened and purified, wielding absolute mastery over the law of the body. "For," as St. Paul says, "to be carnally minded is death; but to be spiritually minded is life and peace."[5] The mystics have held that this mastery must be dearly bought. Their conviction is that of Epictetus: "Life is a soldier's service."

In that warfare, however, the mystic believes that the spirit of man has a powerful ally, for he believes that there already exists a

[4] *Life and Works of Saint Bernard*, editor, Dom John Mabillon; translated and edited by Samuel J. Eales (London, 1896), III, 284.
[5] Rom. 8:6.

relation between the soul of man and the spiritual reality. To the Brahmanic pantheist, man's soul is an emanation, a portion of the Universal Soul or Atman, for the moment of a lifetime imprisoned in the body as a portion of the air in a room may be shut within a vase;[6] to the Christian, the soul is a spirit that God breathed into man, the image of God, in itself the very stuff of reality.[7] It is this relation between the soul of the individual and the World-Soul, the Absolute, or God, that makes possible the soul's attaining to direct and immediate contact with Supreme Reality even in this life. And that contact is the goal of the mystic.

Here the mystic parts company with many whose vagaries have often been laid at his door, the magician, the alchemist, the obscurantist. Where they are seeking for knowledge, or power, or beauty, or mystery, he will have none of these. For his goal is reality itself, or, to use the conception with which the majority of us in the western world are familiar, it is God himself. The testimony of the mystics is unanimous that even the slight knowledge of God that sends the mystic on his long road produces a profound contempt for any other knowledge. As Jami sings:

> All that is not One must ever
> Suffer with the wound of absence;
> And whoever in Love's city
> Enters, finds but room for One.[8]

"God," said Matthew Arnold, "is the power not ourselves that makes for righteousness." The man who made that statement was one of the most spiritual-tempered men of the nineteenth century; there have been few men in any age to whom the spiritual experience of the race was a greater reality; but that definition, in its cautiousness, lacks the accent of certainty, and in the coolness of its precision it wants that emotional warmth that comes only from immediate realization. Yet even to the faith of the mystic the definition of his goal is one of the most difficult tasks that ever the brain of man essayed. For by definition the senses, upon the basis of

[6] "Sacred Books of the East." I. *Upanishads, Khand.*, edited by F. Max Müller (Oxford, 1879), III, chap. xii, pp. 8–9; chap. xiv, pp. 3–4.

[7] *Sancti Bonaventurae, operum tomus septimus* (Lugduni, 1668), p. 126.

[8] Jami, *The Persian Mystics.* II. Translated by F. Hadland Davis (London, 1908), p. 50.

which man has built his very language, cannot compass the spirit. The very rudiments of his thought and language have therefore compelled the mystic to resort to symbol for what is to him the one reality, to synthesis for what is really immanent, to transcendence for that which is of all things the nearest, to negation for the only thing that is positive. In this effort to express what never can be expressed, far more difficult than to give in terms of color the sound of a whisper, in terms of dynamics the impetus of a thought, the mystic has of course failed, but his failure is colored by an imaginative and emotional exaltation not to be found in the definitions of the philosopher. Even translation into an alien tongue cannot take away the light of this litany of Krishna:

> I am the offering, I am the sacrifice, I am the oblation, I am the libation; I am the chant, I am the holy oil, I am the fire, I am what is offered. . . . .
> I am the way, the supporter, the lord, the witness, the home, the refuge, the beloved; the forth-coming, and withdrawing, the place, the treasure, the everlasting seed.
> I give warmth, I withhold the rain and send it forth; I am immortality and death, existent and non-existent, O Arjuna.[9]

Again, the terms may be the terms of philosophy, but the temper is that of religion in words like Krishna's: "I am the goodness of the good,"[10] or Jami's: "The Absolute Beauty is the Divine Majesty endued with [the attributes of] power and bounty. Every beauty and perfection manifested in the theatre of the various grades of beings is a ray of His perfect beauty reflected therein."[11]

This belief of the mystics that God is the source of all that is good or serviceable or lovely in this world has been the basis of the positive, constructive descriptions of God. These descriptions—because of their logical looseness and generality one can hardly call them definitions—have been fruitful in their power to impress the hearer with a sense of the omnipotence of God and to elevate his imagination and to inspire him with devotion, but they leave the heart of the mystery still unexplored. To that mystery those who approach God by the negative path come logically nearer, although they lose much in imaginative suggestion and emotional quality.

[9] *Bhagavad-Gita*, translated by Charles Johnston (Flushing, New York, 1908), IX, 16, 18, 19.
[10] *Ibid.*, X, 36.   [11] *Jami*, p. 57.

The basis of their effort is a frank and consistent recognition of the fact that the Supreme Reality is inaccessible to the senses. For the Christians the pseudo-Dionysius gives the most famous expression to this point of view in that chapter of the *Mystical Theology* where he declares that God is above all human categories and perceptions, and resorts to that famous series of negations that is one of the world's most logical definitions of the Supreme:

> We say that the cause of all things, who is Himself above all things, is neither without being nor without life, nor without reason nor without intelligence; nor is He a body; nor has He form or shape, or quality or quantity or mass; He is not localised or visible or tangible; He is neither sensitive nor sensible; He is subject to no disorder or disturbance arising from material passion; He is not subject to failure of power, or to the accidents of sensible things; He needs no light; He suffers no change or corruption or division, or privation or flux; and He neither has nor is anything else that belongs to the senses.
>
> Again, ascending we say that He is neither soul nor intellect; nor has He imagination, nor opinion or reason; He has neither speech nor understanding, and is neither declared nor understood; He is neither number nor order, nor greatness nor smallness, nor equality nor likeness nor unlikeness; He does not stand or move or rest; He neither has power nor is power; nor is He light, nor does He live, nor is He life; He is neither being nor age nor time; nor is He subject to intellectual contact; He is neither knowledge nor truth, nor royalty nor wisdom; He is neither one nor unity, nor divinity, nor goodness; nor is He spirit, as we understand spirit; He is neither sonship nor fatherhood nor anything else known to us or to any other beings, either of the things that are or the things that are not; nor does anything that is, know Him as He is, nor does He know anything that is as it is; He has neither word nor knowledge; He is neither darkness nor light nor truth nor error; He can neither be affirmed nor denied; nay, though we may affirm or deny the things that are beneath Him, we can neither affirm or deny Him; for the perfect and sole cause of all is above all affirmation, and that which transcends all is above all subtraction, absolutely separate, and beyond all that is. . . . . For God abides above created intellect and existence, and is in such sense unknowable and non-existent that He exists above all existence, and is known above all power of knowledge.[13]

Here is where the western mind, seemingly less at home among abstractions and negations than the eastern (of course this statement is open to the challenge of possible confusion of cause and

[13] A. B. Sharpe, *Mysticism: Its True Nature and Value, with a Translation of the "Mystical Theology" of Dionysius, and of the "Letters to Caius and Dorotheus"* (London, 1910), pp. 220–25.

effect), was more fortunate in Christianity's gift of a mediator, of One who combined both the nature of God and the nature of man. Christ is divine and ineffable, but on one side at least He is knowable. Bernard of Clairvaux recognized this when he said that "a principal cause why God, who is invisible, willed to render Himself visible in the Flesh, and to dwell as a Man among men, was to draw in the first place, to the salutary love of His sacred Flesh all the affections of carnal men who were unable to love otherwise than in a carnal manner, and so by degrees to draw them to a pure and spiritual affection."[14] The more speculative, the more highly intellectual of Christian mystics, while availing themselves of all the opportunities which that relation affords for symbolism, have gone hardily on into the unknowable. But the less intellectual have in that mediator enjoyed an opportunity for mystical life and expression that would hardly be available for the corresponding type in the East. Only the God who had become man could be the object of an address like Richard Rolle's:

> Jhesu my dere & my drewrye,
> Delyte thou arte to synge;
> Jhesu my myrthe and my melodye;
> In to thi lufe me brynge.
>
> Jhesu, Jhesu, my hony swete
> My herte, my comforthynge:
> Jhesu, all my bales thou bete
> And to thi blysse me brynge.[15]

Although it has also opened the way for dubious elements of visions and supernatural appearances, this conception of the Incarnation has in general humanized spiritual life.

But if the spirit be essentially unknowable to the flesh, how is the soul of man to lay hold upon reality? Certainly not through the senses, for they have nothing of kindred nature whereby they may lay hold upon the spirit; certainly not by the routine operations of the reason, for the best that may be achieved by their agency is a scientific or philosophic generalization or analysis of material derived from the senses. How then is man to know God? By that in

[14] Bernard, *op. cit.*, IV, 113.

[15] *Richard Rolle of Hampole*, edited by C. Horstman (London, 1895), I, 365, ll. 65–72.

which he is like unto God. In that all mystics agree. Man will not come to God in vision or audition or revelation, but within his own soul. In varying forms all mystics reiterate St. Paul's "Know ye not that ye are the temple of God, and that the Spirit of God dwelleth in you?"[16] The words that brought light to Madame Guyon: "The trouble is, Madame, that you are looking outside for what you have within. Accustom yourself to seeking God in your own heart, and you will find him there";[17] Law's: "Thou seest, hearest, and feelest nothing of God because . . . . thou seekest for Him in books, in Controversies, in the Church, and outward Exercises, but *there* thou wilt not find Him, till thou hast *first* found Him in thy Heart";[18] St. Augustine's wonder: "And men go abroad to wonder at the heights of mountains, the lofty billows of the sea, the long courses of rivers, the vast compass of the ocean, and the circular motions of the stars, and yet pass themselves by"—[19] all repeat the same story.

The mystic way is therefore essentially an interior way. The external is worthy of consideration only as it affects the internal; it has absolutely no primary or independent value. Consequently, such things as mystic rituals and formulas have no intrinsic significance. For it is by that part of his spirit most like unto reality that man attains to knowledge of that reality. The identification of the faculty by which man attains to reality depends upon the psychology back of the individual mystic's interpretation of his own experience. That in turn varies greatly with the individual. For instance, the psychology of John Gerson, chancellor of the University of Paris, or of Richard, prior of St. Victor, is infinitely more complicated than that of the nun, Mechtild of Magdeburg. The medieval scholastic with his genius for dissecting and labeling was acutely aware of the complexity of the human spirit; the eastern sage, on the other hand, was much less interested in internal machinery. Between these we have all degrees both of psychological complexity and psychological awareness.

[16] I Cor. 3:16.

[17] *La Vie de Madame Jeanne Marie Bouvieres de la Mothe-Guyon, écrite par elle-même* (Paris, 1791), I, 78.

[18] William Law, "The Spirit of Prayer," *Works* (London, 1762), VII, 59.

[19] St. Augustine, *Confessions*, translated by William Watts (London, 1912), II, 99–101.

All mystics recognize in human nature a dualism analogous to that which we have viewed in the universe at large, a higher and a lower part in man. The lower part they usually attribute to man's body, the higher they attribute to reality. The eastern mystics are fond of conceiving of the senses and the passions and the desires of man as spirited and rebellious horses ever straining against the guiding hand of him who drives the chariot, the soul. Should the wild horses slip from the grip of the driver, the soul would be over-powered, and the senses and the passions would rule the whole man. To the Buddhist, to whom the body and the demands it made upon the nature of man always seemed vile and sinful, such a disaster meant the perpetuation of the pain and sin and ignominy of exist-ence. To the Christian mystic the triumph of the natural man has always meant the death of the spiritual, both in this life and in eternity, for the Christian church has always believed with Boehme: "Whatsoever thou buildest and sowest here in the *Spirit*, be it with Words, Works or Thoughts, *that* will be thy eternal House."[20] For every great mystic spiritual progress has required at least perfected self-mastery; for practically all, that degree of abstinence and con-trol that constitutes the less extreme form of asceticism. Note the unanimity of these voices:

Al-Ghazzali:

I saw that one can only hope for salvation by devotion and the conquest of one's passions, a procedure which presupposes renouncement and detach-ment from this world of falsehood in order to turn towards eternity and medi-tation on God.[21]

Thomas à Kempis:

Who is so full of hindrance and annoyance to thee as thine own undis-ciplined heart?[22]

The Master of the *Bhagavad-Gita:*

With soul-vision kept pure, firmly self-controlled, detached from sounds and other sense-objects, and discarding lust and hate;
Seeking solitude, eating little, with speech, body and mind controlled, given up to union through soul-vision, following ever after dispassion;

[20] Jacob Behmen, "The Aurora," *Works,* translated by William Law (London, 1764), I, Bk. I, chap. xviii, 54.

[21] Al-Ghazzali, *The Confessions,* translated by Claud Field (London, 1909), pp. 42–43.

[22] Thomas à Kempis, "The Harvard Classics." VII. *The Imitation of Christ,* trans-lated by William Benham (New York, 1909), I, chap. iii, 3.

Getting free from vanity, violence, pride, lust, wrath, avarice, without desire of possessions, full of peace, he builds for union with the Eternal.[23]

The mystics on the whole have not believed in the natural goodness of man. On the other hand, they have not generally gone to the extreme of denying the reality of man's aspiration to goodness. Most of them have conceived of man as a pilgrim, an exile, a wanderer, in whom for the time being a soul that certainly had the capabilities of a higher life was caught in the net of this existence. "Soul" is, of course, a vague term, any adequate definition of which must take into account a good many different elements. For us only one is important—that faculty by means of which man lays hold upon reality or draws nigh unto God. Plato, for instance, makes the reason the center of the soul. It is therefore by the intellect that the Platonist will apprehend the Idea of the Good. The Brahman and the Buddhist do not localize the faculty, but in their insistence that only the wise man can obtain the knowledge of the supreme, they practically agree with the Platonist. The Christians in general have tended to minimize the intellectual aspect, so that man instead of glorying in his natural faculties might rather render homage to the grace of God, and so that man in his uncertainty amid the data of the senses might rely upon the certainty of faith. It was for this reason that Bernard of Clairvaux worked so hard for the condemnation of Abelard, whom he charged with relying solely upon reason to scrutinize mysteries that were intended to be apprehended by faith alone.[24] For the Christian church has always made much of the words of its Founder to Thomas: "Because thou hast seen me, thou hast believed: blessed are they that have not seen, and yet have believed."[25] The reason for this difference is not hard to guess. The mysticism of the Upanishads is the outgrowth of a system of religious society that had its origin in a conquering race that jealously guarded its sacred lore from the aboriginals around it. The acquisition of that lore certainly involved intellectual discipline; in the long run it undoubtedly involved intellectual superiority. On the contrary, Christianity rises in a revelation delivered to unlettered fishermen. So much for the superficial facts of his-

[23] *Bhagavad-Gita*, XVIII, 51–53.
[24] Bernard, *op. cit.*, II, 872.   [25] John 20:29.

tory. In the sequel the Buddha opened the gates to the lowly of the Hindus, and the wise of this world molded the church.

On the whole, intellectual sans-culottism has not been the characteristic of Christian mysticism. Pride of intellect, like pride of any sort, the Christian church has consistently opposed, but the reason, that holds the passions and the senses in leash, Christian mysticism has not touched. With Aristotle, Bernard of Clairvaux makes the power to govern by reason the distinguishing "endowment and prerogative" of man.[26] What mystics like Richard Rolle of Hampole have arraigned is the reason that rejects every testimony of which the senses cannot bear witness. Unspeculative minds like those of Bernard of Clairvaux and John Tauler have for the most part contented themselves with asserting the existence of a spiritual faculty above the reason, that, unaided by the senses, experiences reality. Bernard of Clairvaux, for instance, contents himself with saying: "These events [the coming and going of the Bridegroom of the Soul] take place by the inward sense of the soul."[27] It is hard to see how this conception differs substantially from what Plato calls the "Soul's own pure apprehension of pure existence."[28] In that sense we may call it intuition. But trained speculators like Richard of St. Victor and St. Bonaventura have organized the inner world, like the outer, into a hierarchy of ascending powers in which the series usually runs in the order of Bonaventura: *Sensus, imaginatio, ratio, intellectus, intelligentia, apex mentis, seu synderesis scintilla.*[29] The last, "the highest point of the mind," we may safely call intuition, if we remember that, contrary to much current misunderstanding, intuition is not an act of the imagination, a faculty of which mysticism has been traditionally suspicious. Intuition is a super-rational apprehension of super-rational truth, an interior enlightenment, what a contemporary philosopher has called "total-working."[30] So defined, it may be

[26] Bernard, *op. cit.*, IV, 232.

[27] Bernard, *op. cit.*, IV, 455.

[28] Plato, *Dialogues*, translated by B. Jowett (Oxford, 1892), II, 227; "Phaedo," 83.

[29] Bonaventura, *op. cit.*, p. 126. We have the best example of the Christian intellectual in what immediately follows: "Hos gradus habemus in nobis plantatos per naturam, deformatos per culpam, reformatos per gratiam, purgandos per iustitiam, exercendos per scientiam, perficiendos per sapientiam."

[30] Charles Bennett, *A Philosophical Study of Mysticism* (New Haven, 1923), p. 97.

questioned if the intuition of the Christian and the knowledge of the Brahman are so far apart as superficially they appear to be.

The practical identity of "knowledge" and "intuition" becomes apparent when we look at the various forms of preparation which they require. The underlying motive of this preparation is probably most clearly revealed in a relatively crude form of mystic effort that will serve as a more tangible analogue for the preparation of the great mystics. To those philosophers of the later days of the Roman Empire who proceeded upon the Ptolemaic view of the universe the soul was a form of matter, originally of etherial purity and lightness, whose destiny was the heights of the fiery empyrean. In its sojourn in this world it inevitably came into contact with heavier and grosser matter. If by scrupulous purity of conduct it retained its pristine lightness, upon its release from the body by death, it immediately sprang to its natural abode; but if in its earthly career it had become clogged with impunity, then its ascent was impeded by the physical weight of its corruption, and it could not join its purer friends.[31] The conception is significant. Sin and earthliness weigh upon the soul's aspiration. Only the spirit free from corruption shall touch the spirit; God will come only into a pure soul.

Therefore all mysticism presupposes an ethical and spiritual discipline. George Fox and Ignatius Loyola would differ perhaps violently on the subject of the candor of the Society of Jesus; Jacob Boehme and John of Ruysbroeck would certainly not be of the same mind about the function of the clergy, and Bernard of Clairvaux might not see at once the difference between Al-Ghazzali and the Muslim against whom he preached a crusade, but all would agree that the discipline of the lower man, or the senses, or the natural man, is essential to mystical achievement. Only to the Brahman whose passions were quieted, whose senses were subdued, whose faculties were uplifted, was the knowledge of the One, the Self (the Universal Soul) possible.[32] Rite or ritual, beauty, wit, learning, or wisdom—none of these would avail if the conflict within had not been adjusted on a firm and stable basis of mastery of

---

[31] This account is indebted to a very interesting lecture which M. Franz Cumont delivered at the University of Wisconsin, March 29, 1921.

[32] *Upanishads, Kath.*, I, 2, 24.

the lower by the higher. For Hindu, Brahman or Buddhist, for Greek and Mohammedan, for Christian, both Protestant and Catholic, that is the minimum requirement. Whether the mystic hoped to proceed by the knowledge of the Brahman, or the love of the Christian, the first step was always an ethical one.

As for the details of that preparation, they vary with the common religious or philosophical life from which the mystic emerges. As noted above, the great mystics have come out of the great movements of the religious and philosophical life of the race. They have not been antinomians. Many of the sages of the Upanishads felt keenly the arid days upon which Vedic inspiration had fallen; yet we have no reason to suppose that they had therefore failed to fulfill the duties of the state of the householder while they were in it, or that they advocated that others should refuse to do so. No reformer of a century and a half later felt more keenly or denounced more bitterly the insufferable corruption of the church of her day than did Catherine of Sienna, and yet the church had no more loyal or energetic supporter and example of the life it was intended to promote. George Fox founded a sect of enthusiasts that gave more worry to the authority of his day, both secular and religious, than most lawbreakers; yet for all its fanaticism of detail, the teaching of his life is the ethics of the great Christian tradition of purity, humility, kindliness, and self-control, and his constant effort is to rest his doctrine upon the one authority the non-conformist of his day could recognize—Scripture. Sects there have been in the Christian church like some of the Brothers of the Free Spirit in the Middle Ages, who, under cover of a mystical pretext, have flouted the common morality of their day for moral license, but they have so far produced no great master of the spiritual life. One may impute this failure to the vigilance of the Inquisition, but the Inquisition has proved singularly unsuccessful in obliterating truth and genius. We may say then that in this region the mystic has not left the way of his fellow-men, but has gone farther in that way.

For that going beyond the common effort, more than the natural strenuousness of the mystic is responsible. It will be remembered that we found that one of his distinguishing traits is a rare ability to concentrate upon the goal of his aspiration. The region of the spirit is a very delicate one, easily disturbed, easily over-whelmed. The very qualities that constitute the great attraction of the mystic's temperament, his sensitiveness, his ardor, are also a menace to his keeping the path upon which he has set out. The world is full of many beautiful and absorbing things that for most men are not only innocent, but profitable; yet they are not what he is seeking. There are people in the world to call forth his great faculty of love, and there is nothing that has done more to make men men than their loving of others; but he is not seeking men. All the things interesting and beautiful and lovable he is gifted to appreciate better than most men; but what he is seeking is incomparably more interesting and beautiful and lovable. "All the riches and glory of the whole creation compared with the true riches, which is God, is supreme poverty and meanness."[33] So he leaves the things that warm the lives of other men and goes forth on a lonelier and a stricter way. Viewed in that light, asceticism has much less in it to touch our pity than we usually think.

But this asceticism of abstinence that all mystics of the great tradition have practised is only one aspect of asceticism. The other is what we may call the asceticism of mortification. It is comparatively easy to renounce all worldly pleasure when one has seen another pleasure that makes the first pale. It is easy to light a candle in a still air, but when all the gusts of the gathering winds beat against it, it is hard to keep that flame tall and clear. So with the law of the spirit and the law of nature: one may pull the rein hard and tight, but at every turn in the road those spirited steeds will jerk and pull. So the mystic sets out to weaken that rebellious strength, to mortify by pain and deprivation the exuberant lusts of mind and body.

The literature of the asceticism of mortification is not pleasant reading; for instance, the autobiography of the Blessed Henry Suso, however edifying to the pious, cannot but be repulsive to any-one with even a spark of imagination. That much of the mortification practised in the interest of mysticism has tended to distraction of interest, that much of it has tended to disturb that inner balance of faculty so essential if the mystic is not to render himself liable to

[33] St. John of the Cross, *op. cit.*, I, 17.

the aberrations of fanaticism and delusion, is evident. In all probability the Middle Ages never went so far as the East, the home of the extremes of luxurious self-indulgence and fanatical self-torture. But the mystics themselves have, most of them, been aware of the dangers of mortification; and most mystical writers, while recognizing it as one of the great resources of the mystic discipline, have cautioned against excess that might weaken the soul's power to work out its salvation. For instance, Catherine of Sienna writes to "Sister Daniella of Orvieto clothed with the habit of Saint Dominic who not being able to carry out her great penances had fallen into deep affliction":

Penance to be sure must be used as a tool, in due times and places, as need may be. If the flesh, being too strong, kicks against the spirit, penance takes the rod of discipline, and fast, and the cilice of many buds, and mighty vigils; and places burdens enough on the flesh, that it may be more subdued. But if the body is weak, fallen into illness, the rule of discretion does not approve of such a method. Nay, not only should fasting be abandoned, but flesh be eaten; if once a day is not enough, then four times. If one cannot stand up, let him stay on his bed; if he cannot kneel, let him sit or lie down, as he needs. This discretion demands. Therefore it insists that penance be treated as a means and not as a chief desire.[34]

But in spite of abuse and excess, and in spite of its seeming superfluity in the face of life's abundant opportunities for vigorous self-denial, there is no doubt that the asceticism of mortification has helped many in their battle against man's worst enemy, the lust within.

While in general this period of preparation has always had a definite beginning, it is difficult to set any precise bounds to it. The Brahman's preparation began when, as little more than a child, he went bearing fuel (the traditional sign of the disciple approaching the master) to the house of his master, where, in the intervals of tending the cattle and building the fire and sweeping the hearth, he learned from his master's lips the Vedas, the divine revelations that his people had for centuries handed down from master to disciple. Arrived at man's estate, he returned to his father's house, took a wife, and began the duties of a householder, and later, of a head of a

[34] *Saint Catherine of Siena as Seen in Her Letters*, translated by Vida D. Scudder (London, 1905), p. 148.

family. When he had seen his son's son on his knee, he disposed of his property, took leave of his family, left behind the complicated rites that he had performed all his life, and went forth without worldly tie to the simple life of the forest for prayer and meditation and conversation of high things.

The preparation, therefore, that the mystic life presupposed among the Brahmans was extensive, arduous, and thoroughgoing. The Buddhist mystic was a monk, a Bhikkhu, devoted to a life of chastity, of poverty, of abstinence, of prayer and meditation. In its primitive simplicity this life went to a degree of rigor and concentration that different external circumstances and a more balanced view of human activity made uncongenial to Christian monasticism, which has in general been mindful of St. Benedict's advice, "To act with prudence and not try too much lest whilst too violently scouring off the rust the vessel itself be broken."

Christian mysticism in the Middle Ages usually had its preparation in the life of the priest or monk or nun, or in the highly developed life of religious activity and observance that the church made possible even for a laywoman. Catherine of Sienna began her strenuous religious career in a cell in her own home, where she seems to have practised a life of more than monastic austerity. Rulman Merswin, the mysterious layman who played so large a part in the career of John Tauler and the evolution of the "Friends of God" in the Germany of the fourteenth century, is the most conspicuous example of a lay mystic in the Middle Ages, and the little we know of his career suggests that his way of life even "in the world" was one of vigorous religious absorption. As for the monk and the priest, whatever the use made of it by the majority, their life certainly offered plenty of opportunity for the development of the mystic.

But striking as is the agreement on the ethical preparations necessary for the mystic life, there is on the surface considerable disagreement among the descriptions which various mystics have given of the way by which the mystic shall set out toward his goal. For Brahman and for Platonist it is the way of knowledge; for Buddhist, the way of renunciation; for Christian, the way of love. On the surface the disagreement is irreconcilable; it would be sophistical to attempt to overlook that disparity; but if one examines into just what each of these terms means, he will find that they are not so far apart as our usual definitions would suggest.

The Brahman at this point speaks much of knowledge, of wisdom. At first the nature of that wisdom seems disappointingly simple, until one remembers that simplicity is one of the characteristics of wisdom. For the most part, it deals with three things: it attempts to express the speaker's experience of what reality is; it reiterates, in terms of varying picturesqueness, in figure, and in parable, the fundamental thesis that reality is to be found only within the spirit; and it offers very general suggestions as to how that difficult feat of reaching reality within one's own soul may be accomplished. Moreover, it is understood that this knowledge is to be imparted only to him who is intellectually ready for it, and that it is of avail only to him who is ethically and spiritually enlightened.

Buddhist renunciation means the absolute liberation—of man's intellect, of his imagination, of his affections—from all earthly liens, essentially an act of the will, as the Buddha said in an address to the band of five priests:

> Perceiving this [that nothing in the world is his; nothing is his ego], O priests, the learned and noble disciple conceives an aversion for form, conceives an aversion for sensation, conceives an aversion for perception, conceives an aversion for the predispositions, conceives an aversion for consciousness. And in conceiving this aversion he becomes divested of passion, and by the absence of passion he becomes free, and when he is free he becomes aware that he is free; and he knows that rebirth is exhausted, that he has lived the holy life, that he has done what it behooved him to do, and that he is no more for this world.[35]

As we have already seen, the Christian possessed what neither Brahman nor Buddhist enjoyed, a personal God whom one might worship as Christ, God, but also man. And He, the Son of God, had so loved fallen humanity that He had left his felicity on high to assume the pain of human life in order that He might make satisfaction on the cross for man's disobedience. Moreover, in so doing He had manifested a most lovable human personality. It would be very easy to exaggerate and to sentimentalize the importance of

[35] Henry C. Warren, *Buddhism in Translations,* "Harvard Oriental Series" (Cambridge, 1900), p. 147.

these factors. But the writings of all Christian mystics show in varying degrees an emotional coloring that is to some extent at least due to their consciousness of the Incarnation and the Redemption. Bonaventura therefore speaks for all the mystics of the Middle Ages in the *Itinerarium Mentis in Deum:* "There is no way except by the most burning love of Him who was crucified,"[36] and John Gerson, in his definition of the *theologia mystica,* confirms him: "The mystical theology [sometimes translated "mysticism"] is the stretching up of the soul into God through the yearning of love."[37] When the Christian mystics, therefore, say "love," they mean to varying degrees love as an emotion. We have an example of the more emotional view in Richard Rolle's *The Form of Perfect Living:* "Luf es a byrnand yernyng in god, with a wonderful delyte & sykerness."[38] Nevertheless, emotion is only a part of what the medievals called the love of God, "charity." Since medieval religion was interested primarily in the soul's relation to God, and only secondarily in its relations to fellow-men, charity meant not what it has come to mean to us—benevolence—but love of God, a turning of the whole man toward God, essentially an act of the will. Practical charity is then a resolution to do the will of God wholly in all things—to surrender one's own will to the will that the mystic believes so infinitely more just and certain than his own. In its significance it is primarily ethical. This view is presented clearly by Tauler in a quotation from St. Gregory:

"Wilt thou know whether thou love God? Take note when cares, troubles, or sorrows overtake thee (from within or from without, whencesoever they come), and weigh down thy spirit so that thou knowest not which way to turn, nor what is to become of thee, and canst find no counsel and art outwardly in a storm of affliction, in unwonted perplexity and sore distress; if thou then remainest inwardly at peace and unmoved in the bottom of thy heart, so that thou dost not in any wise falter, either by complaint, or in word, or work, or gesture, then there is no doubt that thou lovest God."[39]

[36] Bonaventura, *op. cit.*, p. 125: *Via autem non est nisi per ardentissimum amorem crucifixi.*

[37] Joannes Gersonii, *Opera Omnia* (Antwerpiae, 1706), tom. III, pars secunda, col. 384 B, *Theologia mystica est extensio animi in Deum per amoris desiderium.*

[38] *Richard Rolle of Hampole,* I, 36.

[39] *History and Life of the Reverend John Tauler of Strasbourg: with Twenty-five of His Sermons,* translated by Susanna Winkworth (London, 1857), p. 370.

We are apt to think of renunciation and resignation as passive states; they may be, but there is certainly nothing passive about the way to them.

In general, whether the mystic is to attain reality by the road of love or the road of knowledge, it is certain that his path will be a very active one. The grace of God, said the medieval, is a free gift of God to man, but it rests with man whether he shall accept or reject it. All mystics have in one way or another recognized that mystical experience is a very special gift, not to be attained even by purification, but by a more or less definite and prolonged course of work, generally called the "mystic way." Not all mystics have by any means given an account of the mystic way, and not all accounts are in any sense of the word commensurable, either in psychological knowledge or insight. The drama of the mystic way is played out within the soul. Obviously, the ability to recount that inner experience will depend on the powers of introspection of the individual and upon the power of psychological analysis which his age has reached. "God," said St. John of the Cross, "is a well from which everyone may draw water according to the measure of his vessel."[40] Clearly, too, not all mystics, even if they are able to tell, will see any value or interest in recounting the history of their souls. The philosophers of the Upanishads, for instance, did not delve very deeply into the mysteries of the mind. They wrestled manfully with the questions that baffle it; they gave directions for clearing the ground, and they marked out the ground of the great internal effort to reach the reality within. But they had practically no interest in the vicissitudes of that struggle; or if they had, they were not introspective enough; perhaps they were too absorbed in their main purpose to spend much time telling their pupils about them. On the other hand, the medieval Christians, probably encouraged thereto by the institution of the confessional, very often studied what went on within them with extraordinary introspective acumen. And the medieval doctors, like Richard of St. Victor and St. Bonaventura, applied to what they called the mystical theology (recognized by the scholastic as one of the three divisions of theology) the same methods of analysis that produced scholasticism

[40] St. John of the Cross, *op. cit.*, I, 148.

St. Augustine, in his *Confessions,* early gave the main outlines of the story, not from the scientific or the theological point of view, but from the personal, that makes literature. Two later writers, St. Theresa and St. John of the Cross, summed up the experience of all the mystics of their church with remarkable minuteness and detail. It is true that the experience of St. Catherine of Sienna was different, for instance, from that of St. Teresa in details, but in the main lines, we have no reason to think that they differed. And it is significant that the most lucid accounts that the Protestant Jacob Boehme has left of his psychological experiences practically concur with theirs.

Disregarding the subtleties, the various mansions of St. Teresa, and the "dark night," and the "obscure night of the soul," and so forth, of St. John of the Cross, we may discriminate three distinct stages on the mystical way: Illumination, Purgation, Union. The last term we shall have to extend later to include the Nirvana, or release, of the Buddhists and the Regeneration of the Protestants. But the other two will describe accurately the experience of all classes of mystics.

The first of these steps we may define as the glimpse of reality that awakens the hunger of the soul and sharpens all its faculties for the long struggle ahead. Again St. Augustine may speak for all: "Thee when first I saw, Thou liftedst me up, that I might see there was something which I might see; and that as yet I was not the man to see it."[41] The manner of that illumination varies—the tradition is that the Buddha saw three sights typical of the misery and degradation of existence, and one suggestive of the way of escape, and that soon after he resolved to forsake all:

"The time for the enlightenment of prince Siddhattha draweth nigh," thought the gods: "we must show him a sign": and they changed one of their number into a decrepit old man, broken-toothed, gray-haired, crooked and bent of body, leaning on a staff, and trembling, and showed him to the Future Buddha, but so that only he and the charioteer saw him.

Then said the Future Buddha to the charioteer, in the manner related in the Mahapadana,—

"Friend, pray, who is this man? Even his hair is not like that of other men." And when he heard the answer, he said, "Shame on birth, since to

41 St. Augustine, *op. cit.,* I, 373.

everyone that is born old age must come." And agitated in heart, he thereupon returned and ascended his palace. . . . .

Again, on a certain day, as the Future Buddha was going to the park, he saw a diseased man whom the gods had fashioned; and having again made inquiry, he returned, agitated in heart, and ascended his palace. . . . .

And again on a certain day, as the Future Buddha was going to the park, he saw a dead man whom the gods had fashioned; and having again made inquiry, he returned, agitated in heart, and ascended his palace. . . . .

And again on a certain day, as the Future Buddha was going to the park, he saw a monk, carefully and decently clad, whom the gods had fashioned.[42]

The precise nature of his reaction we cannot know, but its strength we may judge from the fact that not even the sight of his beautiful young wife lying asleep on a bed of flowers with his firstborn son in her arms held him from leaping to horse, out of his palace, and away to years of mortification and wandering.[43] The voice on the road to Damascus is another picturesque and dramatic example of illumination.[44] Usually, as in these cases, some external circumstance arouses the forces that produce the change in the man, but the essential and significant feature of the illumination is the internal working that gives the novice a glimpse of a spiritual reality beyond his present ken.

To the mystic, illumination is a supernatural experience; to the Christian mystic, a wonderful grace bestowed upon the unworthy. That an illumination may produce a complete *volteface* and that it may come to one who considers himself the chiefest of sinners there can be no doubt. But the history of the mystics suggests that it usually comes only to the aspiring, however uncertain and intermittent their aspiration may be. In most cases illumination comes only after a period of restless seeking and self-dissatisfaction; in most cases it comes to men who, in the esteem of almost anyone but themselves, would seem to an uncommon degree spiritually mature.

In any case, enlightenment results in conversion—as Henry Suso defines it, a centralization, a withdrawing from the creatures into the soul,[45] and the mobilization of all the forces of the spirit to

---

[42] *Buddhism in Translations*, pp. 56 f.

[43] *Ibid.*, p. 62.

[44] Acts 9:3 ff.

[45] Henri Suso, *Oeuvres*, translated by M. E. Cartier (Paris, 1852), p. 198.

reach the goal that it has for a moment seen. Usually the awakened soul directs its forces first of all toward the extermination of the vices and sins of which it has thus become sharply conscious. Against the purity and splendor of God, those bosom sins stand out dark and hateful. The soul would despair (this is of course applicable to the Christians) were it not for the promise of God that to the repentant sinner all shall be forgiven. And the mystic's penitence is no matter of routine or transitory emotion, if we may accept Ignatius Loyola's description of the process with its three requirements: one, full knowledge and consciousness of sins; two, reformation; three, renunciation of the world.[46]

Not only was the Oriental afraid of the insurrection of the senses, but, particularly in the case of the Buddhist, he was afraid of any attachments to worldly things, of any desires or affections.[47] But the Christian fears pride and self-will. When one remembers the genesis of evil in the Old Testament, he can readily understand why man should fear "the sin by which the angels fell." Pride and self-will are two of the subtlest, two of the most persistent, of human vices; indeed, it may be doubted if any other of man's bosom foes possess such tenacity. Bernard of Clairvaux is very practical: "He who makes himself his own master, subjects himself to a fool as master."[48] Jacob Boehme is very positive: "Men will think to find God in their *own willing*, and he is not therein; for he dwelleth merely and barely in *that willing*, which yieldeth itself with all its reason and knowing wholly to him, and to *that* he giveth knowledge and power to *understand* his Being."[49] And Catherine of Sienna is extraordinarily penetrating in her ferreting out of self-will in the fanaticism of the ascetic, in the depression of the religious enthusiast, or in the despair of the over-conscientious. But the glory of Christian thinking in this field lies not in its analysis of self-will, psychologically meticulous and illuminating as it is, not

[46] *Manresa or the Spiritual Exercises of Saint Ignatius for General Use* (New York, 1914), pp. 59 ff.

[47] *Sacred Books of the East*, X, *The Dhammapada*, translated by F. Max Müller (Oxford, 1881), p. 54.

[48] Bernard, *op. cit.*, I, 310–11.

[49] Behmen, *op. cit.*, Vol. II, Bk. I, "The High and Deep Searching of the Threefold Life of Man," x, 32.

in its program of renunciation, for in that the Buddhists had already achieved a pre-eminence that it would be difficult to surpass, but in its positive conception of joyous conformity to a will that, while infinitely wiser and more satisfying than any human will, was still understandable in human terms, that conception to which Dante gave its most fitting expression in the words of one of his heavenly spirits: "It is the essence of this blessed existence to hold itself within the divine will, whereby our wills themselves are made one . . . . and His will is our peace."

Purgation, however, is only one part of the mystic way. The other is variously described—prayer, meditation, recollection. It is in this direction that man makes his advance upon reality. In the Upanishads we read: "The sages, devoted to meditation and concentration, have seen the power belonging to God himself, hidden in its own qualities";[50] and in St. Teresa: "As far as I can understand, the gate by which to enter this castle [the Interior Castle] is prayer and meditation."[51] However one may describe this aspect of the activity of the illuminated soul, two things are clear as to its nature: It is inward and it is concentrated. The mystics have not denied the merit or the value of all the "good works," of deeds of mercy, of acts of piety, and so on, but it is not by such that the mystic reaches his goal. The reason is obvious—they are all involved in external things: the creatures of the Christian or the illusion of the Brahman. They are outside the region in which the Spirit may be won. It is by concentration of all the powers of his soul in prayer or meditation that the mystic makes his advance.

Vocal prayer is the lowest; as the mystic advances he avoids the inevitable distraction of the physical in this form for the greater concentration of silent prayer. He rises to meditation, a subject upon which mystics and writers on mysticism have expended much thought. It is obvious that the exact nature of meditation will vary with the intellectual and imaginative gifts of the individual, as well as with the religious tradition in which he is working. For instance, the meditations of Richard Rolle of Hampole upon the Passion are

[50] *Upanishads*, XV, Svet., I, 3.

[51] St. Teresa, *The Interior Castle*, translated by the Benedictines of Stanbrook (London, 1912), pp. 9 f.

extraordinarily realistic, obviously the work of a poetical imagination of no mean power. On the other hand, there is much less of the poet and much more of the quoter of fine things finely said in Thomas à Kempis, the reputed author of the *Imitation*, whereas Ignatius Loyola, in the *Spiritual Exercises*, combines imagination, often of a rather terrible complexion that reminds one of Dante, with the logical rigor that one would expect from the founder of the Jesuits. In general, in meditation one brings a subject, for instance, the night in the Garden of Gethsemane, vividly before his mind. The outlines are clear, the work of centuries, but they are as of a picture in the distance. He must come close until every light or shadow is clear, until he feels its significance, until he forgets that it is the picture of what happened a very long time ago, until he is there in the garden, listening in terror to the clatter of the band that has come to take his Master. But he must not linger on the physical details, for that would be to confuse what is only a most inferior means with his end. Consideration of the patience with which Christ laid aside all His power and suffered Himself to be taken will open the gate of the meaning of what followed. Here again the centuries have marked out his way. He will achieve nothing new (novelty is not his goal), but the knowledge that has lain somewhere in the back of his brain will be brought into the very foreground of his consciousness, and what he has known all along, and never regarded, will become of power to influence his conduct and to exalt his spirit. Most of the world's greatest spiritual effort has gone, not to the acquisition of fresh knowledge, but to the realization of knowledge already possessed.

On the physical side of this region of meditation the East has been far more analytical than the West. Many of the prescriptions of the Yoga sages, for instance, deal meticulously with the physiological preparations for meditation: with the selection of the proper place, with the physical circumstances, like the clean sand upon which to sit, with the posture, with the position of the hand, the direction of the eyes, above all, with the regulation of the breath.[52] At first this fussiness over the control of the breath, the methods of inhalation and exhalation, seems absurd, until one remembers that

[52] *Translations from Buddhism*, p. 355; *Svet.*, II, 9.

in the East the physical and the spiritual connotations of the word "spirit" (*Prâsñá*) or "breath" were more immediate than with us,[53] and that the relation between the operations of the body and those at least of the imagination had early been recognized. This physical aspect, it is only fair to say, the great Upanishads did not emphasize excessively, but at least one modern expositor of the *Yoga Aphorisms* of Patanjali expatiates upon the appropriate (from the Western point of view, picturesque) setting for meditation to an extent that in the Western world would run the risk of appealing more to the faddist than to the mystic.[54]

Both East and West have been at great pains to promote concentration. As noted above, that is the motive of much ascetic practice in the Middle Ages. It is the motive of the great emphasis that the Brahman placed upon the repetition of the sacred syllable *Om,* or of the directions that the Master in the *Bhagavad-Gita* gives to the seeker of union:

> In a pure place finding a firm seat for himself, neither too high nor too low, spread with a cloth, a fawn-skin and sacred grass;
> Making his mind one-pointed, controlling thought and powers and acts, seated there let him seek to join himself in union, for self-purification;
> Holding body, head and neck upright, firm and unmoving, fixing his view on the tip of the nose, nor looking this way and that.[55]

All this sometimes savors a little of magic hocus-pocus, but it is really a device to secure concentration. Both Brahman and Christian recognized that the human mind, accustomed as it is to busying itself with the things of which the senses tell it, is only too apt, when held from its usual employment, to sink into formless reverie. Meditation, therefore, is a means of restraining and of elevating it.

Obviously, such violence to nature as is involved in the mystic way would, and did, bring its revenges. The Christians, by the very nature of their method of love, were exposed to difficulties that the intellectual emphasis of the Brahmans to some degree spared them. All Christian mystics bear witness to the succession of periods of "dryness, of seeming aridity" in prayer and meditation (they

[53] *Upanishads,* XV, *Prasna,* II, 2, 13.

[54] *Yoga Philosophy,* lectures delivered in New York, winter of 1895–96, by Swâmi Vivekânanda, on Râja Yoga (London, 1897).

[55] *Bhagavad-Gita,* vi, 11–13.

do not always discriminate between the two) that follows times of great consolation and satisfaction, or, as they say, "sweetness." One might learn much of the psychology of effort and endurance from the pages of Henry Suso, Bernard of Clairvaux, and St. Teresa. All the temptations of the spirit, despair, pride, and their dark train, beset those moments of darkness and emptiness that sometimes stretched into years. Sometimes the mystic seemed to have touched the goal of all his effort; it seemed as if God had come into his soul; and then again all became blackness, and, like the bride in the Song of Songs, to whom he liked to compare himself, he went forlornly up and down seeking Him. Persian mystical poetry bears testimony to the same experience.

With his tendency to see the hand of God in all things, the Christian came to regard these periods of blackness as trials appointed him by God to purify his spirit of its vanity and self-will. He believed that greater effort to purify his own soul and perseverance would then bring back the light. But when they did not, he saw that self-renunciation was what he needed; that lust after sweetness and satisfaction in prayer was seeking something other than the will of God, that he must acquiesce in his darkness, and seek only that the will of God be wholly fulfilled in him. There is no emphasis on passivity in the way the great Christian mystics like St. Bernard and St. Teresa handle this problem, for the task of overcoming the natural impulses of complaint and impatience and rebellion is work in the most strenuous sense of the word.

But while the mystic way is beset with darkness and barrenness, it is also refreshed with various tokens of divine interest. For the Christian believed that he did not seek his Lord any more eagerly than his Lord sought him. "Let none, therefore, doubt that he is loved who already loves."[56] Here we enter into what to the modern must always seem an uncongenial region. The literature of Christian mysticism is full of vision, of apparition, of signs and sounds. No medieval mystic seems to have doubted the possibility of these supernatural manifestations. One must remember, for instance, that one so intellectually gifted and so spiritually distinguished as Henry More, of the Cambridge Platonists, in so rela-

[56] Bernard, *op. cit.*, I, 360.

tively modern a time as the seventeenth century, interested himself in stories of witches as a resource for establishing the supernatural. It is not surprising, therefore, that the record of the thirteenth-century St. Mechtild of Magdeburg, for instance, is a tissue of marvels.[57] But it is significant that there is very little of the miraculous in Bernard of Clairvaux or in John of Ruysbroeck.

For the typical mystics, despite their belief in the possibility of visions from God, are as aware of the weakness of this region as their more scientific critics. In fact their criticism is even more complex, because they recognize a category that scepticism has tended to discard, the devil. St. Teresa and St. John of the Cross are particularly suspicious of visions and signs, because they recognize the infinite possibilities of delusion. They go so far as to suggest that even beneficent visions are probably from good angels rather than directly from God, and in any case they recommend the rejection of signs and visions as matters usually of very dubious character; at best, of little significance.[58] In this attitude St. Teresa and her disciple are securely in the tradition of the great mystics, who have always relegated visions to a relatively low place in the spiritual life. That seems the only consistent position, for apart from the metaphysical inconsistency of mixing the two orders, the material and the spiritual, there can be no doubt that they do not fall under the definition of the mystic's goal, the attaining to union with the spirit in the spirit.

Not by vision or sign, then, does the mystic reach his goal, but by a spiritual activity above meditation, that the medievals called contemplation. While many writers have handled contemplation at great length, the classic treatment is Richard of St. Victor's on the difference between meditation and contemplation. The heart of this distinction is to be found in the following sentence: "The part of meditation is to search into things hidden; the part of contemplation is to behold with admiration things that are clear."[59] Contemplation is a state of peace, possible only when the soul is

[57] For typical visions, cf. *Revelationes Selectae S. Mechthildis* (Coloniae, 1854), in *Bibliotheca Mystica et Ascetica*, X, 96, 102, 122, 149.

[58] St. John of the Cross, *op. cit.*, I, 118, and St. Teresa, *op. cit.*, pp. 154 ff.

[59] Ricardi Sancti Victoris, *Omnia Opera* (Lugdini, 1534), Fo. V, B, Cap. xv: *Meditationis est perscrutari occulta: contemplationis est admirari perspicua.*

perfectly ordered, when the spirit is prepared. The dangers of delusion, of false contemplation, are obvious. The typical mystics again and again enforce the necessity of great care on the part of those responsible for the spiritual direction and guidance of the mystic, that the immature be not promoted to contemplation, lest they lose all the fruits of their labor in idleness. The great mystics have been insistent that peace is not idleness. Bernard of Clairvaux arraigns with unusual severity, "the inane idleness which you call contemplation";[60] and John of Ruysbroeck makes activity the distinction between true rest and false rest, which is simply idleness.[61] In the same spirit, one of the Buddhist scripture writers characterizes a priest who had departed from a conference with the Buddha to devote himself to meditation as "solitary, retired, vigilant, strenuous, and earnest."[62]

But if contemplation is not a state where the imagination fills the mind with its creations, if it is not a state in which the reason maintains its wonted court for the findings of the senses, what goes on there? Obviously, it is illogical for any but the mystic to answer that question. Even the mystics find it hard to do so. Strictly speaking, it is, of course, ineffable and indescribable; therefore they resort to symbolism, always a hazardous expedient, to describe the consummation of their endeavor. The Brahmans, the Persians, practically all the Catholics, have called it "Union." The Buddhists have conceived of it as "Freedom in Union with the Law," and the Protestants, like Jacob Boehme, William Law, and Eckhartshausen have used the figure "Regeneration." George Fox describes the manifestation of his state as being "moved." Since it is not at all clear that the state arrived at by Regeneration differs especially from that represented by the other descriptions, we shall best grasp this difficult matter if we examine the figure of Union.

The Brahman conceived of the individual soul as a portion of the Over-Soul, segregated in the body.[63] Literally, then, the consummation of the mystic's goal was union. So they describe it eloquently and often. The Persian poets consistently use erotic image-

[60] Bernard, *op. cit.*, IV, 284.

[61] John of Ruysbroeck, *The Adornment of the Spiritual Marriage, etc.*, translated by Dom C. A. Wynschenk (London, 1916), p. 155.

[62] *Buddhism in Translations*, p. 162.   [63] *Upanishads*, XV, *Mund.*, III, 2, 7.

ry to describe their pursuit of the Beloved One. It was natural, therefore, for them to use the figure of the earthly union for the union in the spirit. The precise proportion of erotic and spiritual in the poetry of the Persian Sufis is a very difficult matter to determine. Consequently, one is forced to judge each individual separately. The Christian mystics naturally came to use the figure of the mystical marriage because the church has been traditionally denominated the "Mystical Bride of Christ," and the entrance upon the religious life was early looked upon as an espousing of the church or of Christ. But the difference between their use of this imagery and the Persian may be gauged by the fact that the Christians apparently never use the feminine pronoun to designate the object of their search, while some of the Persians do.[64] In fact, one interesting sign of the spiritual power of Christian mysticism is the austerity of its usage of this imagery. Bernard of Clairvaux preached day after day to his congregation of monks on the text of the Canticle of Canticles (the Song of Solomon), but one could never mistake the Bride of his sermons for anything but the soul, and the bridegroom for anyone but Christ, and the result is one of the classics of the monastic life.

Perhaps the word "union" seems a barren term, until one remembers with whom the soul is united. The Brahman in union joined the great World-Soul—"He sees his soul as one with all beings, and all beings as one with his soul; his soul joined in union, beholding oneness everywhere."[65] Plotinus, in those four times of ecstasy of which Porphyry tells us, attained to the Idea of the Absolute Good; into the soul of the Christian came his God. The wisest men might wander the whole world over, seeking all knowledge, but all the knowledge of the universe came into the soul of the all but illiterate Catherine of Sienna as she knelt in her cell. As Henry Suso said, "In that divine Essence in which the three Persons are one and the same nature without diversity, are found also all the creatures according to their eternal ideal, in their essential form."[66] One of the mystics has spoken of the infinite progression in the state of union, of the going on and on in God.

[64] *Jami*, p. 50.   [65] *Bhagavad-Gita*, vi, 29.   [66] Suso, *op. cit.*, p. 234.

But most of them say nothing of that, for their goal is not all knowledge, but God.

As for what this great bliss of the immediate experience of God is like, only the mystic can tell, and, one may add with equal truth, only the mystic can understand. The best we can do is to listen to them for a moment. Plotinus, the greatest of the neo-Platonists, may speak for the philosophic mystics with a fervor that is essentially religious:

When the soul obtains this happiness, and when [the divinity] comes to her, or rather, when He manifests His presence, because the soul has detached herself from other present things, when she has embellished herself as far as possible, when she has become assimilated to Him by means known only to the initiated, she suddenly sees Him appear in her. No more interval between them, no more doubleness; the two fuse in one. . . . . All the things that formerly charmed her, such as commanding others, power, wealth, beauty, science, now seem to her despicable. . . . . Now she fears nothing, so long as she is with Him, and contemplates Him. Even with pleasure would she witness the destruction of everything, for she would remain alone with Him; so great is her felicity.[67]

John Tauler may be taken as the mouthpiece of the German mystical tradition:

It is possible for him to be carried so far that his spirit is as it were sunk and lost in the abyss of the Deity, and loses the consciousness of all creature distinctions. All things are gathered together in one with the Divine sweetness, and the man's being is so penetrated with the Divine substance, that he loses himself therein, as a drop of water is lost in a cask of strong wine. And thus the man's spirit is so sunk in God in divine union, that he loses all sense of distinction, and all that has brought him to this point, such as humility, the seeking of God's glory,—nay, his very self—loses its name and there remains a secret, still union, without cloud or colour. And all good purposes are fused into a true and pure oneness, and a real but silent mystery, such as human powers can scarce apprehend.[68]

But probably the most helpful description is that of Bernard of Clairvaux, in its fullness and its simplicity:

I confess, then, though I say it in my foolishness, that the Word has visited me, and even very often. But although He has frequently entered into my soul, I have never at any time been sensible of the precise moment of His

[67] Plotinos, *Complete Works*, translated by Kenneth Sylvan Guthrie (London, 1918), pp. 756 f.

[68] John Tauler, *op. cit.*, p. 253.

coming. I have felt that He was present. I remember that He has been with me; I have sometimes been able even to have a presentiment that He would come; but never to feel His coming, nor His departure. For whence He came to enter my soul, or whither He went on quitting it, by what means He has made entrance or departure, I confess that I know not even to this day.....
It is not by the eyes that He enters, for He is without form or colour that they can discern; nor by the ears, for His coming is without sound; nor by the nostrils, for it is not with the air but with the mind that He is blended; nor has He merely acted upon the air, but produced it (*infecit, fecit*); nor, again, does it enter by the mouth, not being of a nature to be eaten or drunk; nor, lastly, is it capable of being traced by the touch, for it is intangible. By what avenue, then, has He entered? Or perhaps the fact may be that He has not entered at all, nor indeed come at all from the outside. Yet it has not come from within me, for it is good, and I know that in me dwelleth no good thing (Rom. 7:18). I have ascended higher than myself, and lo! I have found the Word above me still. My curiosity has led me to descend below myself also, and yet I have found Him still at a lower depth. If I have looked without myself, I have found that He is beyond that which is outside of me; and if within, He was at an inner depth still. . . . .

You will ask, then, how, since the ways of His access are thus incapable of being traced, I could know that He was present? But He is living and full of energy, and as soon as He has entered into me He has quickened my sleeping soul, has aroused and softened and goaded my heart, which was in a state of torpor, and hard as a stone. He has begun to pluck up and destroy, to plant and to build, to water the dry places, to illuminate the gloomy spots, to throw open those which were shut close, to inflame with warmth those which were cold, as also to straighten its crooked paths and make its rough places smooth, so that my soul might bless the Lord, and all that is within me praise His Holy Name. Thus, then, the Bridegroom-Word, though He has several times entered into me, has never made His coming apparent to my sight, hearing, or touch. It was not by His motions that He was recognized by me, nor could I tell by any of my senses that He had penetrated to the depths of my being. It was, as I have already said, only by the revived activity of my heart that I was enabled to recognize His Presence; and to know the power of His Sacred Presence by the sudden departure of vices and the strong restraint put upon all carnal affection.[69]

As one reads these accounts, one common element in all three becomes apparent, an element that at first glance seems inconsistent with the stress which all the great mystics lay upon the strenuous activity of the mystic way. It is the unmistakable element of surrender, of yielding the hard-won conscious control of the spirit to a new control that, even though experienced in the

[69] Bernard, *op. cit.*, IV, 457 f.

innermost depths of one's own soul, yet sweeps in with a power and an authenticity beyond the compass of anything one has ever known in himself. And at the same time that this outside control takes possession of the soul it brings implications of ethical activity that makes it seem to the mystic an integral part of the life of ethical strenuousness. All three writers believe that the ecstasy of mystical experience is possible only to a soul that has prepared itself, and on the other hand, all three recognize that the experience in itself is not so much won as bestowed. It is the eternal paradox of inspiration. No amount of work will of itself produce inspiration. It often seems as if inspiration comes rather when one has ceased to work. And inspiration in science or art seems to come, as here, from sources beyond the control of the man himself. But the more common inspiration of science and art affords abundant evidence that the problems which suddenly solve themselves in moments of inspiration are the problems on which the conscious mind has previously concentrated all its energies, and that it very seldom happens that significant inspiration in any field comes to one who has not already been laboring hard in that field. So of the consummation of the mystical way. Whatever elements of surrender, of release, of peace it involves are possible only on the condition of the hard work done before. Such seems to be the significance of the unmistakably ethical implications that distinguish the ecstasy of the mystic from all other forms of ecstasy.

Obviously such a state of supreme concentration could not go on indefinitely without fatal exhaustion of the body. St. Teresa said:

I am not confident that this absorption is genuine when it always remains in the same state, nor does it appear to me possible for the Holy Ghost to dwell constantly within us, to the same extent, during our earthly exile.[70]

Madame Guyon and Miguel de Molinos asserted the possibility of a state of perpetual prayer, of perpetual sanctification and union, but even they did not claim a continual ecstasy. The tradition of the typical mystics from the Buddha down is with St. Teresa. George Fox spent many an hour waiting in the hostile "steeple

[70] St. Teresa, *op. cit.*, p. 60.

house" for the Spirit of the Lord to "move" him before he could preach.[71]

As for the goal of the Buddhists, that is a very difficult matter. It is generally assumed that Nirvana means extinction. It is true that the chief aim of the Buddhist, believing as he did that existence was wholly evil, was to escape from existence.[72] Suicide, at first blush the logical weapon, was useless, for the one reality (in a metaphysical sense) that the Buddhist recognized was that of deeds which bound a man to a round of successive existences, a cycle of rebirth, prolonged according to the evil of his ways.[73]

Whether the desired freedom from rebirth was in view of the fact that the Buddhist denied the existence of an ego,[74] annihilation or not, is a moot question. One can hardly annihilate an ego that never existed. One can hardly conduct life without one, and certainly few have ever conducted life more vigorously than the Buddhist as represented by the *Dhammapada*. Whatever happened to the Buddhist after death, it seems pretty clear that the Nirvana to which the Buddha attained under the Bo tree, the Nirvana in this life (the only one relevant to mysticism), was not non-existence. It was a state of contemplation, the product of strenuous activity, in its very concentration and self-surrender an active state.

As for those like Jacob Boehme, William Law, and George Fox, who use the symbolism of rebirth, a very old one among the German mystics, going back to Meister Eckhart, they recognize substantially the same spiritual process, with less emphasis upon contemplation, and the same spiritual goal. What they do is to emphasize in their theology the Fall and the Redemption. Law expresses the view of all the followers of Jacob Boehme: "The whole Nature of the Christian Religion stands upon these *two great Pillars*, namely, the Greatness of our *Fall*, and the Greatness of our *Redemption*."[75] Adam was created perfect; he sinned and fell. We are all born with the weakness that in our earthly nature is the

[71] George Fox, *Journal* (Philadelphia, no date), p. 265.

[72] *Buddhism in Translations*, p. xiv, "The Three Characteristics."

[73] *Ibid.*, pp. 209–12.

[74] *Ibid.*, p. 144.

[75] William Law, "The Grounds and Reasons of Christian Regeneration," *Works*, V, 56.

inevitable outcome of that fall. We must be born anew. The process of rebirth is the mystic way; indeed, one of the best descriptions of the mystic way of the great tradition is Jacob Boehme's "Way from Darkness to True Illumination."

But when the mystic has reached his goal, what does he then? That depends very much upon his gifts and his circumstances. We may divide the mystics into contemplatives and actives, but that division will be at best a blurred one, for many great contemplatives, like Bernard of Clairvaux and Catherine of Sienna, have been also men and women of action, in every sense of the word, and great actives like George Fox have owed their inspiration and their "openings" to contemplation. The Brahmans regarded contemplation as the goal of life; it was certainly the goal of the Buddhist, and of the philosopher-mystic like Plotinus; it was the goal of the greatest Sufis; however little the average Christian may so regard it, the traditional heaven of the Christians, when it has passed the stage of golden pavements and Elysian fields, has been a state of contemplation. The logical thing, therefore, for a man to do who has reached contemplation would be to stay there, or if he cannot (and the abilities and circumstances of human life make that practically impossible), to bend all his efforts towards recapturing that experience as often as possible. But special attainments have always brought their responsibility for the less gifted, and the mystic has come back from God to his fellow-men. Even in the East, which has certainly surpassed the West in its genius for contemplation, the sage has traditionally become the master. The Buddhists held that a good man by his very presence among men does good,[76] but his spiritual pre-eminence exposed him to the importunities of the disciple in a world that, in certain periods at any rate, valued the inner life more literally and practically than does ours.

In the West the mystic has usually felt that the gifts so freely given were to be shared, that he who loves God must love his neighbor in God, and do all he can to help his neighbor to God. The tradition of mutual serviceableness is one of the oldest of Christian traditions. Therefore the great mystics have been also men and women of action. Of course, there have been apparent

[76] *Buddhism in Translations*, p. 437.

mystics who have been so completely absorbed in their own experiences that they have been of little use to the world, but they are not found among the great mystics. They were useless men and women before they became useless mystics. As Mr. Charles Bennett points out: "The return to the world is not so much part of the mystic's intention as a test of its quality."[77]

The most distinctive activity of the mystic has been, as one would expect, recounting his experience to inspire other men, and giving directions for the guidance of others who are setting out on the road which he knows so well. That is a task to challenge the powers of the most gifted. Upon his success in that effort has to no small extent depended the value of his experience, from the point of view of his fellow-men, and it is largely upon that basis that history has given him his place among the spiritual leaders of men. Of course, the writings of the mystics vary enormously in impressiveness from individual to individual. Even translation cannot quench the ardor that makes John of Ruysbroeck's *The Adornment of the Spiritual Marriage* one of the most glowing of religious writings. One has not gone far in that book before he realizes that he is in the presence of a spiritual master. On the other hand, Julian of Norwich's writings, delightful as they are, leave one dissatisfied with their lack of profundity, and the writings of Angela of Foligno bear the traces of the shallow, rather vain, personality to which enlightenment originally came. Again, not all the repetition and strangeness and prolixity that so appal the reader who stands on the threshold of eastern religious writing can veil the power and beauty of the *Bhagavad-Gita*, for through the worst tangle of alien word and image the winds of the spirit are blowing strong, and to them there is neither East nor West. Here, more than anywhere else, do the gifts of the imagination and the intellect sustain the promptings of the heart.

When he leaves the practical ground of traditional ethics, when he leaves matters of which he may speak directly—and of course, directness is essential to successful treatment of such matters—the mystic usually resorts to symbolism. We have already

[77] Bennett, *op. cit.*, p. 42, footnote.

met the most important of his symbols in the figures used to describe the consummation of his effort, the end of the mystic way. Each of these great figures—that of the rebirth, that of union, that of the mystical wooing and marriage, particularly the last, brings from its natural region its special opportunities for symbolism. The sermons of Bernard of Clairvaux on the Canticle of Canticles and the treatise of Rulman Merswin on the *Nine Rocks* are typical instances of medieval mystical symbolism, in general involved, fairly central, often illuminating, but much of it too highly abstract and allegorical, too involved to be quickening. Whoever the mystic who wrote the Fourth Gospel, he possessed the genius to use symbolism in such a way as to illuminate obscure and difficult matters: "The wind bloweth where it listeth, and thou hearest the sound thereof, but canst not tell whence it cometh and whither it goeth; so is everyone that is born of the Spirit."[78] The comparison upon which that verse rests is with something of universal experience, something that, common as it is, has always piqued the curiosity and stirred the imagination of men. And the expression of that relation, whether the credit be due to the original or to the makers of the King James Version is simple and magical, at once in its sound arousing the sense of beauty, and in its sweep enlarging the imagination. All the while it is at bottom logically sound and spiritually significant. So it is with all successful phrasing of the unutterable.

But after all, what is mysticism worth? That question may be considered from three points of view: from the point of view of absolute truth, from the point of view of the individual, from the point of view of society. From the first point of view no real answer is possible. For by definition the subject is beyond the reach of science; it belongs to faith, and there we can set no criterion that will satisfy one-half of the points of view that would demand consideration. Yet the Christian mystics at least have recognized the dangers of a situation in which every man discovers his own truth, and have usually tried to erect some criterion by which the authenticity of a man's experience might be tried, that the element

[78] John 3:8.

of self-delusion, always to be reckoned with, might be eliminated as far as possible. The Middle Ages, always prolific of safety devices, had three standards by which a new account might be tested —the church as represented both by canon and by ecclesiastical authority, Scripture, and the testimony of other mystics. The Protestants recognized only the Scriptures, a fairly elastic criterion, in view of the latitude accorded to individual interpretation. Lacking these tribunals we shall have to relegate the question as to the absolute truth attained by mysticism, with the question of the status of the supernatural, to the faith or scepticism of the individual. But we may fortify individual judgment to no inconsiderable extent, especially in the region of ethics, if, as we listen to a new mystic, we keep in mind the experience of his predecessors.

As for the value of mysticism to the individual, the experience of every day comes to our aid. Obviously, the person who possesses the qualities that will make a great mystic is an exceedingly rare one, for a great many reasons, probably rarer today than ever before. Obviously, only an individual of very superior inward strength can stand physically, mentally, or spiritually the tax which the mystic way imposes upon the seeker, however specially endowed he may be. What all this amounts to is that the mystic is a genius of a very specialized type, and that real mystical activity is not possible or desirable except for such a genius.

The recognition of this fact is all the more necessary because certain aspects of the superficialities of mysticism are dangerously accessible to the fanatical, the credulous, the emotional, the imaginative. The ability to believe that one has seen visions, the ability to work one's self into an emotional exaltation or hysteria, without any genuine spiritual fruit, and in the long run with very potent intellectual and ethical harm, is too common a phenomenon to be disregarded. Nevertheless, those who have lamented that in our modern world the mystic has had to run the gauntlet of unsympathetic doubt and scepticism have failed to realize that many of the unbalanced and the weak have been protected thereby, and that no real mystic has ever been deterred by such obstacles. The history of the mystics suggests that criticism has on the whole been fruitful for the mystic as well as protective for society.

For the man or woman of religious genius the case is very different. For them the mystic discipline of self-mastery and concentration would seem to heighten rather than to deplete the inborn gifts of character and intellect. The early death of St. Catherine of Sienna may be easily attributed to her very ill-balanced way of living. But her short life is one of the most extraordinarily active and influential in history. And as one reads in her voluminous correspondence, he cannot fail to be impressed by the insight, the practicality, the astuteness, the common sense with which she met the multiplicity of calls upon her powers. That sentence from the *Dialogue:* "And so with love they knew how to be all things to all men, and to give to each one his nourishment," is the most fitting description of her genius.[79] Bernard of Clairvaux is another example of practical abilities of an unusual order. George Fox, one of the first Quakers, spent much time quietly waiting for the spirit to move him, but as one reads of his incessant journeyings, often under the most adverse conditions, that he might bring the Word to the scattered seekers of his day, one marvels at the vitality and the power of endurance of the man. For all of these men and women mysticism afforded what we would call today a very powerful dynamic, for even the affairs of this world.

As for society, the Buddhist sage reminds us that society benefits from the mere presence of a good man. From that point of view society might well cherish a few mystics. Rigorously criticized and preserved from the over-cultivation of the vogue, mysticism might inspire and enkindle as it has in the past. But we must remember that the mysticism that has counted in the past has come out of the spiritual life of its people, and has borne its fruit in revivifying the tradition of their common heritage. Some of the mystical efforts of today are cultivating the strange and the exotic at the risk of ministering to aesthetic and sentimental curiosity rather than to genuine spiritual aspiration. As a matter of fact, the spiritual life is a matter neither of vogue nor of aesthetics. After all, mysticism has performed its greatest service to society

[79] *The Dialogue of the Seraphic Virgin, Catherine of Siena, Dictated by Her while in a State of Ecstasy,* translated by Algar Thorold (London, 1907), p. 254.

in its contribution to the balanced, sane, active spiritual life that, in its requirements, disregards neither the capabilities of human nature nor the lessons of human experience. As a specialization of that life, mysticism has produced personalities of singular spiritual distinction and beauty, but the very nature of the work it exacts places it beyond the reach of the faddist and the connoisseur, beyond the reach of all except him who, in his love of supreme reality, and goodness, and beauty cannot rest, however strenuous the road of discipline and concentration, until in his own spirit he has attained to oneness with that reality, goodness, and beauty, with God.

CHAPTER IV

THE MYSTICAL FIELD

The difference between the typical mystics and "the others" is one of kind and degree with regard to one particular aspect of human activity. For instance, Bernard of Clairvaux comes into practically every list of the typical mystics; Spinoza comes into very few. Viewed simply as a mystic, Bernard of Clairvaux has much greater claims than Spinoza. Viewed as a force in the intellectual life of the race, there can be no question that the philosopher who, for one thing, did more than any other to rouse Goethe to the lifelong quest of the thing-in-itself that makes him still the typical modern man, is second, if second at all, only to the greatest of philosophers. From an absolute point of view, then, to call Bernard of Clairvaux a great mystic and Baruch de Spinoza a mystical philosopher is in no sense to overlook the fact that Spinoza is probably, in independence, originality, and sheer power of mind, a very much greater man than Bernard. That is not the issue.

The main lines of approach to the typical mystics may be used as a starting-point for getting into the much more complicated and less sharply delimited problems of the "mystical field," the general view of the world, the seeking of reality, the method of seeking, the actual experience in various degrees and on various levels of reality, the understanding of reality, the effort to express what has been so discovered, and finally, the various questions of value that inevitably arise out of the effort to bring that very special experience to bear upon the whole body of experience.

To begin, then, at the point at which the typical mystic begins. The point of view that sees behind all this beguiling and absorbing and even blinding world of appearance, a reality which transcends all its phenomena and satisfies all its defects and raises all its promises to a level not dreamed of here, the point of view, in other words, that discerns behind or above or in the material world a spiritual realm is by no means confined to the great mystics. As

95

Mr. Leuba points out in his fragmentary but highly suggestive chapter on "Religion, Science, and Philosophy," "Materialism, as a metaphysical doctrine, has few supporters today, while idealism and spiritualism in their various forms are the dominant conceptions. These doctrines agree in affirming that the ultimate Reality, commonly spoken of as God, is of a mental, a spiritual, nature."[1] But as Mr. Leuba goes on to point out, "The God to which this dominant trend of metaphysics points is an impassible, infinite Being—a Being therefore who does not bear to man the relation which every one of the historical religions assumes to exist and seeks to maintain by means of its system of creeds and worship."[2] The Absolute which Josiah Royce established by his famous argument from error is a mental, even a spiritual, conception, but no one, not even the most passionate of the "meek lovers of the good" could develop a personal devotion to so abstract a perfection. And Mr. Bradley's Absolute, with all its wealth of epistemological meanings, would be equally chilly to an aspiring infatuation. The metaphysical realities with all their beauties of logic and dialectic and all their undeniable resemblances to the unknown gods of the Hindu and the pseudo-Dionysiac traditions are too intellectual, too remote from the fundamental instincts, too far out of reach of those needs of the heart that beset the most sophisticated as well as the savage, ever to give rise to so rich or so profound a life-process as mysticism. They belong to the desk and not to the altar.

Even where the Absolute takes on a more familiar vesture, as in the "higher part of the universe" of William James,[3] or the active "other mind" God of Mr. Hocking, and makes a mystical philosophy which would interpret the experience of any of the great mystics, it still belongs to mystical philosophy and not mysticism. For as Mr. Hocking points out, mysticism is to be defined "not by its doctrine but by its deed, the deed of worship in its fully developed form."[4] The philosophy or even the theology of the mystics

[1] James H. Leuba, *The Psychology of Religious Mysticism* (New York and London, 1925), p. 304.

[2] *Ibid.*, p. 304.

[3] William James, *Varieties of Religious Experience* (New York, etc., 1903), p. 516.

[4] William Ernest Hocking, *The Meaning of God in Human Experience* (New Haven, 1923), p. 355.

is in no sense an exclusive possession, for it is usually such as is shared by a great many people who could not possibly be called "mystics."

Even more interesting for an inquiry into mysticism than any theory of an Absolute or a God is the type of belief in supernal reality that dwarfs all other considerations and makes realization of it and conformity with its nature seem more important than anything else in the world. The Stoics are perhaps the best example of that high fellowship of men who, without any special sense of an individual God with whom they might commune, have yet found in an allegiance to the whole as opposed to the parts, in the surrender of all personal consideration to an interest in a world order or working, the most absorbing purpose of strenuous and noble lives. Epictetus, Seneca, Marcus Aurelius are perhaps the names best known to the general reader, as the Earl of Shaftesbury is to the English student. Marcus Aurelius may speak for all in a sentence or two from his meditations that sum up the creed of the Stoics:

> All parts of the universe are interwoven and tied together with a sacred bond. And no one thing is foreign or unrelated to another. This general connection gives unity and ornament to the world. For the world, take it altogether, is but one. There is but one sort of matter to make it of; one God that pervades it; and one law to guide it, the common reason of all rational beings; and one truth; if, indeed, beings of the same kind, and endued with the same reason, have one and the same perfection. . . . . Now that is always good and reasonable which makes for the service of the universe.[5]

This bears the mark of the mystic's earnestness and concentration; it agrees with his estimate of what is of real importance. But it wants the light and the glow of the mystic's certainty, that actual experience that gives the flash of life to even so brief a phrase as that cry of St. Augustine's, "O Beauty of all things beautiful!" There is in it a defect of energy that justifies Professor Gilbert Murray's description of Stoicism as, heroic as it is, a failure of nerve.

In contrast to the often sadly uncertain and at times half-agnostic spirit of the Stoic is the joyous assurance of the religious

---

[5] Marcus Aurelius, *Meditations*, translated by Jeremy Collier (London, 1887), Book VII, paragraph 9, and Book XII, paragraph 23.

genius. There can be no question of the fullness of assurance or the richness of religious realization in the *Apologia pro Vita Sua* of John Henry Newman, or the intensity of spiritual history so plainly and so movingly recorded in the *Journal* of the Quaker, John Woolman, but a comparison of these with the *Journal* of George Fox, or the story of the conversion of John Tauler in the *Theologia German-ica*, leaves no question of a very real difference in kind. Newman's *Apologia* is a very great document of the religious life, but it is the history of the thoughts and feelings of a man for whom religion was the most interesting object of thought and the dearest object of feeling in his life, and not the story of how a man came to experi-ence God beyond the bounds of human thought or feeling.

The same is true of many men who have played a very large part in the shaping and direction of the religious life of the race. The author of the Fourth Gospel is universally recognized as a mystic; the author of the First is quite as clearly not a mystic. The Buddha was a mystic; Mohammed, for all his angel and the dictating of the sacred books, was probably not, but, like Moses, much more of a lawgiver and an organizer than a contemplative, more interested in hearing the word of his God and making other people keep it than in entering into any protracted or ineffable com-munion with God himself. The author of the Benedictine rule, who has indirectly done more than most mystics to promote mystical life, was in all probability a great reformer rather than a seeker of direct communion with God. It is not always easy to tell with certainty about individuals. Some of Luther's visions are undoubtedly mysti-cal, while the general impression of his mind and of his methods of dealing with religious problems suggests the distinctly non-mysti-cal. Romain Rolland's brief account of Mahatma Gandhi, while leaving no doubt of the fact that our day has known in the Indian prophet a great religious leader and an authentic saint, does not give enough evidence to make clear that Mr. Gandhi is a mystic in either the Hindu or the Christian sense. To sum up, a belief in the existence and supreme importance of a spiritual reality and the de-votion of all the forces of a man's life to the realization and service of such a reality constitute one of the most important elements in the *weltanschauung* of a mystic, but are not of necessity mystical and do not in themselves make a man a mystic in the sense of the typical mystics.

The problem of those who devote themselves to the task of knowing God, while at many points raising the same issues as the preceding, is more complicated. For though apparently in the main a question of purpose, it is to no small extent also a question of method, since the way in which men set about to realize a purpose about which much has been thought and said is often more revealing of its essential nature than any conscious formulation can be. For the problem of knowledge is, whether approached from the epistemologist's point of view or the moralist's, a knotty one. The age-old contention over Socrates' insistence that the root of evil conduct is ignorance and the guaranty of good conduct, knowledge, is but one example of the eternal battle between justification by faith and justification by acts that is still with us in our twentieth-century faith in nostrums, spiritual and intellectual.

The Cambridge Platonists afford an excellent example of those who have sought to know God by methods essentially in no wise different from the way in which man comes to know man and the world about him. The best known is Henry More, whose *Divine Dialogues* are a classic for their type. Henry More wished to know divine truth (his study of witchcraft as an evidence of the existence of God is in itself an interesting evidence of the status of English religious life in the seventeenth century), and devoted no small share of his life's work to a study of the meaning of God and the soul and the possible relations between the two. His highest flight in the envisaging of this quest seems to be his definition of what he calls the "Divine Sagacity," a principle "more noble and inward than Reason itself, and without which Reason will falter, or, at least, reach out to mean and frivolous things."[6] But the "Divine Sagacity" is in its nature but an illuminated reason. For More's approach, even to his beloved supernatural, is thoroughly rationalistic, as is apparent in a sentence from the "Brief Discourse of the True Grounds of the Certainty of Faith in Points of Religion," annexed to his *Divine Dialogues*, which thus lays down the law for

---

[6] Quoted from preface to "General Collection of Philosophical Writings of Henry More," in John Tullock, *Rational Theology and Christian Philosophy in England in the Seventeenth Century* (London, 1872), II, 356.

this curious development of Platonism: "Rightly circumstantiated Sense and Reason and Holy Writ are the truest Grounds of the Certainty of Faith."[7]

But for the seeking to know God as the highest act of the human mind in a larger sense than the rationalism of the preceding, we must go to Spinoza. Spinoza is especially interesting here because there can be nothing abstract or academic about the intellectual pilgrimages of a Jew of seventeenth-century Amsterdam whose divergences from the faith of his fathers led to his excommunication from the synagogue, while his general intellectual and spiritual bias prevented his joining either branch of the orthodox Christianity of the time. Spinoza is by no means indifferent to "the power which clear and distinct knowledge, and especially that third kind of knowledge, founded on the actual knowledge of God, possesses over the emotions,"[8] but his distinctive approach to this field and his dominating interest remain in the philosophic problem. "The mind's highest good is the knowledge of God, and the mind's highest virtue is to know God."[9] And though he recognizes intuition, the third of his classes of knowledge, as the highest, yet his definition of intuition is thoroughly intellectual and in no sense super-rational, like the *apex mentis* of the medievals or the contemplation of the Buddhists: "This kind of knowledge proceeds from an adequate idea of the absolute essence of certain attributes of God to the adequate knowledge of the essence of things."[10] Even Spinoza's idea of God, metaphysically mature as it is among the theological conceptions of all time, belongs to what one of his commentators has called "the distinctive advance of the scientific consciousness,"[11] rather than to the experience of the inner life, to the realistic endeavor of knowing what is, rather than to the mystic endeavor of knowing God.

What is true of one of the greatest of all mystic philosophers is even more true of those philosophers who put their major emphasis not upon knowing reality, but upon the way to know real-

[7] Henry More, *Divine Dialogues* (London, 1668), II, 492.

[8] Benedict de Spinoza, "Ethica," *The Chief Works of Benedict de Spinoza*, translated by R. H. M. Elwes (London, 1891), II, 258.

[9] *Ibid.*, p. 205.   [10] *Ibid.*, p. 113.

[11] Harold H. Joachim, *A Study of the Ethics of Spinoza* (Oxford, 1901), p. 262.

ity, of whom M. Henri Bergson is probably the most distinguished representative of our time. "Reality" is defined by M. Bergson in the most brilliant of modern versions of the flux of Heracleitus as "a perpetual growth, a creation' pursued without end."[12] Such an ever changing reality of becoming constantly eludes the categorical gropings of the intellect, for it is living, while the intellect, by definition, is accustomed and fitted to cope only with the dead, inert mechanisms of matter. To escape from the bondage of the material world and the inevitable limitations of an experience that has been fettered by its constant preoccupation with matter, M. Bergson appeals to psychology. In one of the most brilliant passages of a very brilliant treatise on *Creative Evolution*, M. Bergson urges this escape:

> Let us then concentrate attention on that which we have that is at the same time the most removed from externality and the least penetrated with intellectuality. Let us seek, in the depths of our experience, the point where we feel ourselves most intimately within our own life. It is into pure duration that we then plunge back, a duration in which the past, always moving on, is swelling unceasingly with a present that is absolutely new. But, at the same time, we feel the spring of our will strained to its utmost limit. We must, by a strong recoil of our personality on itself, gather up our past, which is slipping away, in order to thrust it, compact and undivided, into a present which it will create by entering. Rare indeed are the moments when we are self-possessed to this extent: it is then that our actions are truly free. And even at these moments we do not completely possess ourselves. Our feeling of duration, I should say the actual coinciding of ourself with itself, admits of degrees. But the more the feeling is deep and the coincidence complete, the more the life in which it replaces us, absorbs intellectuality by transcending it.[13]

As for the faculty by which this plunge is accomplished and which the plunge in turn cultivates, M. Bergson is more explicit in a later discussion of what he calls the two kinds of knowledge: the first, the knowledge by which we manage the inert world of matter: and the second, the kind of knowledge with which, as in the fore· going passage, we attempt to understand the reality of pure becoming. The second kind of knowledge would set the first aside, for it is not within the habitual world of matter but:

[12] Henri Bergson, *Creative Evolution*, translated by Arthur Mitchell (New York, 1911), p. 239.

[13] *Ibid.*, pp. 199–200.

. . . . within becoming that it would have transported us by an effort of sympathy. We should no longer be asking where a moving body will be, what shape a system will take, through what state a change will pass at a given moment : the moments of time, which are only arrests of our attention, would no longer exist; it is the flow of time, it is the very flux of the real that we should be trying to follow. The first kind of knowledge has the advantage of enabling us to foresee the future and of making us in some measure masters of events; in return, it retains of the moving reality only eventual immobilities, that is to say, views taken of it by our mind. It symbolizes the real and transposes it into the human rather than expresses it. . . . . The other knowledge, if it is possible, is practically useless, it will not extend our empire over nature, it will even go against certain natural aspirations of the intellect; but, if it succeeds, it is reality itself that it will hold in a firm and final embrace. Not only may we thus complete the intellect and its knowledge of matter by accustoming it to install itself within the moving, but by developing also another faculty, complementary to the intellect, we may open a perspective on the other half of the real. For, as soon as we are confronted with true duration, we see that it means creation, and that if that which is being unmade endures, it can only be because it is inseparably bound to what is making itself. Thus will appear the necessity of a continual growth of the universe, I should say of a *life* of the real. . . . . To intellect, in short, there will be added intuition.[14]

These two passages from *Creative Evolution* repay further scrutiny, for they not only analyze and describe the intuition which plays so large a part in contemporary thought, but they give a very glowing sense of how it works and, to put it rather naïvely, of how it feels. Here the poet in Bergson comes to the aid of the metaphysician in a fashion that is responsible for much of the charm of this delightful piece of epistemology. Many elements of the two accounts above will be recognized as in varying degrees mystical— the effort to discover reality not outside of, but within, the human consciousness, the relation of knowledge to its object, not knowing about or of, but knowing reality as it is in itself, the transcendence of ordinary categories, the sense of the ineffable, the conviction of illumination; these are, in a very conspicuous degree, mystical elements. But in its fundamental impulse and in its final claims the intuition of M. Bergson belongs to the realm of the problem of knowledge, of the knowing of reality, rather than to the field of what Mr. Charles Bennett has called the "being Real." It is another way of pointing out the old difference between what depends

---

[14] Bergson, *op. cit.*, pp. 342 f.

on the discipline and energy of the will and what rests on the working of the mind, a difference probably more fundamental than any questions, however engaging, of general feeling or impression.

Practically the same is true, for almost the opposite reasons, of that other great branch of the search for knowledge by super-rational—or, as the sceptic will say, infra-rational—means, represented most dramatically by the long history of alchemy. The roots of alchemy are to be found in the magic practices of savage tribes, probably better represented at the present time by the myths of the least advanced peoples than by any species of primitive man existent today. Those crude beginnings have found issue in developments of the present day of varying degrees of intellectual maturity. In a certain sense modern science is one; in another very different sense modern spiritualism is another; and in still a different sense modern occultism is a third.

For the nature of alchemy we may go to a somewhat confused, but very revealing, definition of the Abbot Trithemius, from whose book, printed in 1506, the following passage is taken:

The art of divine magic consists in the ability to perceive the essence of things in the light of Nature, and by using the soul-powers of the spirit to produce material things from the unseen universe (A'kasa) and in such operations the Above (the Macrocosm) and the Below (the Microcosm) must be brought together and made to act harmoniously. The spirit of Nature is a unity, creating and forming everything, and by acting through the instrumentality of man it may produce wonderful things. Such processes take place according to law. You will learn the law by which these things are accomplished, if you learn to know yourself. You will know it by the power of the spirit that is in yourself, and accomplish it by mixing your spirit with the essence that comes out of yourself. If you wish to succeed in such a work you must know how to separate spirit and life in Nature, and, moreover, to separate the astral soul in yourself and to make it tangible, and then the substance of the soul will appear visibly and tangibly, rendered objective by the power of the spirit. Christ speaks of the salt, and the salt is of a threefold nature. Gold is of a threefold nature, and there is an ethereal, a fluid, and a material gold. It is the same gold, only in three different states, and gold in one state may be made into gold in another state. But such mysteries should not be divulged, because the sceptic and scoffer will not be able to comprehend it, and to him who is covetous they will be a temptation.[15]

[15] Quoted by Franz Hartmann, *The Life of Philippus Theophrastus Bombast of Hohenheim, etc.* (London, 1910), pp. 289–90, footnote.

The classic motives of alchemy may be discerned in this passage: the desire for power, curiosity in its nobler sense, and a philosophic ambition to understand the whole. And there is some suggestion in it, too, of that range of interest which characterized alchemy at all times. The belief that the real mainsprings of nature are kept secret to be surprised only by the fully initiated is there, one of the oldest and most fundamental occultist beliefs. As will be shortly noticed in its due place among the efforts at symbolic interpretation, the *Cabala* and the tradition of biblical study out of which it came also represent such an effort to get at secret meanings. So do the various efforts at symbolic interpretation of scripture which have followed the ambiguous sentence of the founder of Christianity to his disciples:

Unto you it is given to know the mystery of the kingdom of God: but unto them that are without, all these things are done in parables. That seeing they may see, and not perceive; and hearing they may hear, and not understand, lest at any time they should be converted, and their sins should be forgiven them.[16]

So the ancient Gnostics, when challenged to produce the sources of the antinomian beliefs with which they were shocking early Christian orthodoxy, replied that they had "drawn these opinions from certain secret doctrines of Christ, which were not exposed to vulgar eyes."[17] The knowledge of such secrets, as notably in the case of the ancient book of magic called *The Sword of Moses*, which tells how the secret name of the Lord may be used to conjure with, was supposed to confer extraordinary power upon its possessor. Much of this higher magic presupposes an intuition that in some of its elements, especially in the case of the Greek mysteries, involves genuine ethical preparation, in an abbreviated form, much like the more extended discipline of the great mystic. Gnosis, for the alchemist as for the hermetic, is only for the pure of heart, as Ben Jonson's Pertinax Surly puts it in *The Alchemist*, "a pious, holy, and religious man." But the end in magic, as probably in the Greek mysteries, is chiefly power to transcend the limits of unaided

---

[16] Mark 4:11-12.

[17] John Lawrence Mosheim, *An Ecclesiastical History, Ancient and Modern, etc.*, translated by Archibald Maclaine (Berwick, 1809), I, 138.

human life, immortality being the highest manifestation of such transcendence.[18]

Paracelsus is the most famous example of those who have studied alchemy, not merely as a means of transmuting metals, but as a way to understanding nature. The sentence of Paracelsus which the Theosophical Publishing Company chose for the epigraph of the 1910 edition of Franz Hartmann's *Life and Doctrine* is significant of all of Paracelsus' teachings: "The beginning of wisdom is the beginning of supernatural power." Like many of the alchemists, Paracelsus believed that spiritual purification and enlightenment were essential to success in mastering the secrets of nature. And as Browning has drawn his mental portrait in the poem that bears his name, Paracelsus was unquestionably interested in the seeking of that sublime knowledge of the whole which transcends all knowledge of particulars, natural or supernatural. But there seems little doubt that his controlling purposes are fairly revealed in what he says at the outset of the *Archidoxies:*

First, then, we have to consider what is of all things most useful to man and most excellent. It is to learn the mysteries of Nature, by which we can discover what God is and what man is, and what avails a knowledge of heavenly eternity and earthly weakness. Hence arises a knowledge of theology, of justice, of truth, since the mysteries of Nature are the only true life of man, and those things are to be imitated which can be known and obtained from God as the Eternal Good. For, although many things are gained in medicine, and many more in the mysteries of Nature, nevertheless after this life the Eternal Mystery remains, and what it is we have no foundation for asserting, save that which has been revealed to us by Christ.[19]

And when Paracelsus displayed not unboastfully, as might be expected of the strolling doctor, his charter of authenticity, it is interesting that what he most relied upon was his possession of hidden knowledge: "From the middle of this age the Monarchy of all the Arts has been at length derived and conferred on me."[20]

So fundamental is this passion for understanding the secrets of the world that it is one of the hardest things for man to leave behind on his mystical pilgrimages. Even after Saint-Martin had

---

[18] Cf. Leuba, *op. cit.*, p. 49.

[19] Paracelsus, "The Archidoxies," *The Hermetic and Alchemical Writings*, translated by Arthur Edward Waite (London, 1894), II, Bk. I, 4.

[20] *Ibid.*, I, 19.

made his famous progress from occultism to mysticism, he could not rid himself of this instinct for knowing what is behind the veil of the future.[21] And Eckartshausen, who regards union with God as the highest goal of man's endeavors, yet devotes much of his *Mistische Nächte* to a celebration of that divinely shared wisdom which teaches the initiate "to recognize the bonds which join the mental to the physical and through which the understanding of all nature is revealed to him, and he beholds things which the wisdom of man could never come near."[22]

The alchemists, then, even at their highest level in a man of great scientific genius like Paracelsus, and the "seekers" in general are, like the idealistic philosophers and the intuitionists, at one with the great mystics in their dissatisfaction with the ordinary limits of experience and their desire to transcend them, but they differ from the great mystics in the fact that for them the problem remains essentially one of knowledge, that their highest reaches are to see with God, to understand God, to know God, rather than to be one with God. Even though most seekers of the gnosis recognize the necessity of some sort of initiation or transformation or preparation, that means little more than what is implied in the scriptural promise that the pure of heart shall see God. Intellect and imagination are still more important (especially in Paracelsus) than will.

Just as some of the intellectual features of mysticism are common to a larger field than that of the greater mystics, even more so are some of the emotional, the more broadly experiential, aspects. The distinguishing mark of the activity of the typical mystics is, as we have seen, the immediate experience of God. In that complete, fully realized form, it is, of course, peculiar to them. But lesser degrees of that experience and adumbrations of varying degree are by no means confined to them. In a certain sense we have all had some elementary mystical experience; in those moments, for instance, when, looking out upon a world lighted by joy or darkened by pain, we behold a strange reality emerging from the mists of our everyday experience. Again, everyone has known that sudden

[21] Arthur Edward Waite, *The Life of Louis Claude de Saint-Martin, the Unknown Philosopher, and the Substance of His Transcendental Doctrine* (London, 1901), p. 206.

[22] Eckartshausen, *Mistische Nächte oder der Schlüssel zu den Geheimnissen des Wunderbaren, u.z.w.* (München, 1791), p. 270.

poignant moment of insight when another spirit lifts to our short-sighted eyes a glass that commands a far greater sweep upon eternity than any we have yet dreamed of. Again, we have all known those times of stress and doubt when, out of the welter of things tried and rejected or yet unappropriated, there suddenly leaps to the desperate need of the moment a totally unsuspected faith and certainty which, so far as the face of things is concerned, we can in no wise justify and, so far as every prompting of the life within is concerned, we can in no wise reject.

Such seems to be the essential nature of religious conversion, whatever the level on which it occurs or however slight the substance of the immediate experience may be. *The Everlasting Mercy* of Mr. John Masefield is probably the best known contemporary account of a common type of such change of moral and spiritual outlook. And such also seems to be the nature of those experiences hardly to be termed either "religious" or "conversion," wherein the soul suddenly discovers within itself some source of energy hitherto despaired of or unsuspected. Such is the account which one great spirit, who would hardly have called himself a mystic or much more than a lay preacher quite without the joyous fold of those who live in the hearth light of God, gives of an experience which gave him heart to confront his own despair and battle, to no glorious conclusion, perhaps, but certainly to stout, manly fortitude. It is the story which Thomas Carlyle puts into the mouth of his mythical philosopher in *Sartor Resartus,* of how he triumphed over the "Everlasting Nay." He had been living for what seemed years in a state of mind in which

it seemed as if all things in the Heavens above and the Earth beneath would hurt me; as if the Heavens and the Earth were but boundless jaws of a devouring monster, wherein I, palpitating, waited to be devoured.

Full of such humor, and perhaps the miserablest man in the whole French Capital or Suburbs, was I, one sultry Dog-day, after much perambulation, toiling along the dirty little Rue Saint-Thomas de l'Enfer, among civic rubbish enough, in a close atmosphere, and over pavements hot as Nebuchadnezzar's Furnace; whereby doubtless, my spirits were little cheered; when, all at once, there rose a Thought in me, and I asked myself: "What *art* thou afraid of? Wherefore, like a coward, dost thou forever pip and whimper, and go cowering and trembling? Despicable biped! what is the sum-total of the worst that lies before thee? Death? Well, Death; and say the pangs of Tophet too, and all that the Devil and Man may, will or can do against thee! Hast thou not a heart; canst thou not suffer whatsoever it be; and, as a Child of Freedom, though outcast, trample Tophet itself under thy feet, while it consumes thee? Let it come, then; I will meet it and defy it!" And as I so thought, there rushed like a stream of fire over my whole soul; and I shook base Fear away from me forever. I was strong, of unknown strength; a spirit, almost a God. Ever from that time, the temper of my misery was changed: not Fear or whining Sorrow was it, but Indignation and grim fire-eyed Defiance.

Thus had the Everlasting No (*das ewige Nein*) pealed authoritatively through all the recesses of my Being, of my Me; and then was it that my whole Me stood up, in native God-created majesty, and with emphasis recorded its Protest. Such a Protest, the most important transaction in Life, may that same Indignation and Defiance, in a psychological point of view, be fitly called. The Everlasting No had said: "Behold, thou art fatherless, outcast, and the Universe is mine (the Devil's)"; to which my whole Me now made answer: "I am not thine, but Free, and forever hate thee!"

It is from this hour that I incline to date my Spiritual New-birth, or Baphometic Fire-baptism; perhaps I directly thereupon began to be a Man.[23]

Carlyle's experience is more sharply marked than most of our experiences of this type, because it was an intellectual experience in the stress of a battle with his own mind, and that a mind singularly aware of its own movements and uncommonly searching in its self-analysis. But its increased sharpness and substance is not due to any consciousness of strength from outside. In its sense of the necessity of self-reliance it is Stoic rather than religious, and in its self-determination it is purely humanistic.

The average experience, unless falling into some channel already clearly marked out by the religious tradition or environment, as in the case of the revivalist Methodist conversion, is much more diffuse, much more elusive of intellectual scrutiny. It is more nearly expressed by the poets when they strive to grasp "those thoughts beyond the reaches of our souls" that vex our moments of deepest sensitiveness and fullest imagination:

> . . . . Those obstinate questionings
> Of sense and outward things,
> Fallings from us, vanishings;
> Blank misgivings of a Creature
> Moving about in worlds not realized,
> High instincts before which our mortal Nature
> Did tremble like a guilty Thing surprised. . . . .

[23] "Sartor Resartus," *The Works of Thomas Carlyle* (New York, 1897), XII, 128-29.

of Wordsworth's great ode. Or, on the positive side, making for peace and reconciliation with the heart of things, doubtless the type of experience which the same poet describes in *Tintern Abbey* has come, in some more or less conscious form, to hundreds of men who had not the great poet's gift of disburdening the heart in words. It is of the beauteous forms of cliff, and tree, and field that he writes:

> . . . . These beauteous forms,
> Through a long absence, have not been to me
> As is a landscape to a blind man's eye:
> But oft, in lonely rooms, and 'mid the din
> Of towns and cities, I have owed to them
> In hours of weariness, sensations sweet,
> Felt in the blood, and felt along the heart;
> And passing even into my purer mind,
> With tranquil restoration. . . . .
> . . . . Nor less, I trust,
> To them I may have owed another gift,
> Of aspect more sublime; that blessed mood,
> In which the burthen of the mystery,
> In which the heavy and the weary weight
> Of all this unintelligible world,
> Is lightened:—that serene and blessed mood,
> In which the affections gently lead us on,—
> Until, the breath of this corporeal frame
> And even the motion of our human blood
> Almost suspended, we are laid asleep
> In body, and become a living soul;
> While with an eye made quiet by the power
> Of harmony, and the deep power of joy,
> We see into the life of things.

There is much in the elevation of this passage, much in the type of feeling which it describes to justify the adjective "mystical" in defining it. But since this belongs to a class of experience, whether expressed in poetry or not, in which it is rare for its fullness of realization and beauty of expression rather than for its essential nature, it is well to notice at least in passing that full as it is, and even profound in its description of the moment, its meaning for mysticism depends upon its context, and that its context, while more than adequate for great poetry, is tenuous for great mysticism at that point of ethical relation which is so much more consequential for mysticism than for poetry. Here, then, we have a mood, perhaps a disposition of feeling, which is redolent of the mystical, but its power does not go far enough beyond that—indeed, there is no reason for the poem why it should do so—for it to find its place in the revelations of mysticism.

As for the seeing "into the life of things," that is one of the most popular of the reasons given for calling certain great poets like Wordsworth, Shelley, Byron, Tennyson, Browning—the list might be multiplied almost ad infinitum—mystics. There is probably no aspect of the poet's gift, save perhaps the sheer genius for song, that more impresses the nonpoetic observer than this amazing power of discerning in the everyday world a beauty, a meaning, a wonder, which the common mass of uninspired humanity passes daily without seeing. There is no magic so transforming as the magic of the seeing eye in a world of the blind. But here again the element of sheer emotion is likely to be more important than anything else when we try to understand what practically defies understanding. It would be interesting to determine how much of this is due to the sheer magic of the form, the music, the pulse of the verse, and other imponderables of the poetic form. We may go some way toward isolating the noetic elements from the largely emotional by taking a prose example of that sort of transformation. A fair specimen may be found in a very charming passage from a writer who has done much to open the world of physical nature to the inexperienced. It is from W. H. Hudson's *A Hind in Richmond Park:*

> Apart from the aesthetic feelings which the object or scene or atmospheric conditions may rouse . . . . there is a sense of the *thing itself*—of the tree or wood, the rock, river, sea, mountain, the soil, clay or gravel, or sand or chalk, the cloud, the rain, and what not—something, let us say, penetrative, special, individual, as if the quality of the thing itself had entered into us, changing us, affecting body and mind.[24]

Without the magic of poetry that makes any very exacting scrutiny almost impossible, this passage gives a very intelligent and sensitive impression of a type of phenomenon in which lyric poetry, especially the lyric of the so-called "nature poets," whether of the

[24] W. H. Hudson, *A Hind in Richmond Park* (New York, 1923), p. 30.

seventeenth or the nineteenth century, abounds. In its prose it reveals a process which adds much to the sense of the mysterious and the strangely old-and-new which baffles literal-mindedness. But in its essence it is a process which quite exactly reverses the mystical process. It is a simplification, not by transcendence, but by isolation. It does not seek to gather up the detail that it may climb to the whole, or to sweep all the particulars together that it may see the universal, or to eliminate the divisions that it may grasp the meanings of the relations. What it does is to wash out the whole, to sever the connections, to break the threads that bind the individual object to its context, to sweep away the meanings which prevent our seeing the literal data, and to concentrate on them. Of course, there is always something startling and even awe-inspiring in the impact of such a freshly naked phenomenon on our meaning-attuned faculties, but the mystical element in such a case consists rather in our reaction to the experience than in its real nature.

One of the most disenchanting facts about the ineffable experience which seems at first sight to be the most peculiarly characteristic mark of mysticism is that it is by no means peculiar to the mystical experience per se. As an abundant body of evidence scientific and unscientific suggests, and as recent researches on the various drugs, such as mescal, which primitive people use to produce ecstasy make plain, ecstasy can be produced by very humble means, and an at least temporarily satisfying transfiguration of the world effected by nothing more potent than whiskey or surgeons' ether.[25] Happily, no such merely rational consideration can have any power when the mind is in the full tide of the experience of a sunset or a vision or a rapture, but the critic must remember such daylight considerations as part of the penalty he pays for a little curiosity.

One thing more must be included in even a rough sketch of literary mysticism or poetic mysticism, and that is the question of poetic visions as distinguished from prophetic visions, which will be discussed later on, or symbolism, also to be discussed later in its own right. Certain visions are, of course, literary conventions. Chaucer's *Parlement of Foules* is an excellent example of the pure-

[25] Lêuba, *op. cit.*, chap. ii.

ly literary device which, even made real by a master of description, deceives nobody. The great allegories of the race, as distinguished from the fairy stories or the myths, are another example. *The Pilgrim's Progress* is a great presentation of the history of the human soul far vaster and more universal than the experience of one tinker's son of Bedford, transcending in its simplicity and reality any possible intention of even a great creative artist, so that it seems the work of nature herself working with a depth and a surety beyond the power of man, but the miracle of its creation has nothing to do with the supernatural; it is purely a miracle of literary creation. That is, a man with an extraordinary power of visualization suddenly saw human life lie before him simply and concretely, as the author of *Piers Plowman* had seen it lie before him, as the author of the *Inferno* had seen the world of the Middle Ages lie before him, and the lineaments of that imaginative—if you will, poetic—vision became as real to him as the stones about him and the village streets which he had walked beyond the gaol, and he lived with them as the great artist always lives with the people he draws. It is said that for days Flaubert tasted on his tongue the poison with which Emma Bovary had ended her life.[26] All inspiration that carries the human mind beyond the limits of its habitual earth-keeping inertia must seem an influx from a strange world of power without. It is no wonder that in times past men have called it divine. And it is hard to see how even the behavioristic psychologist will be able to explain "the light that never was on sea or land" in terms of pen and ink and aching head, or, to be quite up-to-date, portable Corona and cigarette. But this strange fire that every so often burns human lips does not confine itself to poetic frenzy There is an abundance of evidence that inspiration works so in the solution of mathematical formulas, in the framing of hypotheses in physics, in the elaboration of detective theories, conceivably even in matters of tariff and university curricula. In certain fields it may be distinctly mystical, but here again it looks as if the inspiration were defined by the context, and not the context by the inspiration. For the ineffable experience, then, as for the preoccupation with spiritual reality and the seeking of the knowledge of reality,

[26] Leuba, *op. cit.*, p. 289.

we may say that while there are undoubted elements of the mystical in many of the cases that challenge our definition, they do not in themselves constitute mysticism, appearing, as they do so frequently, in unquestionably non-mystical contexts.

With our approach to the ground of the problem of knowing, with its component problems of vision, of revelation, of supernatural direction, of prophecy, we come to ground less common to ordinary experience and probably of less general interest, but of perhaps even more interest to the special student. It is also more debatable ground than any of that considered before in the present chapter because here the point of view of modern psychological criticism has made certain ground uncomfortable even for the literary student, to whom certain traditional values are dear. To be specific, it is easy to take the text-tagging voices that pursue John Bunyan through the agonies of *Grace Abounding unto the Chief of Sinners* as the projections of his own hypochondriac scrupulosity, but to account in similar fashion for Ezekiel's four beasts by the river Chebar is, whatever the degree of one's personal attachment to these extraordinary beings, to rob the religious traditions of the race of a great deal of their lustre. Fortunately, the question of value does not always depend for its phrasing on the question of literal or metaphysical reality.

What has been said of the sense of the ineffable applies almost as fully to the visions. First of all, they are by no means limited to the experience of the mystic. Leaving out of account the vast class of hallucinations and delusions incident to various mental diseases or to unusual states of nervous tension, there is the great realm of vision opened by drugs. Two men of literary genius, Coleridge and De Quincey, have familiarized the English-speaking world with the often magnificent visions of the opium-eater, while there is an abundance of testimony as to visionary experiences enjoyed under the influence of various other narcotics and even of the more common anaesthetics.

Then, too, visions may have much meaning or none. They may be as trivial, as irrelevant, as dreams. They may be so fantastic, so involved, as to exhaust all the interpreter's energies in their bare decipherment, and when they have been deciphered they may yield meanings no more impressive than those of the Rosicrucian parables which Dr. Silberer expounds in his treatise on the *Problems of Mysticism and Its Symbolism*.[27] Or they may be so simple, so relevant to human nature's most enduring needs, so appealing to imagination and the sense of beauty as well as to the desires, that, like the dream of the City of God which has fired the religious imagination from the days of St. John to Francis Thompson, they may speak to the wise and the simple alike, stimulating the one to the full and direct realization of the vision that makes it potent for the spiritual life, and the other to that appropriation and use which gives vision its substance and its most authentic claim to value.

Visions may be revelatory or not, just as the ineffable mystic experience may or may not be revelatory. But practically all visions, like practically all ecstasies, even those whose physical or mechanical causes are easily ascertainable, come to the consciousness with a sense of meaning. Even when they are apparently fairly simple and self-contained they tease the imagination to find out the significance, just as do vivid dreams. "It must mean something!" is the normal human reaction to the aura which they wear. A sense of being on the threshold of a great discovery, of being just within reach of the solution of some great problem, sometimes even a psychological or scientific problem, seems to be a common experience of yielding to anaesthetics, for instance. There seems to be in this field, at least, abundant evidence to support the conclusions which Mr. Leuba has drawn for trance-consciousness in general:

In the condition of diminished and degraded mental activity characteristic of trance, certain sensations, or the disappearance of certain sensations, certain feelings and certain emotions—which in certain instances have a purely physiological origin—may give rise to the thought of a great achievement.[28]

This noetic quality is one of the most interesting and the most central aspects of mystical experience, but it is interesting to note, as has been noted in the preceding chapter, how little value the great mystics attach to these experiences in comparison with that final experience of union toward which they are working.

Some of the lesser mystics, however, place a great deal of em-

[27] Translated by Smith Ely Jelliffe (New York, 1917), chap. i.
[28] Leuba, *op. cit.*, p. 273.

phasis upon revelation for itself. Swedenborg and his early followers seem especially to have done so. Indeed, in matters of everyday history, Swedenborg's revelations descend even to the level of clairvoyance, as in the account which Kant gives of how Swedenborg, at a time when he was in Gottenburg, nearly three hundred miles away, knew of a great fire that was raging in Stockholm.[29] But for more important matters Swedenborg seems to have believed also that they were directly shown to him, as in the case of the "Universal Theology of the New Church" set forth in *The True Christian Religion,* which was given to him in this fashion:

> Awaking on a time out of sleep, I fell into a profound meditation about God, and when I looked upwards I saw in the heaven above me a most clear shining light in an oval form. As I fixed my eyes attentively upon that light, it gradually receded from the centre towards the circumference; and lo! heaven was then opened before me, and I beheld magnificent scenes, and saw angels standing in the form of a circle, on the southern side of the opening, in conversation with each other; and because I earnestly desired to know what they were conversing about, it was permitted me first to hear the sound of their voices, which was full of celestial love, and afterwards to distinguish their speech, which was full of wisdom flowing from that love.[30]

To something of the same province, at least in outward appearance, belongs the consciousness of heavenly direction which plays so large a part in the history of the Quakers. The *Journal* of George Fox is full of instances in which he felt that he had been directed by heaven to act as he did. Sometimes he speaks definitely of a voice in a sense strongly reminiscent of Bunyan's experience, as in one of his accounts of his earlier history: "I heard a voice which said, 'There is one, even Christ Jesus, that can speak to thy condition.' "[31] But more often it is something more inwardly pervasive than any voice, as when he stood listening to a sermon in a steeple-house, "Now the Lord's power was so mighty upon me and so strong in me, that I could not hold; but was made to cry out, 'Oh! no; it is not the scriptures.' "[32] or when again he stood in a quiet market place where centuries before the blood of early

[29] Nathaniel Hobart, *Life of Emanuel Swedenborg* (Boston, 1845), p. 71.

[30] Swedenborg, Emanuel, *The True Christian Religion; containing the Universal Theology of the New Church, foretold by the Lord* (New York, 1912), § 25.

[31] *Journal* (Philadelphia, no date), p. 60.

[32] *Ibid.*, p. 76.

Christian martyrs had drenched the stones, "Then was I commanded by the Lord to pull off my shoes. I stood still, for it was winter; and the word of the Lord was like a fire in me. So I put off my shoes."[33] But the kind of direction found in these pages which is of the type more common to Quaker experience as represented, say, in the daily experience of a John Woolman, is the "opening," which seems to be a sudden "coming clear" within the mind of the worshiper which makes him see the point at issue clearly and the relevant answer, and makes him yearn to communicate his discovery or to act in accordance with it, a type of mental process probably analogous in a rough fashion to poetic inspiration, although, in cases such as the foregoing, accompanied by a sense of moral compulsion which the habit of the religious specialist naturally refers to a supernatural origin. Here again the question of context is of very great importance.

The same is true in an even more literal sense of prophecy which in a maturer fashion usually combined all three ways of knowing—vision, revelation, supernatural direction—but which in its highest forms has assumed responsibilities for literal reality not usually assumed by the visionary at least. To waive for a moment the question of fact, and to consider prophecy in itself, there are two very distinct ways of approaching the problem of what prophecy is. The first is what we may call the introspective approach. What is a prophet like as seen by himself? In other words, What is the prophetic consciousness? It is the question which Mr. Hocking asks and answers thus:

By the prophetic consciousness I do not mean a knowledge that something is to happen in the future, accomplished by forces beyond myself : I mean a knowledge that this act of mine which I now utter is to succeed and hold its place in history. It is an assurance of the future and of all time as determined by my own individual will, embodied in my present action. It is a power which knows itself to be such, and justly measures its own scope.[34]

So defined, the prophetic consciousness is a consciousness of having seen the truth, of having a message whose authenticity and significance are quite beyond any question of the fitness of the

[33] George Fox, *Journal*, p. 97.
[34] Hocking, *op. cit.*, p. 503.

messenger, being justified by him who sent the messenger. The Old Testament, the richest single mine of prophecy in Western tradition, at least, gives just such a picture of the prophetic calling, of his charter of regency, in the vivid account which Isaiah gives of his calling to prophecy:

In the year that king Uzziah died I saw also the Lord sitting upon a throne, high and lifted up, and his train filled the temple.

Above it stood the seraphims: each one had six wings; with twain he covered his face, and with twain he covered his feet, and with twain he did fly.

And one cried unto another, and said, Holy, holy, holy, is the Lord of hosts: the whole earth is full of his glory.

And the posts of the door moved at the voice of him that cried, and the house was filled with smoke.

Then said I, Woe is me! for I am undone; because I am a man of unclean lips, and I dwell in the midst of a people of unclean lips: for mine eyes have seen the King, the Lord of hosts.

Then flew one of the seraphims unto me, having a live coal in his hand, which he had taken with the tongs from off the altar:

And he laid it upon my mouth, and said, Lo, this hath touched thy lips; and thine iniquity is taken away, and thy sin purged.

Also I heard the voice of the Lord, saying, Whom shall I send, and who will go for us? Then said I, Here am I; send me.

And he said, Go, and tell this people.[35]

In other words, the central fact of the prophetical consciousness is that he has seen the truth, what really is, and it is his part to make that known.

The other approach to the prophet—and here again we have a definition from a purely lay source, who did not himself claim any supernatural call—we may call the objective, the historical, that asks, "What is a prophet as he appears in this world of men; what, in what we can make out of his thought and action, marks him out from other men?" It is Carlyle who answers this question in his discussion of the career of Mahomet:

A Hero . . . . has this first distinction, which indeed we may call first and last, the Alpha and Omega of his whole Heroism, that he looks through the shows of things into *things*. Use and wont, respectable hearsay, respectable formula: all these are good, or are not good. There is something behind and beyond all these, which all these must correspond with, be the image of, or they are—*Idolatries;* "bits of black wood pretending to be God"; to the

[35] Isa. 6:1-9.

earnest soul a mockery and abomination. Idolatries never so gilded, waited on by heads of the Koreish will do nothing for this man. Though all men walk by them, what good is it? The great Reality stands glaring there upon *him*. He there has to answer it, or perish miserably. Now, even now, or else through all Eternity never! . . . . Mahomet was in his fortieth year, when having withdrawn to a cavern in Mount Hara, near Mecca, during this Ramadhan, to pass the month in prayer, and meditation on those great questions, he one day told his wife Kadijah, who with his household was with him or near him this year, That by the unspeakable special favor of Heaven he had now found it all out; was in doubt and darkness no longer, but saw it all. That all these Idols and Formulas were nothing, miserable bits of wood; that there was One God in and over all; and we must leave all Idols, and look to Him. . . . . He is the Reality. . . . . That Mahomet's whole soul, set in flame with this grand Truth vouchsafed him, should feel as if it were important and the only important thing, was very natural. That Providence had unspeakably honored *him* by revealing it, saving him from death and darkness; that he therefore was bound to make known the same to all creatures: this is what was meant by "Mahomet is the Prophet of God."[36]

This definition of Carlyle's is well borne out by what we know of biblical prophecy, Hosea, Ezekiel, Isaiah, St. John the Divine. There is the effort to find out the truth, generally an effort motivated by revulsion from the errors and shams and sins which the prophet sees about him, an effort to get at what, travestied or neglected, lies behind the shallower, hearsay ways about him. Then there is the sudden, dramatic, often visible, answer to his quest, a revelation which fills him not only with a sense of what is real, but with a compulsion to make that known. From whichever angle we approach the matter, that seems to be the essence of the prophet.

In view of the large part which discipline or preparation plays in the history of the mystic, it is interesting to notice the evidences of much concern with spiritual problems, the signs of long struggle with the difficulties involved, the familiarity with practical issues of doctrine, of conduct, of group disposition and tendency which so strongly mark the great prophecies of the Bible, both in the Old and the New Testaments, whether it be Isaiah arraigning the wickedness of the people of Israel or St. John the Divine taking stock of the heresies, the weaknesses, the indifferences of the first-century Christian congregations. There is much here to justify the saying of the great Jewish philosopher of the Middle Ages, Maimonides,

---

[36] Thomas Carlyle, "Heroes and Hero Worship," *Works*, XII, 285–88.

that "Prophecy is impossible without study and training; when these have created the possibility, then it depends on the will of God whether the possibility is to be turned into reality."[37]

It is here in the field of prophecy that the mystical is most dramatically and vigorously challenged by the historical. Joachim de Flore, like many another promulgator of a new gospel, was, if we may believe the somewhat imperfect accounts that have come down to us, perfectly sure that he had grasped the reality which would mend the imperfections of the church of his time. He "foretold the destruction of the church of *Rome,* whose corruption he censured with the greatest severity, and the promulgation of a new and more *perfect gospel* in *the age of the Holy Ghost,* by a set of poor and austere ministers whom God was to raise up and employ for that purpose."[38] So great was the appeal of the rather fantastic form in which he set forth this new gospel of the Holy Ghost which was to supplement the outworn gospels of the Father and the Son that many of the Spiritual Franciscans enthusiastically embraced it. But its grasp of the realities of the life of the age and of the enduring problems of human nature was so imperfect that its once almost revolutionary influence was exhausted, and today it is a curiosity for the student. Here probably the most important and complicated problem of value which we have yet encountered arises. Though the consideration of that is better broached with the questions of value fundamental to the whole field, one thing may be noted in passing: that there seems to be a definite ratio between the power with which a prophet deals with the everyday world of human motive and capacity and action, and the enduring interest of his prophecy beyond the confines of his own cult and his own age.

Like the mystic, the prophet finds the ordinary categories of experience inadequate for the expression of the reality which he has come to know. For language, however rarefied by metaphysics or poetry, is still fundamentally the coin of everyday experience, of the rough interchange of common sense and feeling and thought.

[37] Quoted in Jacob A. Kaplan, *A Study of the Prophetic Mind as Manifested by the Ancient Hebrew Prophets* (Philadelphia, 1909), p. 88.

[38] Mosheim, *op. cit.,* III, 210.

What the prophet has to tell is of what lies at the roots of the everyday far below our superficial delving, of what transcends our world far above the utmost flight of our earth-keeping dreams. His problem, then, is with our earth-grown language to suggest what far transcends it; to put what forever eludes the grasp of the senses into the vesture of this world, that the children of this world may understand it and be won to forsake their lowly haunts for a place of higher reality. Surely it is one of the most heroically paradoxical ventures that man has ever attempted.

So he invokes symbol and parable and myth, that the earth itself may give the fancy a spring to leave it. The most common symbols of the great mystics, the rebirth, the union, represent the effort to communicate the experience of the mystic. Similarly, the symbols of the prophet are efforts to communicate the truth which he has seen. Sometimes the symbols which the prophet uses come to him in a vision, a vision distinguished from the generality of visions in that the meaning is the absorbing thing, rather than the figures seen or the voices heard. This does not mean that they may not be very vivid, and even dramatic. Usually the symbols which the great religious traditions have handed down from generation to generation are of this order. The Revelation of St. John the Divine is an example again of the type of religious symbolism which has exerted a powerful influence on all succeeding mystical writing. Some of the symbolism in this great prophetic vision is very simple, almost to the point of literalness. The vision of the seven candlesticks and the seven stars is immediately explained by the "one like unto the Son of man" as the symbols of the seven churches of Asia and the symbols of the seven angels of the seven churches. And even where the succeeding symbols are not explicitly interpreted, their meaning is made quite apparent.

In some cases these symbols are very old ones. The four beasts, probably going back to symbols of life of ancient Assyria, have already been made famous by Ezekiel; and the symbol of the new Jerusalem gathers up a long and noble tradition of the dreams and the longings of the great prophets, splendid with the genius of Jeremiah and Isaiah, to name only two. Much of the symbolism, too, is not only rich in traditional association, but in itself full of fresh dramatic color—the vivid picture of the woman upon the scarlet beast, the famous four horsemen, the four-and-twenty elders casting down their crowns, to mention only a few of the most notable. And so the vision rises to its great climax in the twenty-first and twenty-second chapters:

And I saw a new heaven and a new earth: for the first heaven and the first earth were passed away; and there was no more sea.

And I John saw the holy city, new Jerusalem, coming down from God out of heaven, prepared as a bride adorned for her husband,

And I heard a great voice out of heaven saying, Behold, the Tabernacle of God is with men, and he will dwell with them, and they shall be his people, and God himself shall be with them, and be their God.

And God shall wipe away all tears from their eyes; and there shall be no more death, neither sorrow, nor crying, neither shall there be any more pain; for the former things are passed away.

.   .   .   .

And he shewed me a pure river of water of life, clear as crystal, proceeding out of the throne of God and of the Lamb.

In the midst of the street of it, and on either side of the river, was there the tree of life, which bare twelve manner of fruits, and yielded her fruit every month: and the leaves of the tree were for the healing of the nations.

And there shall be no more curse: but the throne of God and of the Lamb shall be in it; and his servants shall serve him;

And they shall see his face; and his name shall be in their foreheads.

And there shall be no night there, and they need no candle, neither light of the sun; for the Lord God giveth them light: and they shall reign for ever and ever.

This passage has been quoted at length because it is an example of symbolism on a very high level, symbolism which has entered into the language of the race, still living even today wherever the concepts which it expresses are still of interest. It also shows unusually well certain characteristics of successful symbolism. Its symbols are not peculiar; they are, in general, not new-made for the occasion. They come, for the most part, even when they are given a fresh turn, from a long history of evolution and use. They therefore bring with them a wealth of association, deepened and enriched by the thought and feeling of generations. They have a fragrance of meaning that the cleverest of newly minted symbols can never have. They are rich with the personal consciousness of untold individuals, but they have a larger life than any one individual could give them.

Yet they are fresh, for they are here used to express a very fresh, and in that sense new, experience of truth. There is no question of any conventional literary experience here. They are redolent of the intensity, of the glow of immediacy, of a very fresh personal experience; of the thoughts and feelings of a man who has seen for himself what no hearsay or tradition could tell him. They are therefore concrete and particular, with that amount of detail that particularizes and vitalizes the abstract and the general. But they are also simple and direct in the sense that, with one or two exceptions (notably the description of the gates of the city, omitted from the verses quoted above), no elaboration of detail is suffered to obscure the central meaning. There is little of the working out of detail for detail's own sake that one finds alike in the lesser poetry and the lesser symbolism. Greatness of symbolism seems to be due to the same qualities that make for greatness in allegory and in poetic imagery generally, concreteness, clarity, simplicity, beauty, and meaningfulness for heart and mind.

But here in symbolism, as in all manifestations of the human spirit, the great process of formalistic corruption has been at work. For in symbolism, as in all its other works, it seems to be well-nigh impossible for humanity to avoid confusing the means with the end. It is like the problem of technique in art, the old problem of formalism in religious observance. For one great painter who, having mastered his technique, devotes all his energies to the realization of his vision, there are a hundred brilliant technicians who lavish a wealth of medium and method upon a handful of trivial conceptions. For one genuine saint there are a thousand devotees. So with symbolism. From being a means, a groping, half-conscious effort to achieve an end beyond its powers, it becomes an end in itself. And a Boehme or a Swedenborg or any of a score of lesser heavenly geographers works away at the elaboration of a huge symbolistic system which threatens at any moment to engulf the narrow basis of meaning upon which it arose. This process is the counterpart, in the sphere of the imagination, of the scholastic process in the realm of the intellect.

The imagination under such circumstances becomes liable to the same obsession which sometimes seizes upon the ear when the sound of words becomes more important than their meaning. Almost everyone has had the experience of falling under the spell of some combination of sounds that satisfies an obscure craving of the ear without any regard to what it means. Very much the same sort of thing seems to happen with symbols, like the "beast having seven heads and ten horns, and upon his head ten crowns." They haunt the imagination long after the context which gave them meaning has faded away, until in time they become themselves the occasion of elaborate significations and correspondences which grow, mushroom-like, out of all proportion to their occasion or their meaning.

Or the delight in curious symbolism may give rise to a faith in obscurity for its own sake, and the search for hidden meanings, like the search of the romantic knight for adventure, may end in the conquest of giants that for the normal mind never existed. The elaborate system of signatures and correspondences which Swedenborg worked out is only one example of what has happened in every tradition when the search for hidden meanings has taken the place of the genuinely spiritual activity which created the great symbols and invested them with meaning beyond the chance associations of ear and eye. Much of the commentaries of Shankara for the Hindu tradition, and much of the Cabala for the Hebrew esoteric tradition, noble as is its purpose, "by a subtle understanding of the Scriptures . . . . to trace out the way to God for men, to shew them how they may act with Him, and prophesy from Him,"[39] is devoted to this quest. However inspiriting the results of such multiplications of interpretations may be to those who devote their energies to them, to the average mortal this searching out of hidden meanings will probably always be singularly barren of either spiritual illumination or inspiration.

When one views the field of the mystical in general, from the so-called mystic beliefs in spiritual reality to the colossal brain structures of prophetic and cabalistic symbolism, the variety and the complexity of it all seem overwhelming. And the inevitable

[39] Paracelsus, *The Hermetic and Alchemical Writings*, I, 51.

more-or-less emotional reaction to the impressiveness of the total is the question, "What does it all amount to?" That question has, however, more than emotional significance, for any form of human activity that is so nearly coextensive with human history and that has absorbed so much of human energy inevitably raises the challenge of value. And that, in turn, raises the question of degree of value for the individual manifestation.

To the question of value for the entire field, we need hardly answer. For, in a sense, history has already answered it for us. The mysticism of the typical mystics can be, as we have seen, abundantly justified by the way in which it has still further energized and ennobled personalities of singular human worth. The Middle Ages and Oriental antiquity were probably quite right in their faith that the saint is, in a very literal sense, his own excuse for being Mysticism has, moreover, on the testimony of those who have devoted themselves to it, proved the most satisfactory of all possible ways of life, and here the sceptic must face the fact that very few ways of living have been so enthusiastically called good, first and last, by their exponents as the way of the mystics. Then the contribution which mysticism, in the person of its greatest representatives, has made to the common religious life of the race, surely one of the race's most significant purely human undertakings, puts its historic significance beyond value. For not only the mystic, but humanity in general, has been very much the richer, the surer, the nobler for the great mysticism.

As for the rest of the mystical field, in the person of its greatest representatives, what has already been said of the great mystic holds true. The mystic philosopher and the prophet are at their highest among the greatest of the children of men, among those to whom the human race at large is most heavily indebted. Even the great alchemists like Paracelsus are of importance to the human race, if not in the strictly religious field, then certainly in the history of the search for knowledge. The instincts which prompt men even to the least noble aspects of their search for knowledge are too deep-rooted, too fundamentally essential to human satisfaction, too productive of unexpected and incidental value for the human race at large to need serious defense.

Unfortunately, absolute, mechanical certification of authenticity is no more to be attained in religion than the short cut, the magic formula for which the heart of our self-improving age yearns. When Miss Underhill, whose judgment all humbler students of mysticism must respect, says, "The only interpreters of Christian doctrine to whose judgment we are bound to submit will be those in whom this process of development has taken place; who are proved to have followed 'The Mystic Way,' attained that consciousness, that independent spiritual life, which alone is really Christian,"[40] she offers us a certainty which we must say we have no right to. The great mystic is justified by himself, by his way of life, by the viability of the spiritual patterns which he has followed. For a mystic whom history has not so acclaimed, we can seek the motives of his working, examine his methods, scrutinize the fruits of his mysticism, and say whether or not they belong with those which have already proved so triumphantly successful in the case of the typical mystics. Where he departs, we can, taking all available data into consideration, try to judge whether or not his aberrations tend toward a fresher and fuller realization of their purposes, afford perhaps a new and untried way of reaching their goal, or differ in essentials so completely as to demand a very different sort of classification. But the question of absolute dependability in the field of doctrine is not to be handed over to the mystics without the invoking of considerations of religious truth, the full development of which lies outside the scope of this study.

For the other members of the mystical field, what William James said of what he differentiated as the classic and the lower mysticisms applies throughout the field for ecstasy, for vision, for revelation, for prophecy (for the various levels of the mysticism of the great mystics even):

It is evident that from the point of view of their psychological mechanism the classic mysticism and these lower mysticisms spring from the same mental level, from that great subliminal or transmarginal region of which science is beginning to admit the existence, but of which so little is really known. That region contains every kind of matter: "seraph and snake" abide there side by side. To come from thence is no infallible credential. What

[40] Evelyn Underhill, *The Mystic Way* (London, 1913), pp. 56–57.

comes must be sifted and tested, and run the gauntlet of confrontation with the total context of experience, just like what comes from the outer world of sense.[41]

It is "this confrontation with the total context of experience" that gives its authenticity to any human achievement and ratifies its claim to the name of greatness. Here vision and prophecy meet only the challenge which every human effort in any field must meet. What Dr. H. Crichton Miller says of the spiritual life in general will hold for particular manifestations: "When all has been said it will ever remain true that the paramount criterion of a man's spiritual life will be the validity of his contact with the eternal."[42] "By their fruits shall ye know them."

To particularize, many hysterics duplicate certain stages of mystic experience: the perception of the unsatisfactoriness of life on its ordinary terms or the craving for a spiritual fellowship, but in the hysteric these elements become the sources of disintegration, while in the mystic they are the sharpest of goads to integration of thought and feeling and purpose. An ordinary love affair on a relatively low level, the use of certain drugs, the following of certain kinds of mind-cure formulas may produce a certain temporary enhancement of life, but they are not sufficient in themselves to produce that transformation of the whole being, that irresistible dynamic which the great mystics wrest from their experience. The effort alone is not sufficient for value in the spiritual life or in any other life. The quality of the effort, the objective of the effort, the kind of life it achieves are much more important than its superficial character.

So of the prophets. The sense of a prophetic mission is no rare phenomenon in ordinary human experience. Neither is the inner consciousness of the truth of what one professes. Verily, there are false prophets, and wise is he who can, by the garments they wear, tell the sheep from the ravening wolves, or—what is perhaps more to the point in our Laodicean age—the wise from the foolish. Here again, however roughly or blindly he can, one must invoke the

[41] William James, *The Varieties of Religious Experience: A Study in Human Nature* (London, 1903), p. 426.

[42] H. Crichton Miller, *The New Psychology and the Preacher* (New York, 1924), p. 157.

"whole context of human experience." The prophet says he has the secret of it all. How sound is he on the ground which we know, and on which we can follow him? As we look into his life and scan his personality, how much of life does he know? Upon what stores of experience does he draw in his inevitable criticism of custom and institution? And for his prescriptions for our ills, how well does he understand fundamental human nature, as the wise men and the poets and our own unenlightened experience may help us to judge? Does he know the things we know already before he invites us to leave them for higher things? And finally, in the way he talks do we hear the accent of the masters of prophetic speech, not only certainty, but simplicity, clarity, the beauty of meaning surely and fully realized so that to hear is to want to do?

These are rough tests, depending much upon the experience and the insight of him who applies them. But some test is essential, for to hearken to a false prophet is to shut one's ears to a true. And these are the tests which the experience of the race in matters not only religious, but aesthetic and intellectual and moral, suggests. And if we view the new prophet not only in himself, but against the background of the great prophets who have gone before him, with the help of their example and their experience, we shall be able to find some better solution of the problem than blindly rejecting or equally blindly accepting. And if we fail in our endeavor, we shall at least have defined the issues and cleared the ground for those wiser than we, who, in reversing our judgment, shall more fully have realized our purpose.

CHAPTER V

THE TENDENCIES OF BLAKE'S LIFE AND READING

The external facts of William Blake's life are so simple and so familiar, and the main lines of his character so well known, that any systematic outline of his life is unnecessary. Yet some aspects of this material bear so directly upon the course of his thinking and his imagining that they must be considered if we are to understand his mystical development. First of all, the fact that William Blake was born in the year 1757 is an item of great importance. For it means that he was born in time on the one hand to feel keenly the peculiarly positivistic qualities of eighteenth-century thought, whether expressed in art, or literature, or religion, or politics; and on the other hand, to respond to the first airs of that wind of revolt that ushered in the new century. The general period was, therefore, one to encourage a man of strongly individual genius to strike out his own way.

This general impulse was reinforced by the peculiar circumstances of Blake's life. All that we know of the family into which he was born goes to show that from the start he was helped little by his relations to other people. His father was a thriving, but by no means affluent, tradesman, a hosier; according to tradition, a nonconformist. While he seems to have displayed rare intelligence in having at least not interfered with his second son's marked artistic proclivities, he seems to have left no mark on that son's thought or work. Two of Blake's three brothers appear to have been positively uncongenial to his temperament; the third he loved devotedly, but Robert died when William was thirty. William believed that he had learned the curious process by which the *Songs of Innocence and of Experience* were engraved from this dead brother in a dream. His name occurs several times in Blake's letters and works, but it is impossible to establish that Robert Blake had any real influence on the thought of his brother, who was five years older.

The fact that Blake, apprenticed at the age of fourteen, missed

128

the social opportunities of school is also suggestive. It is interesting to hear that Blake's master, to prevent his quarreling with his less strenuous fellow-apprentices, sent him to work alone in Westminster Abbey at sketches of the effigies on the tombs. Probably this solitary work among the dead only deepened the tendencies to imaginative brooding in the boy who already at the age of four had seen his first vision.

His young manhood gave Blake a brief contact with the world of polite culture in his intercourse with the brilliant and somewhat sophisticated group that gathered about the wife of a fashionable city preacher, Mrs. Mathew, at Rathbone Place. But this relation with the elegant bluestocking hostess and her friends was of short duration, probably because, as Gilchrist suggests, the young poet who at first delighted all by his singing of his own songs came not to be taught, but to teach. We have no certain evidence on this point, but there is much in what we do know of the Blake of later years to suggest that this is the attitude Blake early took toward the world about him.

His marriage, when he was twenty-five years old, to pretty, unlettered, sympathetic Catherine Boucher brought him as devoted a wife as man ever had, but it brought him no extension of intellectual vision and no possibility of real interchange of ideas. He loved his wife, but he always regarded her as by nature his inferior, destined to follow his lead and to accept his judgment in all things. So perfectly did Mrs. Blake fulfil these expectations that, it is said, she even came, under her husband's influence, to see visions.

The various contacts that Blake made with other people during his long life of seventy years brought him machinery for his visions and animus for his opinions, but they do not seem ever to have really penetrated into the world of his own peculiar inner life. We cannot point to any of his various friends and acquaintances and say that this man or that ever made any substantial difference in Blake's way of thinking.

The nearest approach to such an influence is probably to be found in Blake's association with the group of radicals whom he met about 1791 at the house of Johnson, the publisher. Gilchrist tells us that at that time Drs. Price and Priestley, Holcroft, Godwin, Mary Wollstonecraft, and Tom Paine used to gather there for the hospitable publisher's dinners and interchange of ideas.[1] Gilchrist reports that while in general Blake agreed with this group on politics, he staunchly defended Christianity when they began to air their infidel tenets.[2] How far Blake was influenced by this group is uncertain, especially in view of the fact that, like other generous young Englishmen of the period, he was for a time swept off his feet by the French Revolution. According to Gilchrist, he boldly donned the *bonnet rouge* and wore it openly in the street at a time when to do so was to invite the wrath of more conservative mobs, but when September of 1792 brought the excesses of the Terror, then Blake, like other famous Englishmen, revolted from the French Revolution in horror and disgust.[3] However great or small the influence of the Johnson circle on Blake's ideas, it is certain that then for the first and last time in his life Blake found a publisher for his verse. For Johnson brought out in 1791 the first, and so far as what remains of his work is concerned, the last, book of the *French Revolution*. While this work was a direct reaction to the events and the interests of the moment, much more significant evidence of Blake's response to the spirit of the time is to be found in the pleas for liberty of every sort and the enthusiasm for utterly unrestrained impulse that begin to appear in the works of these years. Especially is this true of the *Marriage of Heaven and Hell*, of 1790, and the *Visions of the Daughters of Albion*, of 1793.

While it is perfectly true that Blake never enjoyed the recognition which his rare gifts of fancy deserved, he seems not to have lacked interested friends who endeavored to help him to sell his works and to secure congenial and lucrative commissions. Blake never won public interest largely because, beyond the ill-fated exhibition of 1809, he never did very much to woo public interest. But from time to time various people like Dr. Trusler made some effort to patronize his abilities, efforts which usually came to little because Blake was most emphatically a man who must do things in his own way. In early years George Cumberland seems to have made especial efforts to help Blake, and so does Flaxman, the well-

---

[1] Alexander Gilchrist, *Life of William Blake* (London, 1880), I, 92–93.

[2] *Ibid.*, p. 94.

[3] *Ibid.*, p. 94.

known sculptor and member of the Royal Academy, with whom Blake seems to have maintained about as intimate and as enduring relations as with any of his friends. About 1800 Flaxman introduced Blake to William Hayley, a wealthy, benevolent, but intellectually commonplace and pretentious squire dilettante who enjoyed a considerable vogue among the fashionable of the time. For three years Blake lived near Hayley at Felpham. The chief result, for Blake's intellectual development, of this sojourn in a world different from his own was the reinforcement of his own independence of temper that made him withdraw the more profoundly into the world of his dreams. What Hayley tried to do, it would seem, was to shape up in what he would consider a more cultivated and acceptable fashion a genius which he seems never in the least to have understood. Blake's side of the matter as he saw it in 1802 in the very midst of his troubles becomes clear in the following passage from a letter to Thomas Butts:

My unhappiness has arisen from a source which, if explored too narrowly, might hurt my pecuniary circumstances; as my dependence is on engraving at present, and particularly on the engravings I have in hand for Mr. H[ayley] : but I find on all hands great objections to my doing anything but the mere drudgery of business, and intimations that if I do not confine myself to this, I shall not live. This has always pursued me. You will understand by this the source of all my uneasiness. This from Johnson and Fuseli[4] brought me down here, and this from Mr. H. will bring me back again. For that I cannot live without doing my duty to lay up treasures in heaven is certain and determined, and to this I have long made up my mind. And why this should be made an objection to me, while drunkenness, lewdness, gluttony, and even idleness itself, do not hurt other men, let Satan himself explain. The thing I have most at heart—more than life, or all that seems to make life comfortable without—is the interest of true religion and science. And whenever anything appears to affect that interest (especially if I myself omit any duty to my station as a soldier of Christ), it gives me the greatest of tor-

[4] Fuseli, a native of Zurich, came to England as a young man and won such distinction in his painting that he became professor of painting to the Royal Academy. Of his relations to Blake, Mr. A. B. G. Russell says (in his edition of *The Letters of William Blake*, London, 1906, in a footnote to p. 66): "He [Fuseli] is likely to have made Blake's acquaintance in 1780, when he returned from Italy and settled down in Broad Street, Carnaby Market, close to Blake's own home. It was under Blake's influence that his imaginative quality first began to develop itself, and that his style underwent a change in the direction of restraint and refinement. He remained Blake's constant friend and admirer. He is said to have been the author of the *Advertisement* of the designs to Young's *Night Thoughts*, and he afterwards composed the prospectus of the illustrations of Blair's *Grave*. Several of his designs were engraved by Blake's hand."

ments. I am not ashamed, afraid, or averse to tell you what ought to be told: that I am under the direction of messengers from heaven, daily and nightly.[5]

The *Milton* shows what Blake thought of his experience with Hayley after it was over. Then it had become a transaction of universal scope and significance, but the notebook epigrams and verses show how very human was the irritation to which it gave rise in a man always possessed of a very limited amount of patience with the stupid and unsympathetic. Blake still maintained relations with Hayley after his return to London, as the fifteen notes that we have from Blake to Hayley for the year 1804 show. But these notes do not suggest any real intellectual communion. That was impossible.

The years that followed were years of deepening neglect. Blake's exhibition of his drawings in 1809 attracted the interest of Henry Crabb Robinson to whom we owe some of our most interesting glimpses of Blake's last years, but while Crabb Robinson was able to secure Blake some customers, he could bring him little of understanding or fellowship. Gilchrist, who uncovered so much gossip about Blake's life, was unable to find much of anything for the seven years that followed the failure of the exhibition. Mr. Russell's collection of Blake's letters has added practically nothing for that period. During those years Blake seems to have worked on in increasing poverty and isolation. Toward the end of this period even Major Butts, who had been Blake's most satisfactory and dependable patron for many years, failed him.

It is interesting that it was a very young painter, John Linnell, afterward moderately distinguished for his landscapes, who rescued Blake from poverty and neglect. With a disciple's admiration he assured Blake's meager livelihood by contracting to purchase anything he chose to do in the way of painting or design. This arrangement, which left Blake free to do exactly what he wished in his own way, was the kind of patronage he liked.

It is also significant for Blake's whole life that the group of young men, practically all artists, to whom Linnell introduced him at his home in Hampstead and who came to regard Blake as their prophetic center gave Blake probably the most satisfactory social

[5] *Letters of William Blake*, p. 99.

relation he ever enjoyed. But it was essentially a master-and-disciple relation, such as, even if it could have come earlier, would never have proved of any substantial consequence for the forming of his point of view.

The human relations that life brought to Blake were none of them, therefore, powerful enough to break through the essential isolation of spirit which only deepened as the years went on. But it must never be forgotten that Blake's character was largely his fate. The peculiarities of his temper and personality had their large share of responsibility even for the isolation that superficially seemed attributable to the external circumstances of his life. The letter that Blake wrote to John Linnell in 1827 on the subject of a contemplated removal from London to Linnell's more rural home goes deeper than an old man's aversion to change; it reveals something that determined Blake's entire life:

> I have thought and thought of the removal. I cannot get my mind out of a state of terrible fear at such a step. The more I think, the more I feel terror at what I wished at first, and thought a thing of benefit and good hope. You will attribute it to its right cause—intellectual peculiarity, that must be myself alone shut up in myself, or reduced to nothing. I could tell you of visions and dreams upon the subject. I have asked and entreated Divine help; but fear continues upon me, and I must relinquish the step that I had wished to take, and still wish, but in vain.[6]

That inner necessity of being shut up within himself seems to have affected all Blake's life. Indeed, he was far better equipped to preserve his own peculiar powers among the ignorant and unsympathetic than to achieve that ability to understand and make understood that is indispensable to any fruitful contact with one's peers.

In spite of this social isolation Blake's activity as an artist should have carried him beyond himself, for art is in general a liberalizing and depersonalizing element in men's lives, however secluded they may be. And Blake was probably as whole-hearted an artist as ever lived. Indeed, his approach to everything in life, both human and non-human, secular and religious, was the artist's. But here again the same uncongeniality of circumstance and independence of spirit that isolated him from his fellows in general social intercourse isolated him in his art. He had very early manifested

[6] *Letters*, p. 219.

his aptitude for drawing and painting, but his definite training in creative art was meager. He enjoyed some drawing lessons from Pars when he was ten, but when, at the age of fourteen, the time came for his choice of a profession, he was, by his own generous desire to spare his parents expense, apprenticed to the engraver, Basire. Such a choice would normally have condemned him to a craftsman's existence. Under Basire Blake received thorough training for the next six years in the hard, dry, but very painstaking and exact method of engraving that Basire followed, a style of engraving that was already passing out of fashion. From Basire Blake probably derived that intense emphasis on the importance of the firm sharp outline in drawing which characterizes all his utterances on art. And his experience of Gothic art in Westminster Abbey, where he was sent to copy ancient monuments, undoubtedly helped to form his peculiar style in the handling of figure and drapery.

This apprentice period gave him a thorough training in his craft; but his creative impulses found neither master nor companion. For his dearest aspirations Blake was left to his own devices. It is interesting to note that already his tastes were very different from those of his day. Even as a child he expended his few shillings on prints from Raphael and Michael Angelo at a time when the fashion was for Titian and Rembrandt. And when the great Sir Joshua Reynolds was delighting all England with the luxurious richness of his portraits of fashionable beauty, the young engraver's apprentice was emulating the sterner power of Michael Angelo or the barer dignity of the Gothic sepulcher. That is one of the most consequential elements in Blake's life: that in his own chosen field, where his gifts were so distinguished, he began life with a set of tastes and principles quite out of any relation to the prevailing interests and tastes of his time.

When his apprenticeship ended, in his twenty-second year, Blake studied for a while in the newly established Royal Academy. But the amount of help that he derived from the experience may be gauged by an incident he recounts in his commentary on Reynolds' *Discourses:*

I was once looking over the prints from Raffael and Michael Angelo in the Library of the Royal Academy, Moser came to me, and said, "You should not study these old, Hard, Stiff, and Dry, Unfinished Works of Art. Stay a little, and *I* will show you what you should Study." He then went and took down Le Brun's and Rubens' *Galleries.* How did I secretly rage. I also spoke my mind. . . . . I said to Moser, These things that you call Finished are not even Begun, how then can they be finished? The man who does not know the Beginning cannot know the End of Art.[7]

For a while Blake tried drawing from life, but the posed artificiality of the academic studies disgusted him. And probably even more fundamentally he revolted from these long hours of practice because they bound the fancy to the tyranny of external appearance. "Natural objects," he tells us to the close of his life, "always did & now do weaken, deaden, & obliterate Imagination in me!"[8] From that time on Blake used only his wife's figure and his own (which he came to regard as the standard of manly vigor and beauty) for his models. And more and more did he rely on his fancy for the lineaments of things as they really are. There was emphatically nothing of the disciple in Blake, to either man or nature.

Under such circumstances it is not difficult to see why Blake, with all his unremitting toil, never achieved anything like public recognition. The drawings that now form some of the choicest treasures of the collector's portfolio created no stir in their own day. For years Major Butts was almost the sole purchaser of Blake's original creations. When at last, goaded by disappointment at Cromeck's transferring the commission for the *Canterbury Pilgrimage* to the popular favorite, Stothard, Blake appealed to the public in his exhibit of 1809 with its now famous *Descriptive Catalogue* and a group of pictures that might be counted upon to prove "caviare to the general," he received no response. After that Blake made no further effort. He executed rare commissions, like the illustrations to Dr. Thornton's *Vergil,* with spirit and power; he undertook the *Illustrations to Dante* for Linnell, but his happiest, his most thoroughly satisfying, work was that on his own designs, especially his designs for the so-called "Prophetical Writings."

[7] "Marginal Notes to the Discourses of Sir Joshua Reynolds," Ellis and Yeats, *op. cit.,* II, 321.

[8] MS notes on Wordsworth. Quoted, Henry Crabb Robinson, *op. cit.,* p. 24.

In his poetry Blake was even more driven in upon himself by his circumstances and his peculiar genius. He had no regular education in the humanities. He had at best very little reading. He had read Shakespeare, according to Malkin, Ben Jonson's *Underwoods* and *Miscellanies*, Spenser, Chatterton's *Rowley Poems*, and above all, Macpherson's *Ossian*, in those years between fourteen and twenty when, in the leisure of his apprenticeship, he wrote his extraordinary *Poetical Sketches*. He had probably read very little more when, in 1789, he printed and engraved the *Songs of Innocence*. These he published in so laborious and costly a fashion, ironically enough on account of his poverty, that they were available only for the art collector, and in no way for the general reader of verse. With the exception of the *French Revolution*, which, from all the evidence available, came stillborn from the press, all his works were published in this fashion. The result was, as we have seen, that even the *Songs of Innocence* and the *Songs of Experience* (published in 1794), that have given Blake his enduring place in English literature, were almost unknown to his contemporaries. And, of course, the later books, with their increasing obscurity and symbolism, never had the slightest chance of extending Blake's contacts with the world about him. Here again Blake had to rely upon his own practically unaided genius, with no possibility of the stimulation and the enrichment of power that one derives from the impact of other minds and personalities upon his ideas. But even had circumstance been more generous of this aid, there is no reason to believe that Blake would have welcomed it. Here, as in his drawing and painting, Blake placed his faith in the power of his own genius, and probably before all else prided himself upon his independence and his originality.

This extraordinary self-confidence of his springs, of course, from the fact that he always felt he had a source of life and truth beyond the judgment of the world that neglected him. This source lay in his visions. According to the account which his wife gave to Tatham, they began when he was four years old, with the face of God looking in at a window. When he was eight or ten he narrowly escaped a whipping from his matter-of-fact father for claiming to have seen a tree full of angels. After his brother Robert's death he felt that he still enjoyed converse with him in heaven. In one of the "Memorable Fancies" of the *Marriage of Heaven and Hell*, Blake speaks of an occasion on which the prophets Isaiah and Ezekiel dined with him, and at the beginning of *Jerusalem* he expressly claims daily converse, "as man with man," with the "Friend of Sinners," who dictates the poem to him. Other examples of similar tendency might be instanced to show that he actually "saw" what he painted and wrote.

For many people this is the most interesting issue about William Blake, on counts varying all the way from insanity on the one hand, to supernatural authenticity on the other. To take up first the question most commonly raised on this aspect of Blake's work —Was Blake insane? Practically all Blake critics are agreed that he was not, in our ordinary sense of the word. He was able to look after himself, as the writings of his friends and his own letters testify. He seems to have conducted himself calmly and sensibly on the occasion of his trial on a trumped-up charge of treason, for instance. And he does not seem ever to have aroused any apprehension of irresponsibility on the part of those who knew him intimately. In that sense we may say he is sane. On the other hand, there does seem to be considerable evidence, in his letters as well as in his notebooks, that he was of a rather unstable temperament: what Dr. Collins, in a very lively discussion of the case, has called "psychotic."[9] A good many of his letters express an exaltation, an optimism about, say, the attitude of the public toward his work, or the prospects of patronage opening before him, for which at this day of a hundred years later we can find no evidence, and which all the evidence we do possess goes to contradict. And with all possible allowances for inevitable vicissitudes of liking and dislike incident to any close association of men of fundamentally different temperaments, the accounts which Blake gives in his letters, his notebooks, and *Milton* of his relations with Hayley are very difficult to reconcile on any fundamental hypothesis of seeing life steadily or seeing it whole. In this sense, then, there is much to suggest that Blake was subject, probably more than most men but probably not more than many other artists, to startling variations of mood and feeling that made him see the external world out of all proportion to literal fact. It is almost unnecessary to point out that

[9] J. Collins, "The Sanity of William Blake," *Bookman*, LXI (July, 1925), 553–55.

while such oscillations can hardly be called sound, they do not in themselves constitute insanity.

As for the visions themselves, they are clearly no mere figure of speech. He speaks of them too simply, in too matter-of-fact a fashion for that, and he gives them an importance that a poetic convention could hardly enjoy. On the other hand, they do not seem ever to have involved any confusion of what other people would call external reality with internal reality. He talked and wrote about visions as other people write about objective realities, but there is no evidence to contradict the conclusion that he was aware of the difference, even though he reversed the usual estimate of value.

Two well-authenticated items in his biography shed very interesting light upon this problem. The first is that series of sketches of historical personages which Blake drew for the painter, Varley. The method followed seems to have been this: Varley would ask to see what someone, say the "Man who Built the Pyramids," looked like; Blake would "look," and then would quickly draw a portrait, as if from an actual presence. Of these so-called "visionary portraits," the most famous is the "Ghost of the Flea," a terrible apparition of blood-thirsty evil. As Mr. Darrell Figgis has pointed out, Blake had already drawn the same figure in form and motion in his preternatural "Pestilence," of some fourteen years before.[10] What this suggests is not hallucination, as has sometimes been thought, but an uncommon power of visualizing, and of remembering what has once been so visualized.

The other item that seems to offer a key to this problem is to be found in some verses which Blake sent from Felpham to Major Butts. They contain the most explicit record we have of what Blake himself has to say on this subject:

> A frowning Thistle implores my stay.
> What to others a trifle appears
> Fills me full of smiles or tears;
> For double the vision my eyes do see,
> And a double vision is always with me.
> With my inward eye, 'tis an old Man grey;
> With my outward, a Thistle across my way.[11]

[10] Darrell Figgis, *op. cit.*, p. 97.　　　　　[11] *Letters*, p. 109.

Here Blake is certainly clear about the difference between the inward and the outward eye. At the same time what, if it came to most people at all, would be a passing fancy, remains with him and is recognized as a revelation of significance.

But Blake's relation to these visions is not always so perfectly voluntary as the foregoing suggests. There are indications in his letters, as well as in his writings, of visions which by no means waited upon his pleasure, but forced themselves upon his attention when he was trying to hold himself to more material pursuits. It is of this that he complains to Thomas Butts in a letter of 1801:

> I labour incessantly. I accomplish not one half of what I intend, because my abstract folly hurries me often away while I am at work, carrying me over mountains and valleys, which are not real, into a land of abstraction where spectres of the dead wander. This I endeavor to prevent; I, with my whole might, chain my feet to the world of duty and reality. But in vain! the faster I bind, the better is the ballast; for I, so far from being bound down, take the world with me in my flights, and often it seems lighter than a ball of wool rolled by the wind.[12]

This expression of a sense of division and struggle within himself belongs to the Felpham period, when Blake was trying to force himself to do the uncongenial work which his patrons and advisers forced upon him for what they considered his practical advancement. It would be interesting to know just how long this lasted, or whether, after the triumphant sense of being himself again that attended upon his emancipated return from Felpham to London, it ever recurred. All we can do in the face of lack of positive evidence is to judge from the amount of work he did and the picture of content which his friends and less interested observers like Crabb Robinson have left of his later years. That would suggest that when he had definitely given up the struggle to make his way in this world and devoted himself entirely to the visions he found peace.

Whether or not this followed, it is clear that the story of his life from this point of view is the story of increasing devotion to the life of what he called "the inward eye." To begin with the first literary work of his maturity, the *Songs* clearly suggest his peculiar way of looking at the world, but they can scarcely be called "vi-

[12] *Letters*, pp. 90–91.

sionary." It is certainly possible both to understand and to enjoy them without any puzzling reference to an underlying system. But there is no question of the symbolism of *Tiriel*, written at the time of the first *Songs* in 1789; and in 1797 the beginning of *Vala*, chaotic as it is, marks the full maturity of Blake's symbolical system. He was then forty-two. The remainder of his writing, apart from mere exposition of his theories, is devoted to accounts of visions and things seen and heard in the world of vision. From the point of view of the student of literature, this use of Blake's poetic gift is an artistic tragedy; for the visionary it was the fulfilment of his destiny. To it he joyfully consecrated his happiest energies. But here again Blake was working in a world limited by its very nature to the purlieus of his own imagination. His wife could sit by his side during the long night hours when the heavenly spirits were dictating to him, or Varley could watch while Blake drew those strange visitants that he summoned from the "vasty deep" to please his friend's curiosity, but they had, in the nature of things, no power of sharing or even understanding the strange workings within that vision-filled head.

Indeed, Blake's isolation in his visions was more complete than that of the visionary monk of the Middle Ages in his cell. For the visions of the monk always must bear the scrutiny of his directors and the challenge of the experience of his church. But William Blake, although he had declared that his purpose in life was to advance "true religion and science," belonged to no church or religious group. His father was a Dissenter. He himself was buried in that great field of the dissenting dead, Bunhill Fields, and when asked what service he would have for his funeral, he is said to have expressed a preference for the Church of England burial service. His brother James is reported to have been much interested in the visions of Swedenborg; his friend, Flaxman, was certainly a member of the New Church. But we cannot discover any such religious affiliations for Blake. He obviously was deeply interested in religion as viewed from his own individual position. But here again Blake lived within himself. The result is that at all points he elaborated his view of life without any effective critical impact from the minds of his contemporaries. Any modification of that proud isolation and self-dependence is, therefore, to be sought in his readings.

From Blake's own testimony, in various passages of his works, we know that he was familiar with, and made use of, the writings of Swedenborg, Boehme, and Milton, and that he was above all a zealous reader of the Bible. He also refers to Dante, Shakespeare, Paracelsus, and other writers both literary and mystical, but it would be impossible in any reasonable space to examine all these suggestions, and, so far as Blake's mysticism, our present subject, is concerned, irrelevant and unremunerative. It will be sufficiently illuminating to examine some of the most outstanding suggestions of sources upon which Blake may reasonably have drawn in the elaboration of his own highly individual view of life.

With the exception of the Bible, probably no source afforded Blake more help than the writings of Swedenborg. The best known of Blake's explicit references to Swedenborg are to be found, of course, in the *Marriage of Heaven and Hell,* where his estimate of Swedenborg runs from slighting aspersion to vigorous repudiation. In the following passage he mildly suggests that Swedenborg is superseded:

> As a new heaven is begun, and it is now thirty-three years since its advent, the Eternal Hell revives. And lo! Swedenborg is the Angel sitting at the tomb; his writings are the linen clothes folded up.

Later on in the same work he makes the downright statement of "plain fact" that "Swedenborg has not written one new truth . . . . he has written all the old falsehoods," a verdict which he goes on to justify on this ground: "He conversed with Angels who are all religious, and conversed not with Devils who all hate religion, for he was incapable thro' his conceited notions."

It is always difficult to determine with any precision a man's indebtedness to his predecessor, and especially so when, as in this case, we know that both men drew upon common sources of inspiration. But when we find in Swedenborg already elaborated some very salient features of Blake's belief and teachings, and when we discover therein terms and formulations that appear often in Blake's writings, we may be sure that whatever the literal indebtedness, we have here valuable evidence as to the materials actually at Blake's disposal when he set out to master the world of his dreams.

First of all, it is interesting to note that Swedenborg claims a heavenly mission very similar to Blake's, in essence, if not in terms, when he says:

> Since the Lord cannot manifest Himself in person [to the world], which has just been shown to be impossible, and yet He has foretold that He would come and establish a New Church, which is the New Jerusalem, it follows, that He will effect this by the instrumentality of a man, who is able not only to receive the doctrines of that church in his understanding, but also to make them known by the press. That the Lord manifested Himself before me his servant, that He sent me on this office, and afterwards opened the sight of my spirit, and so let me into the spiritual world, permitting me to see the heavens and the hells, and also to converse with angels and spirits, and this now continually for many years, I attest in truth; and further, that from the first day of my call to this office, I have never received anything relating to the *doctrines* of that church from any angel, but from the Lord alone, while I was reading the Word.[13]

When one remembers the undoubted rôle that suggestion plays in all mystical vision, it is interesting to notice the theory of vision that Blake found already recorded in Swedenborg's writings. The Swedish philosopher claims constant discourse with spirits "even in full wakefulness of the body, and this now during many years."[14] But, in addition to this, Swedenborg recognizes two very special types of vision which he calls "the states" of man "when he is in his interiors, or, what is the same thing, when he is in the spirit."[15] The first is a very special state that Swedenborg admits he has enjoyed only three or four times, and then for very definitely catechetical purposes, and which he thus describes at some length:

> As to what concerns the first point, viz. being withdrawn from the body, the case is this: man is brought into a certain state, which is a middle state between sleep and waking, and when he is in this state he cannot know any other than that he is altogether awake, all his senses being awake as in the highest wakefulness of the body, both the sight and hearing, and, what is wonderful, the touch, which, on this occasion, is more exquisite than it is pos-

---

[13] Emanuel Swedenborg, *The True Christian Religion, Containing the Universal Theology of the New Church, Foretold by the Lord*, § 779.

[14] "Tract 4," *New Jerusalem Tracts* (Boston, 1830), I, 10, quoted from "A Treatise concerning Heaven and Its Wonders, and also concerning Hell, Being a Relation of Things Heard and Seen," by Swedenborg.

[15] *Ibid.*, p. 10.

sible to be in the wakefulness of the body: in this state, also, spirits and angels are seen altogether to the life; they are likewise heard, and, what is wonderful, touched, and in this case scarcely anything of the body intervenes: this is the state which is called being *withdrawn from the body,* and of which it is said by one who experienced it, *that he knew not whether he was in the body or out of the body.* Into this state I have been let only three or four times, that I might just know what was its quality, and at the same time that spirits and angels enjoy every sense, as does man also, as to his spirit, when he is withdrawn from the body.[16]

The second extraordinary state was apparently of more frequent occurrence and, apparently, of less consequence for spiritual enlightenment, although a stranger to Swedenborgianism can never be sure that he is appreciating at full value some apparently trivial detail that seems of deep significance to the genuinely enlightened. At any rate the description is clearer:

Walking through the streets of a city and through fields, and on this occasion being engaged also in discourse with spirits, I knew no other than that I was thus awake with my eyes open as at other times, thus walking without error, and in the mean time I was in vision, seeing groves, rivers, palaces, houses, men, and several other objects; but after I had thus walked for some hours, suddenly I was in bodily vision, and observed that I was in another place, at which being greatly astonished, I perceived that I had been in a state similar to that of those of whom it is said that they were *translated by the spirit into another place;* for, during the process, the way is not attended to, though it be of several miles, neither is time reflected on, whether it be of several hours or days, neither is any fatigue perceived; on such occasions, also, the man is directed through ways, which he himself is ignorant of, without error, till he reaches the place of his destination.[17]

Swedenborg's accounts of his excursions into the world of spirits and into heaven are too well known to need more than cursory mention here. There is nothing ineffable about these experiences. Even though Swedenborg expressly denies body in a material sense to the angels, he says over and over again that they look like men and behave like men. The result is that however edifying Swedenborg's visions undoubtedly have proved to his followers, they do not escape the incongruity inevitable to any effort to describe too literally and particularly the celestial world. The account of the occasion on which the good little angels received robes, caps, and wreaths of laurel as a reward for their endeavors in

[16] *Ibid.,* pp. 9–10.   [17] *Ibid.,* p. 10.

the school of wisdom may stand as an example.[18] Sometimes such visions take on a spiritual affinity to *Alice in Wonderland,* as, for instance, in the case of the vision of the turtles with the faces of men.[19]

We have no evidence as to whether or not Blake knew of Swedenborg's spiritualistic powers, but the reader of Varley's accounts of those midnight sittings in which Blake called from the world of spirits the ghost of the flea or the man who built the Pyramids and limned their invisible faces will be interested in contemporary accounts of how Swedenborg hunted up the dead friend of a German merchant and discovered the subject of his last discourse with his parted friend,[20] or received, at the very moment of its occurrence, tidings of the death of the Emperor of Russia,[21] or, as no less a person than Kant records for us, became aware of a great fire[22] that was raging nearly three hundred miles away.

From one point of view these resemblances are trifles. They certainly do not prove direct borrowing, but they do shed valuable light on the sort of thing which fed Blake's mind and imagination in the critical years of his early manhood.

Much more important for our purposes are the great truths which Swedenborg believed he discovered in these visions, truths which at some very important points strikingly anticipate Blake's own discoveries. M. Berger has noted three which he believes indelibly impressed Blake: "the likeness of man to God; the perception that the Invisible had a real existence, outside of time and space; and the correspondence between the material and spiritual worlds."[23]

A more accurate statement of the first of these beliefs would undoubtedly be the likeness of God to man. Not only do the angels look like men,[24] but "all the angels who are in the heavens never

[18] Swedenborg, *The True Christian Religion,* § 48.

[19] *Ibid.,* § 462. It is only fair to add that the "spiritual-minded" reader of such a passage would remember the symbolism undoubtedly inherent in such a fancy.

[20] Nathaniel Hobart, *Life of Emanuel Swedenborg* (Boston, 1845), pp. 57 f.

[21] *Ibid.,* p. 59.

[22] *Ibid.,* p. 71.

[23] Berger, *William Blake,* p. 205, in his very brief but exceedingly suggestive chapter on "The Sources of His Doctrines."

[24] "Tract 2," *New Jerusalem Tracts,* I, 15–17.

perceive the Divine under any other form than the human,"[25] and, "it is accordingly implanted in every man who receives any influx from heaven, to think of God under a human shape."[26] So heaven appears as one man whom the angels call "the Grand and Divine Man."[27] Indeed, so important is the doctrine, that "knowledge of this arcanum . . . . is the chief article of the intelligence of the angels," as Swedenborg tells us in his *Heaven and Its Wonders*.[28]

Quite as important for Blake as this actual belief that God is like man is the physiological symbolism to which it gives rise. A by no means insignificant portion of Blake's symbolism is definitely forecast in that section from *A Treatise concerning Heaven and Its Wonders*, which describes how heaven is distinguished into members and parts as man is, and concludes by its division of heaven into three anatomical sections: "In general, the supreme or third heaven forms the head to the neck; the middle or second heaven forms the breast to the loins and knees; the ultimate or first heaven forms the feet to the toes, and likewise the arms to the fingers, for the arms and hands are the ultimates of man, although at the sides."[29]

The second point on which Swedenborg may have helped Blake is his belief in a world of spirit really existent quite apart from this world of matter, yet possessing claims upon man's knowing quite as imperative as the claims of the world of sense. To this belief is due much of Swedenborg's spiritualistic activity. This involves what Swedenborg calls the "world of spirits":

> The world of spirits is not heaven, neither is it hell, but it is a middle place or state between both; for thither man first comes after death, and then, after a stated time, according to his life in the world, is either elevated into heaven, or cast into hell . . . . it is a middle state, from this circumstance, that man, so long as he is there, is not yet in heaven, neither is he in hell.[30]

Apparently, however, Swedenborg also conceives of a spiritual world which may be defined in more conventional terms, as in the

[25] *Ibid.*, p. 19.

[26] *Ibid.*, p. 20.

[27] *Ibid.*, p. 9.

[28] Emanuel Swedenborg, *Heaven and Its Wonders, The World of Spirits and Hell: from Things Heard and Seen*, translated by Samuel Noble (New York, 1872), § 59.

[29] "Tract 2," *New Jerusalem Tracts*, p. 12.   [30] "Tract 4," *op. cit.*, p. 1.

following passage: "There are two worlds, a spiritual world for angels and spirits, and a natural world for men."[31] But even the spiritual world presented in such passages must have much of the physical about it, for there is nothing of the ineffable in man's contact with that sphere. The nature of that contact may be seen in Swedenborg's definition of the vision of God: "Since by a man's spirit is meant his mind, therefore by *being in the spirit*, which is a phrase that sometimes occurs in the Word, is meant a state of the mind separate from the body; and as in that state the prophets had a sight of such objects as exist in the spiritual world, therefore that state is called *the vision of God.*"[32] Only to those possessed of such a special illumination is the knowledge of genuine truth possible.[33]

Of course, such a view of the spiritual realm is, in a certain curious fashion, still very much of this material world. Like Blake, Swedenborg objected to the domination of "the senses five" in man's life and to the rationalism that the world had reared upon those narrow foundations; but, like Blake, he tended to substitute different data rather than a different method when he attempted to transcend the habitual workings of the reason.

The same difficulty which Blake's injunction to put on mind, later met, infects Swedenborg's definition of spirit, as in the following:

> By a man's spirit in the concrete, nothing else is meant but his mind, for it is this which lives after death and is then called a spirit. . . . . The mind of every one is his internal man, which is actually a man, and dwells within the external man, that makes its body; therefore, on the rejection of the body by death, it is in a complete human form.[34]

The insight accessible to this spiritual mind consists chiefly of recognition of those correspondences between the spiritual and the natural worlds which Swedenborg considered one of the most important of his doctrines, and which later played so considerable a part in Blake's mystical view of the universe. The "spiritual world, which is heaven," says Swedenborg, "is conjoined to the natural world by correspondences; hence by correspondences communication with heaven is given to man . . . . wherefore when

[31] *The True Christian Religion,* § 75.
[32] *Ibid.,* § 157.   [33] *Ibid.,* §§ 231–33.   [34] *Ibid.,* § 156.

man is in the science of correspondences, he may be together with the angels as to the thoughts of his mind, and thus be conjoined with them as to his spiritual or internal man."[35] This correspondence is not limited to the correspondences to be found in man's body that have already been noted; it extends to the animal, even to the mineral, kingdom. In view of Blake's use of animals, familiar and strange, for the expression of truths in the human field, it is interesting to note Swedenborg's statement:

> The animals of the earth in general correspond to affections, the tame and useful ones to the good affections, the savage and useless ones to evil affections: oxen and bullocks specifically correspond to the affections of the natural mind; sheep and lambs to the affections of the spiritual mind; but winged animals, according to their species, correspond to the intellectual things of each mind.[36]

Likewise, in the common metals, gold, silver, and copper, Swedenborg, like the alchemists for centuries before, discovers symbols of celestial, spiritual, and natural good, respectively; and finally, in iron, he discovers in very Blake-like fashion the symbol of the "last age," signifying "hard truth without good."[37] Again like Blake, he finds a correspondence of deep spiritual significance in the four points of the compass. Much as Blake later came to associate the South with the illuminated intellect in his conception of the unfallen Urizen, the Angel of the Presence, Swedenborg discovered that the South was the direction of wisdom and intelligence.[38] In the perusal of such correspondences did Swedenborg find the highest life of the spirit of man.

And in a similar spirit he found, in the highly intricate interpretation of the hidden meanings buried in the Scriptures, the chief spiritual sustenance and devotional exercise of man. It is probable that Blake, particularly after he had got clear his own position on the subject of the Ten Commandments, paid very little attention to Swedenborg's study of the Decalogue for its literal, natural, spiritual, and celestial meanings,[39] but it is hard to believe that he was not impressed by Swedenborg's interpretations of the Apoca-

[35] "Tract 3," *New Jerusalem Tracts*, p. 7.

[36] *Ibid.*, p. 5.

[37] *Ibid.*, p. 8.

[38] *Heaven and Its Wonders*, § 150.   [39] "Tract 1," *New Jerusalem Tracts*.

lypse, especially since his own symbolism is so heavily indebted to the latter. The following passage from Swedenborg's explication of chapter 21 is an unusually lucid and characteristic example:

> By the new heaven and new earth they [the angels] understand a new church; by the city Jerusalem descending from God out of heaven, they understand its heavenly doctrine revealed by the Lord; by its length, breadth, and height, which are equal, and twelve thousand furlongs, they understand all the goods and truths of that doctrine in the complex; by its wall, they understand the truths protecting it, ...[40]

The more abstruse explanations of "signification" found in the *Arcana Coelestia* are interesting because they show the type of elaborate spinning out of interpretations to which Blake's mind had become accustomed before he came to work out his own symbolic system. It would take more time than would serve our purposes to go into the detail of Swedenborg's interpretations, but a mere glance at the space assumed by such undertakings will suggest something of the elaborate complexity of the results. In the sixth volume of an American edition a little over three pages are devoted to the reproduction of the text of Gen. 41:1–57, and one hundred and thirteen pages, to the exposition of the "internal sense" of those verses.[41]

But more important than any of these conceptions (M. Berger notwithstanding) for shedding light on the material Blake found to hand when he started on the task of creating his universe is the peculiarly congenial analysis of man's nature and man's state that Swedenborg had already completed. First of all, his conception of man's nature is strikingly like Blake's: "There are . . . . with every man two gates, one of which opens towards hell, and to the evils and falses thence issuing, the other opens towards heaven, and to the goods and truths thence issuing."[42] Consequently:

> It is so provided and ordered by the Lord, that so far as man thinks and wills from heaven, so far the internal spiritual man is opened and formed. . . . . But, on the contrary, so far as man does not think and will from

[40] "Tract 10," *op. cit.*, p. 20.

[41] Emanuel Swedenborg, *Arcana Coelestia. The Heavenly Arcana Contained in the Holy Scriptures or Word of the Lord Unfolded, Beginning with the Book of Genesis; Together with Wonderful Things Seen in the World of Spirits and in the Heaven of Angels* (New York, 1870), VI, 5–118.

[42] "Tract 4," *New Jerusalem Tracts*, p. 5.

heaven, but from the world, so far his internal spiritual man is closed, and his external is opened; it is opened into the world.[43]

The author then proceeds to define the opposite type in terms that strongly suggest some of Blake's most vigorous denunciations of his age: "He whose internal is so far external, that he believes nothing but what he can see with his eyes and touch with his hands, is called a sensual man; this is the lowest natural man, and is in fallacies concerning all the things which are of faith and the church."[44]

Like so many of the German religious enthusiasts, Swedenborg uses the symbolism of the re-birth for the salvation of this natural man: "Unless a man be born again, and as it were created anew, he cannot enter the kingdom of God."[45] This regeneration is of interest to students of Blake only in its stress on knowledge of spiritual things, as in the following: "No man can be regenerated unless he knows such things as belong to the new life, that is, to spiritual life; and the things which belong to the new life, which is the spiritual life, are truths which are to be believed and goods which are to be done."[46] And like Blake, Swedenborg makes love and faith the two distinguishing features of his conception of practical good.[47] Indeed, it is in the failure of these two powers that he finds the cause of the end of the present church,[48] and in terms of their triumph he defines his heaven.[49]

It would be easy to point out many other conceptions and terms and points of view afterward used extensively by Blake that were suggested and often explicitly developed by Swedenborg.[50]

[43] Emanuel Swedenborg, *Of the New Jerusalem, and Its Heavenly Doctrine, as Revealed from Heaven* (Boston, 1829), p. 19.

[44] *Ibid.*, p. 20; *The True Christian Religion*, §§ 401-2.

[45] *The True Christian Religion*, § 572.

[46] *Of the New Jerusalem*, p. 48.

[47] It would probably be nearer the truth to say "the feature," for Swedenborg makes them inseparable: "Where there is no charity there is no faith, forasmuch as charity makes one with faith as good does with truth" (*Of the New Jerusalem*, p. 33).

[48] *Ibid.*, p. 12.

[49] "Tract 2," *New Jerusalem Tracts*, p. 4.

[50] One of these terms has been mentioned so often in these last pages that it would hardly seem necessary to mention it again were it not of such frequent occurrence in Blake's work as to merit special notice: the word "church," in the sense of fresh enlightenment or revelation.

But they would add little to the conclusion already apparent: that, however uncertain the facts as to precisely what Blake thought of Swedenborg beyond those few occasions on which he expressed a definite judgment of his work, and however uncertain the facts as to his actual contact with Swedenborgianism as a practical religion, Blake found in Swedenborg, already elaborated with extraordinary minuteness and perspicuity, many of the elements of his own mystical doctrine. To say that where we have found salient resemblances Blake is indebted to Swedenborg is to run all the hazards of exaggeration attendant upon any effort to establish definite "influence," especially when the ideas involved are by no means unique. There is much to suggest Swedenborg's own indebtedness to Boehme, with whose thought Blake was familiar. This general difficulty is further augmented by the fact that everything that came into Blake's consciousness was transformed by the point of view of the creative artist into the stuff of his own religion of art. Consequently, where Swedenborg worked out a view of the universe that recognized to a considerable extent the traditional emphasis of will and ethics, Blake elaborated a not dissimilar view in terms of imagination and art. But when it is remembered that Blake actually studied Swedenborg, it is difficult to refrain from suggesting that in Swedenborg's works we have a potent source of stimulus and encouragement and suggestion for Blake's mysticism. They help us to understand what Blake had to work on when he set out to express his own vision of the world.

In a very well-known passage of the *Marriage of Heaven and Hell* Blake declares that "Any man of mechanical talents may, from the writings of Paracelsus or Jacob Behmen, produce ten thousand volumes of equal value with Swedenborg's, and from those of Dante or Shakespear an infinite number." It is well to consider the entire passage before we hastily conclude that Blake preferred Boehme to Swedenborg or was more indebted to Boehme than to Swedenborg. Again the actual evidence we have to go on as to just how much Blake read and under what circumstances and with what effect he read Boehme is very scanty. That he read Boehme is beyond question and that he read Law's translation of

Boehme is very likely, for Law was quite the most distinguished and talented disciple of Boehme in the England of his time.[51]

There was much in Boehme's circumstances and temper that Blake must have found congenial. A humble and unlearned shoemaker earning a modest living by his craft in a small town near Görlitz, Jacob Boehme could say with pride:

> I am only a layman, I have not studied, yet I bring to light things which all the High Schools and Universities have been unable to do. . . . . The language of Nature is made known to me so that I can understand the greatest mysteries, in my own mother tongue. Though I cannot say I have *learned* or *comprehended* these things, yet so long as the hand of God stayeth upon me I understand.[52]

Under such circumstances it is not surprising that Boehme came to scorn the learning which he had so well spared. Sometimes he displays an antipathy to all the works of the learned, especially those involving reason, which is in many ways suggestive of Blake's. Indeed, his view of the fruits both of reason and learning is strikingly like Blake's arraignment of the reason for the unspiritual state of humanity in his age. Boehme says: "We see clearly, that hitherto we have been *locked up,* and led as it were blindfold; and they are even the Wise of this world, who have shut and barred us up in their Art and Reason, so that we *must* [be tied to] *see with their Eyes, both in* Philosophy *and* Theology."[53] Consequently: "We are all asleep in the outward Man, we lie in the Cradle, and suffer ourselves to be *rocked asleep* by Reason."[54]

This attitude brings with it a revolt against institutionalism, which he protests against sometimes under the name of Cain, sometimes under the title of Babel, as in the following repudiation of the prevailing historical and legalistic Christianity: "Whatever Babel teaches of external imputed righteousness, or of external assumed

---

[51] M. Berger's suggestion (*op. cit.*, p. 203) that the fascinatingly ingenious illustrations to this edition may have suggested to Blake the main theme of his *Jerusalem* would be illuminating were it not that a story so well known as that of man's fall and redemption hardly needs so ingenious a source, especially when it is explicitly developed in the Bible.

[52] Rufus M. Jones, "Jacob Boehme: His Life and Spirit," *Spiritual Reformers in the Sixteenth and Seventeenth Centuries* (London, 1914), chapter ix, p. 152.

[53] Jacob Behmen, "The High and Deep Searching of the Threefold Life of Man," *Works,* translated by William Law (London, 1764), II, Bk. I, chap. vi, 10.

[54] Jacob Behmen, *ibid.*, p. 62.

adoption is without foundation or footing."[55] To the conventional formulas and observances of institutional Christianity he opposes the pristine reality of his own revelation. He was about twenty-five years old (in or about the year 1600) when he experienced his first great illumination which he so eloquently describes in *The Aurora* as a breaking through the gates of Hell:

> But the Greatness of the Triumphing that was in the Spirit, *I cannot express* either in Speaking or Writing; neither can it be compared to any Thing, but with *that*, wherein the Life is generated in the Midst of Death, and it is *like* the Resurrection from the Dead.
>
> In this Light my Spirit suddenly saw through all, and *in* and *by* all the Creatures, even in Herbs and Grass, it knew God, who he is, and how he is, and what his Will is: And suddenly in that Light my Will was set on by a mighty Impulse, to describe *the Being of God*.[56]

The fruit of that impulse was Boehme's first book, *The Aurora*, written in a fashion very much like that which Blake later described in his account of the composition of his works. Boehme says in one of his epistles:

> Art has not written here, neither was there any time to consider how to set it down punctually, according to the understanding of the letters, but all was ordered according to the direction of the Spirit, which often went in haste, so that in many words letters may be wanting, and in some places a capital letter for a word; so that *the Penman's hand*, by reason that he was not accustomed to it, did often shake. And, though I could have wrote in a more accurate, fair, and plain manner, yet the reason was this, that the burning fire often forced forward with speed, and the hand and pen must hasten directly after it; for it goes and comes like a sudden shower.[57]

Like most mystics, Boehme was profoundly impressed by the oneness of the universe. He accounted for what he conceived to be the fact by saying that the world arose out of the effort of God to realize himself. But

> behind the visible universe and in it there is an invisible universe; behind the material universe and in it there is an immaterial universe; behind the temporal universe and in it there is an eternal universe, and the first business of the philosopher or naturalist, as Boehme conceives it, is to discover the essential Nature of this invisible, immaterial, eternal universe out of which this fragment of a visible world has come forth.[58]

[55] Jones, *op. cit.*, p. 192, quoted from *Mysterium Magnum*, chap. xxvii.

[56] Behmen, "The Aurora," *Works*, I, Bk. I, chap. xix, 11–12.

[57] Jones, *op. cit.*, p. 162, quoted from Boehme's *Third Epistle*, 35.

[58] *Ibid.*, p. 172.

The relation between these two worlds is made clear in the following passage: "The whole outward visible world, with all its being, is a 'signature' or figure of the inward, spiritual World, and everything has a character that fits an internal reality and process and the internal is in the external."[59]

Jacob Boehme, as the great mass of alchemistical interpretations that obscure his writings testify, was a sedulous student of Paracelsus and other partly mystical and partly alchemistical and partly scientific seekers of nature's mysteries. It was probably the influence of these studies that led him to lay such stress on the possibility of discovering in external nature the secrets of God's working.

While Blake certainly made no effort to emulate the complexities of Boehme's analysis of the forces that compose the universe, the student of Blake will recognize in Boehme's description certain elements which later play such a conspicuous part in Blake's account of the world. The first of these forces is "in its inmost essence *desire,* the egoistic tendency, the focusing of will upon a definite aim so that consciousness contracts from its universal and absolute possibilities to a definite, limited, concrete *something in particular,* and thus negates everything else. The second

is the attractive, gravitating tendency which binds whole with whole as an organizing, universalizing energy. . . . . It is a fundamental love-principle in the inner world—the foundation, as Boehme says, of sweetness and warmth and mercy—and at the same time is a structural, organizing law of nature, which tends out of many parts to make one universe. . . . . The tension occasioned by these opposite forces gives rise to the third "quality," which is a tendency toward movement, oscillation, rotation—what Boehme often calls *the wheel of nature,* or the wheel of motion, or the wheel of life. . . . . The fourth "quality" is the *flash,* or ignition, due to collision between nature and spirit, in which a new principle of activity breaks through what before was mere play of *forces,* and reveals something that has activity in itself, the kindling, burning power of fire, though not yet fire which gives light. . . . . The fifth "quality" is Light, springing out of the "flash" of fire and rising to the level of illumination and the revelation of beauty. . . . . It is the dawn and beginning of the triumphing spirit of freedom which wills to draw all things back to one centre, one harmony, one unity, in which wild will and selfish passion and isolating pride, and all that springs from the dark fire-root are quenched, and instead the central principle of the spiritual world—Love—comes into play. [The] sixth "quality" [is] voice or sound, but he means

[59] Jones, *op. cit.,* p. 174, quoted from *Signatura Rerum,* ix, 1–3.

by it the entire range of intelligent expression through tone and melody, music and speech, everything in the world, in fact, that gives joy and beauty through purposeful utterance. . . . . The seventh, and final, "quality" is body or figure, by which he means the fundamental tendency or energy toward expression in actuality and concrete form.[60]

The first of these seven qualities or forces of the universe finds a striking parallel in Blake's conception of the narrow, egoistic desire of the soul that is imprisoned in the close fetters of this world. The second is substantially Blake's principle of union, the sympathetic love that binds the whole universe together. The fourth is suggestive—but only suggestive—of Blake's conception of energy, while the fifth is in much the same way suggestive of his conception of imagination. The sixth reveals, of course, a friendliness to beauty and the arts that Blake would find acceptable, and the seventh gives that recognition to form, or outline, or embodiment that Blake so vigorously insisted on.

This analysis of Boehme's "qualities" also suggests that recognition of the necessity of opposites for the life of the whole, of the eternal presence of the positive and negative, even within God's own hidden nature, that Boehme believed essential for the manifestation of the nature of God in the world.[61] Here one may believe Blake found warrant and encouragement, if not the hint, for his oft-repeated dictum: "Without contraries is no progression."

Again, like Blake and like Swedenborg, Boehme believed that man is a microcosm containing within himself the universe.[62] Consequently, when man "knows himself aright, he knows also his Creator, and all the Creatures, too."[63]

In order to know himself aright, the first thing for man to do is to discover his own history. In the beginning he was created perfect, a higher being even than the angels, for he was complete.[64] But: "He broke the perfect temperature—or harmonious balance of qualities—and turned his will toward the dark world and the

[60] Jones, op. cit., pp. 180–82.
[61] Ibid., pp. 177–78.
[62] Ibid., p. 184.
[63] Behmen, "The Three Principles," Works, Vol. I, Bk. II, p. 8, Preface.
[64] Margaret L. Bailey, Milton and Jakob Boehme (New York, 1914), p. 29.

light in him grew dim."[65] Here is one of the most striking points of agreement between Boehme and Blake, for the latter likewise makes the fall of man as prefigured, say, in the revolt of Urizen, a disturbance of the initial harmony of the qualities that constitute man's soul and a turning of man's spirit in the direction of the lower life. In both systems the result is blindness, as Boehme says: "We Men with our [Earthly] eyes which we have from this world, cannot see God and the Angels, which yet are every moment present to us."[66] To save man from this blindness is the mission of Christ the Redeemer—"therefore God has made his *Covenant* with us in Christ, that we should be *new born* again in Christ: for he hath given up his life into Death for us, and hath brought our soul again quite through the Eternal Fire and turned it about."[67] There is a strong suggestion of Blake's favorite picture of the human soul with gates opening on eternity in another of Boehme's descriptions of the work of the redemption:

Christ in the human Essence hath broken up and opened the gates of our inward Heavenly Humanity, which was shut up in *Adam;* so that nothing is now wanting, but that the Soul draw its Will out of the Vanity of the corrupted Flesh, and bring it into this open Gate in the Spirit of Christ.[68]

To be saved, Boehme believes, man must be born anew into God.[69] His statement of the process of regeneration is a fairly conventional presentation of the view current among German mystics from the time of Tauler:

The poor soul must watch and pray, and continually put its will into God's will, it must not give way to the body in anything except it hath *yielded itself* to God *first:* the soul must not please itself at all in its own power; but cast itself merely upon God, as being itself weak and able to do nothing, (though it be strong), and so continually *go out from itself,* from its natural will, and so *fall into the will of God,* and then the Devil cannot meddle with it.[70]

[65] Jones, *op. cit.,* p. 185, quoted from *Mysterium Magnum,* xviii, 31–43.

[66] Behmen, "The High and Deep Searching of the Threefold Life of Man," *Works,* II, Bk. I, ii, 51.

[67] *Ibid.,* xi, 27.

[68] Behmen, "The Third Book of Regeneration," *Works,* IV, Bk. III, chap. iv, 88.

[69] Behmen, "The High and Deep Searching of the Threefold Life of Man," *Works,* II, Bk. I, chap. xi, 48.

[70] *Ibid.,* chap. viii, 23.

Like Blake, Boehme lays great stress on believing, on vital faith, but he defines faith in a fashion that may be taken to epitomize the differences between his teaching and that of the later writer, for he says: "To know only, is not Faith, but an Hunger and Thirst after that which I want, so that I draw it in thereby to myself, and lay hold on it with the Desire and Imagination, and make it my own; this is the Truth and Essence of a Christian's Faith."[71] As here, the central and the decisive element in human destiny for Boehme is will. For Blake it is imagination. Read "imagination" where Boehme says "will," and very often you have Blake's teaching, but always within very definite limits.

Finally, and perhaps most important of all, when Blake read Boehme he found, as in Swedenborg, that pervading consciousness of hidden significance in the world of men and words and things that led Boehme to appropriate the strange pseudo-chemistry of the alchemists and explain in its murky terms the evolution of the universe. Likewise in the Scriptures Boehme found strange, esoteric meanings of the sort that Swedenborg later more extensively pursued in his endless pages of scriptural interpretation, of the type that Blake at least once projected in his plans for an interpretation of Genesis. In view of Blake's own devotion to symbolism it is interesting to know that in Boehme he found a temper sympathetic with his own in the unwearying pursuit of strange revelations of meaning that led ever farther and farther beyond the bounds of literal reality into an infinitely expanding and perennially elusive world of mystery. Like Blake, Boehme found it very difficult to achieve anything like lucidity in his pursuit of this strangely veiled and maniform truth, and like Blake, Boehme possessed absolute confidence in the substantial reality of the significances he so faithfully pursued.

Here again we see at work Blake's peculiar faculty of selection. There was much in Boehme that ran counter to Blake's purposes and interests. It may be seriously questioned whether the central characteristics of Boehme's work were not essentially alien to Blake's endeavor. But those aspects seem to have been quite destitute of any influence on his ways of thinking. He seems to

---

[71] Behmen, "The Third Book of Regeneration," *Works*, IV, Bk. III, chap. iv, 89.

have appropriated what he found congenial, and passed the rest by as if unaware of its presence.

Blake himself commemorates his study of Milton in the title of the prophetic book that recounts his experiences with Hayley at Felpham. He also makes several references to Milton elsewhere. Of these the most famous is the passage in the *Marriage of Heaven and Hell* that concludes with this note: "The reason Milton wrote in fetters when he wrote of Angels and God, and at liberty when of Devils and Hell, is because he was a true Poet, and of the Devil's party without knowing it." M. Denis Saurat has made a very detailed and thoughtful study of this subject, in which, very wisely, he has laid more stress upon likeness of temperament and correspondence of point of view than upon direct influence. For, as he notes, some of the most striking parallels to Blake's ideas are to be found in Milton's *Treatise of Christian Doctrine,* which was not made known to the world until 1825.

In his approach to the subject M. Saurat stresses the fact that probably the most outstanding characteristic of both poets as thinkers was the spiritual pride or egotism[72] that made both seek to justify in their theories the desires and instincts that they recognized in themselves.[73] The direct influence of one poet upon the other he finds most evident in *Vala* and in *Milton*. Blake's Urizen impresses him as a transposition of Milton's Satan into another world.[74] And many of his adventures are to be referred to *Paradise Lost*: for instance, Urizen's conspiracy with Luvah is reminiscent of Satan's with Beelzebub.[75] And in details less striking M. Saurat finds what he defines as "a parallelism of poetic invention which probably was hardly conscious in Blake's mind."[76] So he finds the whole of the sixth night of *Vala* "hardly more than a splendid paraphrase of Milton's description of the voyage through Chaos."[77] But in every case M. Saurat finds that Blake has transformed what he borrowed into the stuff of his own imagination, so vastly more chaotic and suggestive than Milton's. As for the poem which bears Milton's name, there can be no doubt that the Milton of Blake's

[72] Denis Saurat, *Blake and Milton* (Bordeaux, 1920), p. 5.
[73] *Ibid.,* p. 9.
[74] *Ibid.,* p. 15.   [75] *Ibid.,* p. 16.   [76] *Ibid.,* p. 17.   [77] *Ibid.,* p. 18.

conception is the embodiment of many principles that would have shocked the Milton of history.

In the consideration of morality M. Saurat believes that Blake found the same fundamental problem that Milton did: the struggle between desire and reason, but that he solved it in a reverse fashion, "so that Blake is intellectually a sort of inverted Milton."[78] When it came to a more specific handling of the moral problem, in the explanation of man's fall, both poets found it a disturbance of the original harmony of man's nature, but Blake differed radically from Milton in his refusal to recognize the necessity of the supremacy of reason, upon which Milton grounded his entire treatment of the subject.[79] That fundamental difference conditions all Blake's appropriation of what we might otherwise call Miltonic material. Again, Blake probably found here, in his reading of Milton, as elsewhere, stimulus for his own thought rather than definite sources of doctrine and idea.

As for minor and less certain possible influences, the resemblance of some of Blake's teachings to those of the Gnostics of the first and second centuries has been noticed so often that it has become a commonplace in Blake criticism. It is most unlikely that Blake ever saw any of the actual documents of Gnosticism, but it is quite possible that he knew the English version of Mosheim's *Ecclesiastical History*, which first appeared in 1764.[80] There seems to be no way of settling the question of whether Blake ever saw this book, but it is interesting to note that the points which the author stresses in his account of these early heretics are for the most part points in which one may detect a marked similarity to Blake's views. Mosheim's attitude is, of course, unfriendly to these "enthusiastic and self-sufficient philosophers," but in view of the independence Blake displayed in the formation of artistic opinions

[78] Saurat, *Blake and Milton*, p. 39.

[79] *Ibid.*, chap. iv, § 1.

[80] The nature of this work may be most briefly suggested by the following transcript of the title-page of a later edition: "*An Ecclesiastical History, Antient and Modern, from the Birth of Christ, to the Beginning of the Eighteenth Century.* In six volumes. In which the rise, progress, and variations of church power are considered in their connexion with the state of learning and philosophy, and the political history of Europe during that period, by the late learned John Lawrence Mosheim, D.D. and Chancellor of the University of Gottingen. Translated from the original Latin, and accompanied with notes and chronological tables, by Archibald Maclaine, D.D., Berwick, 1809."

radically contravenient of the opinions of Sir Joshua Reynolds and the Academy of his day, it would not be surprising if he read "white" where the more orthodox Mosheim read "black." The fundamental claim that gave these early dissenters their name was one that would arouse the sympathetic interest of Blake—that they were "able to restore mankind to the knowledge [gnosis] of the True and Supreme Being, which had been lost in the world."[81] Their fundamental insistence upon an essential dualism of good and evil in the universe would not interest Blake, but their belief that this world was created, not by God, as orthodox Christianity taught, but by an inferior being, evil or at least imperfect in nature, the demiurge, was one that may be paralleled in Blake's presentation of the Jehovah of the Old Testament in just such a rôle.[82] This led them to what Mosheim describes as a "frantic aversion" to the books of the Old Testament—an aversion so strong as to make them lavish "their encomiums upon the *serpent,* the first author of sin."[83] Again one is reminded of Blake, of the strong admiration he expressed, for instance, for the Miltonic Devil. This aversion also led the Gnostics, as Mosheim goes on to say, to an

abhorrence of Moses and the religion he taught, and made them assert, that, in imposing such a system of disagreeable and severe laws upon the Jews, he was only actuated by the malignant author of this world, who consulted his own glory and authority, and not the real advantage of men.[84]

This position is strongly suggestive of Blake's own rejection of the Ten Commandments and arraignment of Urizen-Jehovah, the lawgiver. While many of the Gnostics went to extremes of asceticism, there were others who "maintained that there was no moral difference in human actions; and thus confounding right with wrong, they gave a loose rein to all the passions, and asserted the innocence of following blindly all their motions, and of living by their tumultuous dictates."[85] Again, if Blake read these lines, he must have found at least encouragement for promulgating that theory of the holiness of impulse and the beauty of spontaneous energy that gives the *Everlasting Gospel,* for instance, its characteristic animus. For the

---

[81] Mosheim, *op. cit.,* I, 133.

[82] *Ibid.,* p. 135.

[83] *Ibid.*   [84] *Ibid.*   [85] *Ibid.,* p. 137.

authority of these novel beliefs some of the Gnostics took refuge in "certain secret doctrines of Christ which were not exposed to vulgar eyes." The more hardy declared "that they had arrived at these sublime degrees of wisdom by an innate force and vigour of mind."[86] This was a manner of justification with which William Blake's mind was thoroughly at home both by natural inclination and by study.

The early Gnostic explanation of the creation of the world was brought closer to Blake by Marcion, who attributed it to an intermediate kind of deity, "The God and legislator of the Jewish nation" (substantially Blake's conception), who "wages perpetual war with the evil principle" to usurp the place of the Supreme Being and to subject to their tyrannous authority the human race.[87] This sounds very much like Blake's arraignment of the usurping Urizen.

Another of the Gnostic group, Valentine, directly or indirectly, probably, gave Blake the term "aeon," although in a rather different sense from that which Blake employed.[88] He also stresses, in a fashion suggestive of Blake's explanation of Urizen's pretensions to power, the arrogance which led the "demiurge" to attempt the usurpation of supreme power, and represents the other angels that preside over the various regions of the universe as emulating his example.[89] This view may very well have suggested to Blake the series of individualistic insurgencies of the various powers of the universe which constitute the central theme of his "Prophetical Writings." Altogether, the resemblances between Blake's teachings and those of the Gnostics are so striking that even the possibility of his having thus indirectly come into contact with these early exponents of some of his favorite ideas must be considered.

As for the influence of various medieval seekers after the hidden truth of life, it is even more difficult to discover whether Blake knew anything of their works directly. There is no reason to think he knew much. Of some he might read in Mosheim, who makes brief mention of Joachim de Flore, the reputed author of the famous *Everlasting Gospel*. This is the book which made such a

[86] Mosheim, *op. cit.*, p. 138.

[87] *Ibid.*, p. 219.   [88] *Ibid.*, p. 229.   [89] *Ibid.*, p. 230.

great stir among the Spiritual Franciscans,[90] and may have suggested the title of Blake's own *Everlasting Gospel*. Joachim is
more famous for the reported fantasy of his prophesies than for
anything he actually said. The item of Mosheim's brief report that
might catch Blake's attention would, of course, be Joachim's assertion (or his Franciscan promulgator's—for our purposes the dis-
pute as to the authorship of the whole work is irrelevant) that "the
gospel of Christ was to be abrogated" and "the true and everlasting
gospel of God" was to rule in its stead.[91]

Mosheim says very little of the Fraticelli who so enthusiastically spread Joachim's prophecies, beyond noticing their refusal to
acknowledge hostile ecclesiastical authority.[92] But he does consider
more fully the so-called "Brethren and Sisters of the Free Spirit,"
a sect in some ways resembling the more extreme wing of the Spiritual Franciscans, which gained ground in the thirteenth century
in Italy, France, and Germany. Mosheim thus describes them:

> This new sect took their denomination from the word of St. Paul [Rom.
> 8 :2, 14], and maintained that the true children of God were invested with the
> privilege of a full and perfect freedom from the jurisdiction of the law . . . .
> "that every man by the power of contemplation, and by calling off his mind
> from sensible and terrestial objects, might be united to the Deity in an inef-
> fable manner, and become one with the Source and Parent of all things: and
> that they, who, by long and assiduous meditation, had plunged themselves, as
> it were, into the *abyss* of the Divinity, acquired thereby a most glorious and
> sublime liberty, and were not only delivered from the violence of sinful lusts,
> but even from the common instincts of nature."[93]

Indeed, they believed that such a person " 'was the *Son of God* in
the same sense and manner that Christ was, and was thereby raised
to a glorious independence, and freed from the obligation of all
laws human and divine.' "[94] Consequently, these Brethren of the
Free Spirit regarded with contempt all ecclesiastical regulation and
all church observance, and even the ordinary practices of prayer
and fasting of the private Christian life. When one recalls certain
aspects of Blake's antinomianism that have attracted much attention in this century, it is interesting to think that Blake may have

[90] *Ibid.*, III, 209.
[91] *Ibid.*, III, 213.
[92] *Ibid.*, III, 223 f.   [93] *Ibid.*, III, 279 ff.   [94] *Ibid.*, p. 281.

read of these antinomians of the Middle Ages in a source that selected so aptly the aspects of their teachings that would have interested him.

A very interesting article in *Englische Studien* for 1920 suggests that Blake had also come into contact with the traditions of the Cabala that had been built up by the Jewish scholars during the Middle Ages. The author of this article is quite sure that Blake had read some one of the cabalistical books by this time accessible at second-hand to Englishmen in various works on the Cabala, and more directly accessible in German versions available in Blake's time.[95] It is not certain that Blake could actually read German well enough to find his way in the highly complicated paths even of the *Kabbala Denudata*. But Herr Fehr certainly presents a convincing case for Blake's having in some way got hold of cabalistic ideas. Blake's use of the "blue Mundane Shell" for the whole visible world of appearance, as in *Milton* I, 19 (Ellis' edition), is one example that he points out. Another is the indebtedness of Blake's handling of Albion in the *Jerusalem* to the cabalistic doctrines of the Adam Kadmon who, symbolically, contained in his members all the world.[96] Herr Fehr says:

> Blake had in his mind some such cabalistical conception of Adam Kadmon and his significance when he planned the great prophetic poem *Jerusalem*. Here he astounds the critics by an incomprehensible symbolical geography. Poplar, Paddington, Malden, Canterbury, appear as members of the giant Albion, and the mystification becomes still more confusing when we look at one of the illustrations which he has added to the poem. Here he exhibits on a large scale his own body which comprehends the whole universe with Sun, Moon, and Stars. It is of course Adam Kadmon—as Albion translated from the Jewish into the British—that meets us here.[97]

Herr Fehr points out other striking resemblances, but these are the most important. Again it is very difficult to prove anything, but it is interesting to note the possibility of such a contribution to the resources upon which Blake could draw for his own work.

Finally, in all Blake's writing and in all his reading and think-

[95] Bernhard Fehr, "William Blake und die Kabbala," *Englische Studien*, LIV (1920), 139-48.

[96] *Ibid.*, p. 142.

[97] *Ibid.*, p. 144.

ing one influence was beyond any question constantly at work: that of the Bible, both the Old and the New Testaments. To trace such an influence in detail is impossible because of its all-pervasive character; to suggest its main lines is to develop the subject of Blake's religious belief, the business of another chapter. Here it is possible to notice only two things about Blake's reading of the Bible: First, that the sections of the Bible that seem most to have impressed his imagination are not the more lucid and humanly simple passages like the Psalms of David or the Parables of the New Testament. Rather, Blake's imagination seems to have been caught by the whirling denunciations of Isaiah or those strange visions of horned beast and jeweled wall that have made the Revelation of St. John the Divine the delight of visionaries of all ages. Much that seems unbelievably strange in Blake's *Jerusalem* may be traced back to those visions of Patmos in which finally the aged apostle is supposed to have seen "that great city, the holy Jerusalem, descending out of heaven from God."[98]

And the second thing is that just as Blake's imagination sought out and appropriated what was most congenial to its own native workings, so Blake's general point of view colored and interpreted all he read. The *Everlasting Gospel* of 1810 shows what the central figure of the New Testament became in his hands. In the light of his own inspiration he seems to have read his own Bible. Indeed, in a certain sense Blake may be said to have made his own gospel and his own Christianity. M. Berger has pointed out that Blake's religion of art carries to a superlative degree ideas already current even in his own lifetime in the various romantic groups of England, France, and Germany.[99] But, as the French critic recognizes, there can be no question of Blake's pre-eminence in thoroughness and energy of conviction.

From this inquiry into the elements of Blake's life and reading that may have influenced his mysticism two things emerge into certainty: The first is the extraordinary isolation of spirit in which he passed his life, an isolation that confirmed the bias of his own temper without that enlargement and enrichment that results from

---

[98] Rev. 21:10.
[99] Berger, *op. cit.*, p. 207.

really effective and critical contact with one's peers. And the second is the fact that in his reading, where he enjoyed practically his sole opportunity for receiving influence from other minds, he seems in general to have paid faithful attention only to writers of a persuasion congenial to his own. Where they have confirmed his own leanings there is reason to think he has appropriated; where they have differed, he has often transmuted the alien conception into a form more harmonious with his own view; but there is practically no evidence to suggest any real modification of his way of thinking. In his reading as in his social contacts, where he encountered disagreement Blake seems to have summarily rejected what displeased him and stood firm in his own conviction.

CHAPTER VI

BLAKE'S MESSAGE

William Blake set forth his vision of man's life in a series of works, almost all in verse, extending from the years just before 1789, the date of the *Songs of Innocence,* to 1820, when *Jerusalem* was engraved. Practically all of these works are accompanied by illustrations, from one point of view an integral part of the text, but often so loosely related that they may in general be left for consideration with Blake's pictures by any study which is primarily concerned with the content of the writings themselves. These may be roughly classified into three main groups: the lyrics—the *Songs of Innocence and of Experience;* the treatises—the *Marriage of Heaven and Hell* and the *Everlasting Gospel;* and the symbolic narratives. The last group, by far the largest and, for our purposes, the most important, falls into three natural groups: first, the so-called "Minor Prophetical Writings," beginning with *Tiriel,* in 1789, and running through the *Song of Los,* in 1795, and comprehending in all eleven distinct poems or fragments of poems; second, the *Nine Nights of Vala,* a huge agglomeration of between four and five thousand lines, which Blake seems to have worked on between 1795 and 1804, which he never completed or even fully organized, and which he seems later to have used as a sort of quarry, not only retelling the stories, but transposing whole passages into *Milton* and *Jerusalem;* and third, the most complete and mature of his "Prophetic Books," *Milton,* some two thousand lines long, written between 1804 and 1808, and *Jerusalem, The Emanation of the Giant Albion,* carried from 1804 to 1820, a fairly complete work of about five thousand lines.

Any complete study of Blake's literary work must also take into account several more miscellaneous but very important sources: his letters, of which about eighty-seven are known, centering, because of the chance of appreciative preservation, about three

165

periods of Blake's life, the first with a group of some eleven letters written to various people from 1800 to 1803; the second with thirty-two letters addressed to William Hayley, written at various times from 1803 to 1805; and the third, more than twenty years later, with twenty-four written between 1824 and 1827 to John Linnell. In general, the third group is of less interest than the first two groups, which throw very important light upon Blake's temperament and his relations to other people, to say nothing of the important matter of vision. Then there are his marginal comments on other writers, notably on Bacon, Swedenborg, Reynolds, and Wordsworth, and some incidental critical writings like the *Descriptive Catalogue* of 1809 and the "Public Address" of 1810, and, finally, what is for the student of Blake's mind and temper the most important of all, Blake's private notebook, chiefly contained in that famous collection of poems, epigrams, and fragments, ranging all the way from the grossly indecent to the delicately poetic, known as the "Rossetti Manuscript."

Superficially viewed, this appears to be a very heterogeneous mass of material. But if one disregards differences of form and discrepancies in detail and is careful to take into account the relation to context as well as the apparent meanings of terms, he soon finds that these various works do make a whole so far as fundamental point of view and controlling energy are concerned. To take an extreme example, it would seem as if no two things could be more unlike both in theme and in form, than the *Songs of Innocence*, 1789, and *Jerusalem*, 1804–20, but the point of view revealed in the "Voice of the Ancient Bard," which closes the *Songs* in the particular copy which Dr. Keynes uses for his text, is the point of view of *Jerusalem*. Again, the plea for enfranchised love in the *Visions of the Daughters of Albion*, of 1793, arises out of the same faith in unrestricted energy that inspires the antinomian Christ of the *Everlasting Gospel* of twenty-five years later.

The same is true of the complicated symbolism through which the majority of Blake's visions are expressed. At first it seems so complicated, so obscure, so incoherent, so utterly unrelated to any world of meaning with which the reader is familiar, that his first impulse is to dismiss it as mad nonsense. But the more the prophetic writings are studied, the clearer it becomes that, however fragmentary and even inconsistent a particular "song" or "vision" or "book" may be, its symbolism comes out of the same body or world of symbol as that out of which the rest of Blake's work comes. In other words, even if the system revealed in these writings is neither logically exact nor well-articulated, it is fundamentally organic. For example, the Urizen of the *Book of Urizen*, of 1794, is the same Urizen as the foe of Los in *Jerusalem*, ten to twenty years later, and behaves in much the same characteristic fashion. And even a less uniform character, like Urthona-Los, goes through changes that are not so much alterations as modifications and amplifications, such as are familiar to the student of any mythology. That word "mythology" is probably the best term to use for the group of symbolic persons and incidents that fill Blake's visions, if we remember that here we have not the unconscious working out of meanings by a people for several centuries, but a curious condensation in the imagination of one man of what is in essence probably pretty much the same process, extending in this case not over centuries, but over a span of at most forty years.

It is true that one may note differences in the work of different periods. The symbolism of *Tiriel* is more obscure and less complicated than the symbolism of *Jerusalem*. It is as if the author had been trying a piece of his myth out, and somehow it did not move to his liking, for he seems to have discarded it soon after. The *French Revolution* dallies with historical characters who have been so transformed that even their enemies would not have known them in the somewhat windy pages of Blake. But with the first book of *Urizen* the ground plan for all the stories is completed and the villain's portrait fully drawn. There will be developments in the next twenty years, genealogies will be multiplied and complicated, new characters will appear and new localities, but one feels it is all an unfolding rather than a building-up. It is as if Blake were letting the reader more fully into the story, rather than elaborating his story. Nowhere is this more clearly shown than in those places where, under the influence of various crises in Blake's own affairs, new characters such as Scofield or Kox are introduced. They find their place in the Pantheon introducing not new elements, but a multiplication or a fresh exemplification of that with which we are already well acquainted.

What makes possible this elaboration of the essentially unchanged is the nature of this mythology, in some ways the most distinctive aspect of Blake's achievement. That may be examined in two fundamental aspects: first, the nature of the protagonists, and second, the nature of their adventures. For the first, the nature of Blake's protagonists, the most striking thing about them is that they have no vesture of particular body or particular personality. They come before us with the clarity and the intensity of a dream, but when we would lay hands upon them, they remain fast in the impressive generality of the dream. We recognize them no matter where we see them, but we recognize them by their accompanying properties, by their symbolic meanings, by their established relations to recognized issues and situations, not as we recognize people in poetry or life by the idiosyncracies of their appearance, the play of individual mind and feeling, the characteristic look or gesture— what we may call personal flavor. Of dramatic life they have none. They remain fast in their meanings.

The reason for this skeletal quality is that they are not people at all, but psychological diagrams that play the rôle of mythological actors. Sometimes, Blake speaks of them as universes, and in many ways that term, "universes," describes them even better than a term which, like "actors," for instance, suggests human personality. For each of these universes represents some aspect of human life: Urizen is the intellect; Luvah, the emotions; Tharmas, the instincts; and Urthona, the dark earth passion, with at the center the sublime universe of Los and Enitharmon, the powers of inspiration. Around these protagonists centers all the complexity of Blake's vast mythology, for in each of these four universes Blake has worked out an amazing set of correspondences and significances on the initial principle of correspondence among all the different orders of existence. Of these the simplest and most germane to our purpose are presented in the following table[1] based on the convenient summaries of the Ellis and Yeats interpretation:

[1] Edwin J. Ellis and William Butler Yeats, *The Works of William Blake: Poetic, Symbolic, and Critical* (London, 1893), I, 254, 257, 260.

Urizen	Luvah	Tharmas	Urthona
Reason..................	Emotion	Sensation	Energy
Mind...................	Feeling	Instinct	Matter
Eyes...................	Nostrils	Tongue	Ears
Light..................	Air	Water	Earth Darkness Dark Fire
Head..................	Heart	Loins	Stomach and Womb
South..................	East	West	North
Translucence or Zenith...	Center	Circumference	Opaque or Nadir

This table omits one significant factor in the history of these four powers, and that is the vehicular form of Urthona, Los, or Inspiration. At his highest, Los is the creative imagination; sometimes not very different from Christ. With Enitharmon, his "emanation," Los plays a very large part in the action of the "Prophetic Books," the part with which Blake most warmly sympathized.

But these universes or powers are not mere allegories or symbols. They are the realities beyond the curtain of sense, the spiritual essentials which his enlightened vision has seen and which he has presented in translation for other men to see. He has not, so far as the conscious powers of the mind are concerned, created these meanings. They have come to him. The rather equivocal state of the text of *Vala* is proof of this, for the fact that he seems not to have been certain of the order of various episodes suggests that they came to his mind in the rather haphazard fashion in which the spontaneous fruits of the imagination come to the relaxed and passive consciousness.

Many of the correspondences which Blake elaborates are by no means original with him. In one way and another, a large number of them were known to the medieval alchemists and to the cabalists. The Four, whom he came eventually in *Jerusalem* to call "Zoas," probably go back to the four living creatures whom Ezekiel saw by the river Chebar. As Mr. Darrell Figgis has pointed out, the term "Zoa" comes from the Greek ζῶον, which is the word for what the Authorized Version of the Apocalypse calls beasts.[2] But the mythology is original with Blake in the sense that

[2] Figgis, *op. cit.*, note to Plate IV.

in the form of his system it laid hold upon his imagination, and was there developed and complicated and set in action in a series of episodes quite his own.

It is very difficult to give in a few words any idea of these episodes, because the variations and ramifications of detail are endless. But at bottom they are nearly all fundamentally the same. They tell the story of the fall of man, the whole spiritual man, into division, into a state of bondage to the materialistic reason which knows only the life of the senses and suppresses all spiritual aspirations by the oppression of the moral law. The first *Book of Urizen*, for instance, to take one of the simplest examples, tells the story of how the "primeval priest," or Urizen, instead of remaining in his own proper place, the region of the illuminated intellect, in the South, assumed power to which he had no right in the North, the province of Urthona, or Energy. In the agony of trying to usurp power in a region where he did not belong, he resorted to laws and set up his prescriptions of one king, one god, one law, and so forth. A vast globe then formed around Urizen, and Los, or Inspiration, from whose side Urizen had been born, "went howling," frightened at the formless death of Urizen. Then the separated Urizen underwent a series of changes which left him with a new set of sense powers, but with his old spiritual sensitiveness and perception dead, in a dark and cold void. Horrified by the undivided space that had opened round them, Los pitied, and in pitying, divided; the globe of life took the form of woman, and the first female fled and tried to hide herself in curtains of darkness of which she had woven the woof and called it science. Los, pitying the female (Enitharmon, Space, etc.), embraced her, but she refused him. He, however, begot upon her, his own divided image, a child, whom they named Orc (Revolutionary Ardor or Energy). When this child tried to embrace his mother, Los became jealous, so that an iron girdle of jealousy grew and tightened round his bosom. Enitharmon and Los then took Orc to the top of a mountain and there bound him with the chain of jealousy. Meanwhile Urizen, stung with the odors of nature, started out exploring his realm. The first book ends with the sons of Urizen withered and deafened and cold, and the Salt Sea (Materialism) rolling "englob'd."

The rest of this story, if Blake ever finished it, has been lost. For some time Blake spent his energies telling various aspects of this story as it affected various protagonists. Not till *Vala,* or, more completely, *Jerusalem,* with the building of Golgonooza, or the City of Art, can he be said really to have told how man was to be saved, a process to be summed up as a restoration to the life of vision. But crude and hurried and in some ways confused as this early version is, it may be taken as the type of the stories of the "Prophetic Books," all of which have the common theme of how man fell into the bondage of the world of unilluminated materialism, and, where the story is completed, of how he was restored to the life of vision, of contact with the spiritual world from which he had fallen. This transaction is not viewed historically, but eternally, beyond the limits of time and space—which Blake regards as the creation of the fall—as it takes place constantly in every human spirit and in the world to which the spirit belongs.

It is through these stories, in the main, that Blake's message finds expression, and it is interesting to note that where the stories and the treatises and even the lyric poems trench on the same ground, they confirm each other to a very striking degree, and that, in general, regardless of the time at which they were written. Critics have tried to discern stages of development in Blake's thought. The endeavor has been made to show that the French Revolution may be taken to mark a dividing line in the history of his opinions, but there is very little evidence for that. And it is interesting that, if we take, for instance, the theme of freedom in love, which has been cited as an evidence of revolutionary influence, we have no reason to think that Blake's views had changed very much in essence by the time he wrote the *Everlasting Gospel,* in 1818, from what they were in 1793. Moreover, even Blake's poem, *The French Revolution,* while showing a sympathetic attention to the events of the day, was far more concerned with the Revolution as a manifestation of eternity than with its historical aspects.

It is true that in the decade from 1793 to 1803 the various aspects of the sex problem: hypocrisy, jealousy, chastity—to name a few—play a much larger part in Blake's work than they do after that time. The problems of the artist, the indifference of the majority of men to the artist's purposes, the vindication of the artist's right to follow his own inspiration unfettered by the stupidity of the world about him, the insistence that all men should be artists, for instance, play a larger part in *Milton*, for example, than does sex. That does not mean that sex is forgotten, nor does it mean that when the subject comes up for consideration Blake's point of view has changed. The presence of the *Everlasting Gospel* of 1818 is proof to the contrary.

A fuller knowledge of Blake's life than any we possess would probably account for this shift in emphasis. What we know of Blake's history from 1800 to 1804 and of the relation of that history to *Milton*, written between 1804 and 1808, is very suggestive. In the years immediately preceding the writing of *Milton*, Blake had had one of the most disappointing experiences of his life in his relations with his unenlightened patron, William Hayley, who had felt himself qualified to judge of Blake's work, treating with half-contemptuous condescension the visionary efforts in art which Blake considered his mission in life, and trying to drive him into more conventional fields, like miniature-painting, which he felt would insure Blake's having bread and butter, and which Blake, after his first effort to conform, rejected as utterly alien to his nature. Blake's letters and his notebooks show how bitterly he had suffered during this period. It is this experience, highly generalized and symbolized, that, with Blake's reaction to it, forms the basis of the story of *Milton*, which may be taken as an introduction to *Jerusalem*.

This suggests the question, Is the predominance of sex in Blake's writings of the years about 1793 also to be traced to Blake's personal experience? At least one critic has thought so, Mr. Edwin J. Ellis, in *The Real Blake*. But the picture which he draws of the problems of Blake's marriage has no certain evidence to support it, and in some particulars at least must be dismissed as pure fantasy. Of objective, external evidence there is none. But the fact that the majority of the verses, epigrams, and fragments scribbled in the "Rossetti Manuscript" for those years betray a burning absorption in sex, that over and over again they plead for freedom from selfish jealousy and the restrictions which morality-bound chastity places upon the free realization of sex desire and the free play of sex energy, suggests that Blake had been moved to what amounts to an obsession by some very stirring experience of his own.

With this difference in emphasis in mind, then, we may proceed to the gleaning of Blake's message from his work.

That message is, first of all, a revolutionary message, from the *Songs of Experience* to the "Ghost of Abel," a message of impassioned and sustained criticism of his own age. The core of his arraignment is the rationalism of the eighteenth century, that overweening trust in the power of the human reason that in his judgment restricted man's faith and allegiance solely to what could be verified by the senses of man, that in the same spirit rejected as foolish or false all that man could not immediately comprehend and pigeonhole, that scorned everything savoring either of imagination or feeling.

This indictment of rationalism is based on two counts: its preference of the material to the spiritual, and its restraint of the energies of man's nature, two counts which may be taken as the cornerstones of his philosophy of life, so fundamental are they to all his thinking in every field. His objection to what he conceived to be the inevitable intellectual fruits of rationalism is put into brilliantly epigrammatic form in one of the most poetic of the little poems of the "Rossetti Manuscript":

> Mock on, mock on, Voltaire, Rousseau;
> Mock on, mock on; 'tis all in vain!
> You throw the sand against the wind,
> And the wind blows it back again.
> And every sand becomes a gem
> Reflected in the beams divine;
> Blown back they blind the mocking eye,
> But still in Israel's paths they shine.
> The Atoms of Democritus
> And Newton's Particles of Light
> Are sands upon the Red Sea shore,
> Where Israel's tents do shine so bright.

In this defiance two objects of attack are implied: the sceptical infidelity of the mockers of religion, and the materialism which Blake believed was the consequence of the faith in reason recently nourished by the growing interest in scientific speculation. The same objects of attack were in Blake's mind when he wrote what is probably the most deliberate and most constructive presentation of his indictment of rationalism in the long speech in which Milton, or Poetic Inspiration, explains the purpose of his coming to earth in the poem which bears his name:

> I come in Self-annihilation & the grandeur of Inspiration,
> To cast off Rational Demonstration by Faith in the Saviour,
> To cast off the rotten rags of Memory by Inspiration,
> To cast off Bacon, Locke & Newton from Albion's covering,
> To take off his filthy garments & clothe him with Imagination,
> To cast aside from Poetry, all that is not Inspiration
> That it no longer shall dare to mock with the aspersion of Madness,
> Cast on the Inspired by the tame high finisher of paltry Blots:
> Indefinite or paltry Rhymes: or paltry Harmonies:
> Who creeps into State Government like a catterpiller to destroy,
> To cast off the idiot Questioner who is always questioning,
> But never capable of answering, who sits with a sly grin
> Silent plotting when to question like a thief in a cave:
> Who publishes doubt & calls it knowledge: whose Science is Despair:
> Whose pretence to knowledge is Envy: whose whole Science is
> To destroy the wisdom of ages to gratify ravenous Envy,
> That rages round him like a Wolf day & night without rest.
> He smiles with condescension; he talks of Benevolence & Virtue:
> And those who act with Benevolence & Virtue they murder time on time.
> These are the destroyers of Jerusalem, those are the murderers
> Of Jesus, who deny the Faith & mock at Eternal Life:
> Who pretend to Poetry that they may destroy Imagination,
> By imitation of Nature's Images drawn from Remembrance.
> These are the Sexual Garments, the Abomination of Desolation,
> Hiding the Human Lineaments as with an Ark & Curtains
> Which Jesus rent: & now shall wholly purge away with Fire
> Till Generation is swallow'd up in Regeneration.[3]

Some of the passion of this arraignment is probably due to Blake's recent experience with Hayley, an experience which, as is well known, left him with even less confidence than he possessed before as to either the intelligence or the disinterestedness of the prevailing patronage of art. But the main lines of the passage give the reasons for Blake's habitual war upon the reason. The reason was the foe to the life of vision, for it suppressed whatever possibilities

---

[3] *Milton*, edited by E. R. D. Maclagan and A. G. B. Russell (London, 1907), p. 43, ll. 2–28. Undoubtedly the most complete arraignment of rationalism is to be found in the *Song of Los*, but the symbolism of that poem makes successful quotation impossible.

man might have of freeing his spiritual vision from the tyranny of the senses; the reason tended to displace simple faith in religious matters; in its backward-looking subservience to memory, to clip the forward-soaring wings of inspiration; the reason was always with its scepticism dampening the ardor of faith, and with its cold calculation and literalness of mind warring on the imagination essential to the creation of real art. Only the poetic inspiration could free mankind from its devastating tyranny.

For Blake grew increasingly, as time went on, more concerned about the damage rationalism did to art even than about its consequences for religion.

The average Englishman of his age, even the cultivated Hayley, was far too sunk in the literalness of materialism to see that the prosperity of a nation depends on its regard for art.[4] And even those who affected to prize the arts were not very forward to indorse Blake's assertion that:

> It is the greatest of crimes to depress true art and science. I know that those who are dead from the earth, and who mocked and despised the meekness of true art (and such, I find, have been the situation of our beautiful, affectionate *Ballads*),[5] I know that such mockers are most severely punished in eternity. I know it, for I see it and dare not help. The mocker of art is the mocker of Jesus.[6]

Even more direct and vigorous in its condemnation of this indifference of the age is the Preface to *Milton*, with all its bitterness of the neglected artist who for years has been watching the popularity of inferior artists:

> Rouze up O Young Men of the New Age! Set your foreheads against the ignorant Hirelings! For we have Hirelings in the Camp, the Court, & the University: who would if they could for ever depress Mental & prolong Corporeal War. Painters! on you I call. Sculptors! Architects! Suffer not the fashionable Fools to depress your powers by the prices they pretend to give for contemptible works or the expensive advertizing boasts that they make of

---

[4] In the "Address to the Public" that opens the *Jerusalem* Blake says: "Nations are Destroy'd, or Flourish, in proportion as Their Poetry, Painting and Music, are Destroy'd or Flourish" (*Jerusalem*, edited by E. R. D. Maclagan and A. G. B. Russell [London, 1904], p. 3, ll. 41–43).

[5] The *Ballads* referred to are thus described by Mr. Russell in his edition of Blake's *Letters*: "*Ballads*, by William Hayley, Esq., founded on Anecdotes relating to Animals, with prints designed and engraved by William Blake" (p. 179, Note 1).

[6] *The Letters of William Blake, Together with a Life by Frederick Tatham*, edited by Archibald G. B. Russell (London, 1906), p. 189.

such works; believe Christ & his Apostles that there is a Class of Men whose whole delight is in Destroying. We do not want either Greek or Roman Models if we are but just & true to our own Imaginations, those Worlds of Eternity in which we shall live for ever, in Jesus Our Lord.[7]

But the text of these appeals explains the reason why even the artists of his day would hardly have satisfied Blake's demands. For the art in which he was interested was what he loved to call "visionary art," art that in very definite, even hard, lines, with very "minute particulars," bodies forth what is seen in vision. In a very squeamish age he maintained that "Art & Science cannot exist but by Naked Beauty display'd."[8] As for technique, his age at almost every point failed to meet his requirements. As he was wont to point out with indignation, Rubens, Rembrandt, the Venetians, and the Flemish held the field among the connoisseurs.[9] Such homage seemed to him a criminal infringement upon the just claims of his masters, Raphael and Michael Angelo.[10] The popular taste of the day reveled in the delicate, often vague and evanescent, lines, and the full, even unctuous, massing of color of Sir Joshua Reynolds, and the fascinating subtleties of chiaroscuro in Rembrandt. To Blake, who delighted in the dry, hard line of the graver and who insisted upon the momentous consequence of detail, especially for visionary significance, these fashions of the day seemed another proof of the blind perversity of his age. For he believed that they were suited to, and served only, the art of this world, the art of the sense-bound materialist. They could only blind people to that form of art which he described in a letter to the unenlightened Dr. Trusler:

. . . . that species which gives existence to every other, namely, visions of eternity. . . . . What is it sets Homer, Virgil, and Milton in so high a rank of art? Why is the Bible more entertaining and instructive than any other book? Is it not because they are addressed to the imagination, which is spiritual sensation, and but mediately to the understanding or reason? Such is true painting.[11]

---

[7] *Milton*, p. 2, ll. 9–18.   [8] *Jerusalem*, p. 36, l. 48.

[9] An example of this indignation is "A Pretty Epigram for the encouragement of those who have paid great sums in the Venetian and Flemish Ooze," *The Poetical Works of William Blake*, edited by John Sampson (Oxford University Press, 1914), p. 207.

[10] Probably the pithiest of his many outbursts on this point is the epigram "To English Connoisseurs," beginning: "You must agree that Rubens was a fool" (Sampson, p. 206).

[11] *Letters*, pp. 60–63.

This visionary art was the type of art which he wished to bring his world to understand, to support, to devote itself to, the kind of art which would restore man to the lost life of vision.

Quite as fundamental as this is Blake's arraignment of rationalism on the score of its restraint of the fundamental energies of man's nature, perhaps most simply and strikingly apparent in his never ceasing attacks upon the church of his day. As might be expected from the foregoing, he objected to the lack of fresh religious inspiration in its teachings, and to its consequent deficiency in human warmth and sympathy. But these charges paled beside his onslaught upon restrictions which the church had formulated, and still relentlessly maintained, upon the natural impulses and graces of man's nature, especially the sex impulses. His arraignment of the church on this score is fully drawn up by the time of the *Songs of Experience*. It is, for instance, the thesis of one of the best-known of these *Songs*, the "Garden of Love":

> I went to the Garden of Love,
> And saw what I never had seen :
> A Chapel was built in the midst,
> Where I used to play on the green.
> And the gates of this Chapel were shut,
> And "Thou shalt not" writ over the door;
> So I turn'd to the Garden of Love
> That so many sweet flowers bore;
> And I saw it was filled with graves,
> And tomb-stones where flowers should be;
> And priests in black gowns were walking their rounds,
> And binding with briars my joys and desires.

And this attack upon the church occurs over and over again in the manuscript notebooks and in the "Prophetical Writings." It is the theme of *The Visions of the Daughters of Albion;* it is the battle-cry of Orc (Passion or Revolt) in *America:*

> The fiery joy, that Urizen perverted to ten commands,
> What night he led the starry hosts thro' the wide wilderness,
> That stony Law I stamp to dust; and scatter Religion abroad
> To the four winds as a torn book, and none shall gather the leaves.[12]

[12] *America,* edited by Sampson, *op. cit.,* p. 296, ll. 61–64.

It constantly recurs in the later "Prophetic Books," sometimes by implication, sometimes directly expressed, as in the following passage from *Jerusalem:*

> . . . . The Satanic Holiness triumph'd in Vala,
> In a Religion of Chastity & Uncircumcised Selfishness
> Both of the Head & Heart & Loins, clos'd up in Moral Pride.[13]

That is what he most objected to in the religious work of his day: its maintenance of the stultifying "Thou Shalt Not" of the moral law. We have the testimony of Blake's friend and biographer that even as a boy Blake so despised all restraints and rules that his father did not dare send him to school.[14] This objection to the restraint which rationalism imposes is one of the most essential characteristics of Blake's temperament and Blake's philosophy. Indeed, more space in Blake's "Prophetical Books" is devoted to the indictment of his age on the two scores of materialism and restraint than to anything else.

In this world of cold, rationalistic indifference to the higher spiritual truth of vision, and of repression of all of man's finer instincts and energies, Blake early felt that he had a very special mission to perform. As we have seen, he was apparently much impressed by Swedenborg's belief that the old "church," or order of religious observance and teaching, had outlived its original truth and potency, and that it must consequently give place to a new "church" or revelation. But he drew from that belief conclusions very different from Swedenborg's. Near the beginning of the *Marriage of Heaven and Hell,* Blake announces: "As a new heaven is begun, and it is now thirty-three years since its advent, the Eternal Hell revives." When he wrote that, Blake was thirty-three years old, and although he was later, in *Milton,* to call Swedenborg the "strongest of men, the Samson shorn by the Churches!"[15] he had already discovered that "Swedenborg has not written one new truth . . . . he has written all the old falsehoods."[16] In other words, Blake was

---

[13] *Jerusalem,* p. 60, ll. 47–49.
[14] Tatham's *Life of William Blake,* in Russell's edition of *Letters,* pp. 3–4.
[15] *Milton,* p. 20, l. 50.
[16] *The Marriage of Heaven and Hell,* Sampson, *op. cit.,* p. 259.

quick to see that Swedenborg, for all his novelty, had in most essentials conformed to the conventions of his tradition. Therefore it seemed to Blake that the work of rebuilding the heavenly city of Jerusalem on earth was yet to be done, and he knew that he was the man to do it.

Perhaps the simplest and most direct avowal of his belief in his divinely appointed mission occurs in that letter in which he explains to his old friend and patron, Major Butts, the difficulties he had encountered in his relations to his new patron during the three years at Felpham. He was then almost forty-four years of age. In telling his friend of the threats that he has been receiving from heaven on the subject of his forsaking his visionary undertakings to comply with Hayley's more mundane wishes, he quotes directly the words of one of his heavenly friends:

"If you, who are organised by Divine Providence for spiritual communion, refuse and bury your talent in the earth, even though you should want natural bread, sorrow and desperation pursue you through life, and after death shame and confusion of face to eternity. Everyone in eternity will leave you, aghast at the man who was crowned with glory and honour by his brethren, and betrayed their cause to their enemies. You will be called the base Judas who betrayed his friend!"[17]

There is a moral fervor to the conviction of that passage that suggests something more even than a heavenly commission to "Renew the Arts on Britain's shore."[18] It is the conviction that something more even than artistic illumination is at stake. That high purpose Blake reveals probably most clearly in the opening pages of *Jerusalem*:

> Trembling I sit day and night, my friends are astonish'd at me,
> Yet they forgive my wanderings, I rest not from my great task!
> To open the Eternal Worlds, to open the immortal Eyes
> Of Man inwards into the Worlds of Thought: into Eternity
> Ever expanding in the Bosom of God, the Human Imagination.[19]

[17] *Letters*, p. 101.
[18] "Now Art Has Lost Its Mental Charms," Sampson, *op. cit.*, p. 141.
[19] *Jerusalem*, p. 5, ll. 16–20.

As he says in the quatrain from the "Address to the Christians" that ends the third chapter of *Jerusalem*, four lines known to thousands who never heard of the poem from which it is taken:

> I give you the end of a golden string,
> Only wind it into a ball:
> It will lead you in at Heaven's gate,
> Built in Jerusalem's wall.[20]

As these and other passages in Blake's letters and visions make clear, Blake was certain that he not only had seen the truth for himself, but had seen it for other men as well. It is with all the confidence of a prophetic revelation that he gives the charter of his authenticity at the beginning of *Jerusalem*: "I am perhaps the most sinful of men! I pretend not to holiness! yet I pretend to love, to see, to converse with daily, as man with man, & the more to have an interest in the Friend of Sinners."[21] And the first chapter of the poem tells us how that revelation was given:

> This theme calls me in sleep night after night, & ev'ry morn
> Awakes me at sun-rise, then I see the Saviour over me
> Spreading his beams of love, & dictating the words of this mild song.[22]

Likewise he says of the "immense poem," that may be *Jerusalem, Vala,* or even *Milton,* of which he tells Major Butts in a letter of 1803: "I have written this poem from immediate dictation, twelve or sometimes twenty or thirty lines at a time, without premeditation, and even against my will. The time it has taken in writing was thus rendered non-existent, and an immense poem exists . . . . without labour or study."[23]

The *Marriage of Heaven and Hell* suggests one or two sidelights on this subject that should perhaps be considered here. In that "Memorable Fancy" which relates how the prophets Isaiah and Ezekiel came to dinner with him and conversed about prophecy, Blake "asked them how they dared so roundly to assert that God spake to them," and Isaiah answered: "I saw no God, nor heard any, in a finite organical perception; but my senses discover'd the infinite in everything, and as I was then persuaded, and remain confirm'd, that the voice of honest indignation is the voice of God, I

[20] *Jerusalem,* p. 77, ll. 1–4.
[21] *Ibid.,* p. 3, ll. 13–16.   [22] *Ibid.,* p. 4, ll. 3–5.   [23] *Letters,* pp. 115–116.

cared not for consequences, but wrote." And then Blake asked: "Does a firm persuasion that a thing is so, make it so?" And Isaiah answered: "All Poets believe that it does, and in ages of imagination this firm persuasion removed mountains; but many are not capable of a firm persuasion of anything." This passage acquires fresh significance in the light of what Blake has said elsewhere of the possibility of all men's attaining to vision if they but cultivated their innate abilities. But this should not be emphasized unduly in the study of Blake's account of his mission, for he seems to have believed that in his visions, whether or not they were dictated by a specific agency, he received, quite beyond any agency of his own, an influx of supernatural truth, of vision.

The world of this vision is not easy to describe, because so often Blake shifts rapidly from one order of being to another without giving any warning. It is perfectly clear that for Blake there are two universes, the world in which we live, and of which our senses bring us report, and the spiritual world beyond their ken. It is to the latter that he devotes most of his effort.

As we have seen, the spiritual world is quite independent of the ordinary categories of space and time. It is all about our material world, and it is within the human bosom at the same time. Its characters are psychological powers more than anything else, and its episodes exist from all eternity and yet are being constantly evolved. Moreover, it is to be discovered in the material world when the enlightened eye looks beyond its vesture into the essential spiritual meaning. In even the tiniest of existences all eternity opens out; in the microcosm the macrocosm is always present in its entirety. So Milton tells "Albion's Sleeping Humanity" when he begins to turn upon his couch:

> Seest thou the little winged fly smaller than a grain of sand?
> It has a heart like thee: a brain open to heaven & hell,
> Withinside wondrous & expansive: its gates are not clos'd:
> I hope thine are not.[24]

For although Blake said it in a jesting epigram against the vogue of the detested Venetian and Flemish art, or "ooze," as he called it, he

[24] *Milton*, p. 18, ll. 27-30.

certainly gave evidence of a tendency toward the point of view expressed in: "What is most grand is always most minute."[25] Perhaps the most famous passage in all his work is the four lines from the "Auguries of Innocence" usually cited as proof of Blake's quality as a mystic:

> To see a World in a grain of sand,
> And a Heaven in a wild flower,
> Hold Infinity in the palm of your hand,
> And Eternity in an hour.[26]

It is a beautiful passage with a certain piquancy of paradox that has done quite as much as the idea to insure its currency. And it merits the attention that has been given to it, for not only is it a masterly version of one of the most significant of Blake's ideas, but it is in style and spirit one of the most characteristic passages he ever wrote.

The secret of this importance of the small is to be found in the famous theory of correspondences. This is in no sense of the word original with Blake, for, as we have seen, Swedenborg had already worked out the idea even more elaborately than Blake did. But the latter's handling of the theory is interesting and of consequence for all his thinking.

The theory is that everything in the universe, animate or inanimate, conscious or unconscious, is bound together in a number of orders, of which the individual members have very definite and significant relations to members of other orders. That is, a certain metal fills the same place in the order of metals that a certain vegetable fills in its order, or that a certain animal fills in the animal kingdom, or that a certain human faculty fills in the human mind. The value of this theory is that of the argument from the known to the unknown. If it is difficult to understand a certain element of human nature or of angelic nature, one may gain light from the study of the corresponding member of the mineral order. Blake gives this a prevailingly anthropomorphic cast, as in a passage which throws light on a good deal of his symbolism and makes clear not only his anthropomorphic handling of nature, but also the large

---

[25] "On Art and Artists," XXVII, Sampson, *op. cit.*, p. 207.

[26] Sampson, *op. cit.*, p. 171.

part which the human plays in his drawing and painting even of the abstract or the heavenly or the inanimate. It is from some verses inclosed in a letter to Thomas Butts that we learn:

> . . . . Each grain of sand,
> Every Stone on the Land,
> Each rock & each hill,
> Each fountain & rill,
> Each herb & each tree,
> Mountain, hill, earth, and sea,
> Cloud, Meteor, and Star,
> Are Men seen Afar.[27]

As the theory of correspondences implies, the universe is essentially one. First of all, all men are essentially one, when viewed spiritually:

> We live as One Man: for contracting our infinite senses
> We behold multitude: or expanding, we behold as one.
> As One Man all the Universal Family: and that One Man
> We call Jesus the Christ: and he in us, and we in him,
> Live in perfect harmony in Eden the land of life,
> Giving, recieving, and forgiving each other's trespasses.[28]

But this essential unity of the universe goes even farther:

> So Man looks out in tree, and herb, and fish, and bird, and beast,
> Collecting up the scattered portions of his immortal body
> Into the elemental forms of everything that grows.[29]

On the relation of external or inanimate nature to this spiritual unity Blake is not entirely clear, because he does not seem to use the word always in the same sense, or always to look at the subject from the same point of view. In his letters, for instance, he says in defense of his visions:

> To the eyes of the man of imagination, Nature is Imagination itself. As a man is, so he sees. As the eye is formed, such are its powers. You certainly mistake, when you say that the visions of fancy are not to be found in this world. To me this world is all one continued vision of fancy or imagination, and I feel flattered when I am told so.[30]

[27] *Letters*, pp. 82–83.
[28] *Jerusalem*, p. 38, ll. 17–22.
[29] *Vala*, edited by Ellis and Yeats, *op. cit.*, Vol. II, Night VIII, ll. 553–55.
[30] *Letters*, p. 62.

That letter was written in 1799. In a letter of nearly thirty years later (1827) Blake writes:

> Flaxman is gone, and we must soon follow, every one to his own eternal house, leaving the delusions of Goddess Nature and her laws to get into freedom from all the laws of the numbers—into the mind, in which everyone is king and priest in his own house.[31]

Furthermore, Crabb Robinson reports Blake as condemning Wordsworth's attitude toward nature as idolatry.[32] The truth is probably that Blake felt that the physical world was spiritual if looked at with eyes of vision, and material if looked at in the spirit of rationalism. Probably for Blake, as for so many of the nature-worshipers, nature was not imagination, as he loved to say, but nature, plus what he brought to it of fancy or imagination, was imagination and spiritual.

And in this as in other things we must remember Blake's tendency to find common ground between things usually conceived of as different, if not entirely to obliterate distinctions. In this unity of all things the conventional antipathy between good and evil is swept away, and, as Blake announces in triumph at the beginning of *Jerusalem:*

> Heaven, Earth & Hell, henceforth shall live in harmony.[33]

We find, then, at the heart of Blake's universe a very comprehensive unity. Literally, God and the Devil embrace, for as Blake so often said, "Without Contraries is no progression."[34] In this unity the small is of as much significance as the large, and the minute and the infinite and the fleeting and the eternal exchange places almost at will. The non-human prefigures the human, and throughout the universe runs a series of gigantic correspondences, for after all, all things are one in God.

It is not enough, however, to know that all things are one in God; the nature of such a unity to no slight extent depends upon the conception of God involved. Significantly, this is a subject on

[31] *Letters*, p. 224.

[32] Arthur Symons, *William Blake* (London, 1907), p. 299, quoted from Crabb Robinson's *Diary, etc.*

[33] *Jerusalem*, p. 3, l. 27.

[34] *Marriage of Heaven and Hell*, Sampson, *op. cit.*, p. 248.

which Blake has very little to say. It is illuminating to note that the Russell and Maclagan edition of *Jerusalem* does not contain any heading in the index for God; under the heading "God," in the same editors' companion edition of *Milton*, but two references are noted. From representations in the illustrations to the *Book of Job*, Blake's masterpiece as an artist and a very wonderful series of visions, and from passages in Blake's writings, we learn that his conception of God was at times primitively anthropomorphic. But the essential thing about Blake's God is that Blake says very little about him. He is not interested in God the Father in the traditional trinitarian sense, at all. His main interest is in Christ, and, interestingly enough, Christ is the divine humanity far more than he is the Son of God. It is true that in one passage there is a suggestion of reaches of subtlety unusual to Blake, when, at the very beginning of *Milton*, he speaks of Jesus as "the image of the Invisible God,"[35] but that is an aspect that Blake does not emphasize and the implications of which he entirely rejects. In the "Prophetical Writings" God is not of primary or special interest, and where God does come into the story he is either the antinomian Christ whose characteristics will be developed later, or that very abstract and general divine humanity in whom all men are united.

The reason is that the center of Blake's universe is man rather than God. Indeed, in the *Marriage of Heaven and Hell*[36] he says: "Where man is not, nature is barren," and again: "God only Acts and Is, in existing beings or Men," and still again, "The worship of God is: Honouring his gifts in other men, each according to his genius, and loving the greatest men best: those who envy or calumniate great men hate God; for there is no other God." In general too much emphasis must not be placed on the testimony of the *Marriage of Heaven and Hell*, but here there can be no doubt. The heart of Blake's philosophy is to be sought in what he said about man.

Traditionally, religion has begun its account of man with a division of man's being into soul and body, a dualism important from our point of view because of its implication of the contrast of

[35] *Milton*, p. 3, l. 12.
[36] Sampson, *op. cit.*, pp. 252, 255, 259.

a lower and a higher nature. Blake's response to this conventional division is significant for his whole psychology. In the *Marriage of Heaven and Hell* the Voice of the Devil is unmistakable:

> All Bibles or sacred codes have been the causes of the following Errors:
> 1. That Man has two real existing principles, viz. a Body and a Soul.
> 2. That Energy, call'd Evil, is alone from the Body; and that Reason, call'd Good, is alone from the Soul. . . . .
> But the following Contraries to these are True:
> 1. Man has no Body distinct from his Soul; for that call'd Body is a portion of Soul discern'd by the five Senses, the chief inlets of Soul in this age.
> 2. Energy is the only life, and is from the Body; and Reason is the bound or outward circumference of Energy.

This means virtually a denial not only of the old dualism of soul and body, but also of the dualism of the higher and the lower nature, and an assertion of fundamental unity that will be very significant for Blake's ethics. One of the motives of this denial is probably to be found in the theory of correspondences, as is implied in a passage from the "Auguries of Innocence":

> God appears, and God is Light,
> To those poor souls who dwell in Night;
> But does a Human Form display
> To those who dwell in realms of Day.[37]

The body seems to be in the world visible to the senses the "correspondence" of the soul; ultimately, of God. That undoubtedly explains the emphasis Blake places upon the body in his art, when he insists that true art can flourish only "by naked beauty display'd," and certainly makes clear why the center of Blake's pictorial art is the naked human body.

This somewhat obscure matter is chiefly of importance because of the effect it has had on the psychological analysis of man's nature that constitutes the heart of Blake's work. For this is after all the primary significance of the Four Zoas whose world, in the more literal sense, is the brain of man. Since the significance of each of the Four Zoas has been already considered, it is necessary to review only their main psychological meanings. Albion, an obvious piece of geographical symbolism, represents the common hu-

[37] Sampson, *op. cit.*, p. 175.

manity. Usually conceived of as a giant, he is the main figure in many transactions in the "Prophetical Writings." Albion contains within him his Humanity, or common human capability of the higher life of imagination; his Emanation, or imaginative nature; his Specter, or rational power; his Shadow, or purely instinctive nature, and then his energy, which is not personified in this particular view of the analysis. As Blake develops this psychology, he makes very clear three characteristics which distinguish it essentially from much of the conventional Christian psychology of his day. The first is that each of these powers, in its unfallen state—that is, before Albion has lost contact with the world of vision, and while it still remains in its proper place—is good, and each out of its place in the fallen man may become evil. This is reminiscent of the Greek ideal of moderation and temperance in all things, and suggestive of the modern psychology of normality. It is unlike most of the Christian psychologies in its refusal to enter into the discussion of relative values. But it must be remembered here as elsewhere that anything suggestive of balance holds true of Blake's theory only when it is most directly and fully expounded. In practice, throughout his work Blake dwells upon the perversion of the intellect, with very much less attention to the possibility of perversion of the other elements of man's nature. Indeed, in a large part of his work Blake presents only the perversion of the intellect, because, as we have seen, the prevailing rationalism of the day made that the most important issue for him.

In the light, then, of this evaluation of the constituents of the human personality, the harmonious character will be conceived of in a fashion very different from that, say, of the Aristotelian psychology that has exercised such an influence on European thinking. It will not be an aristocracy under the benevolent despotism of the reason, but rather a democracy in which all the powers co-operate on pretty much equal terms.[38] In that co-operation, however, one faculty will enjoy a primacy not usually accorded to it:

> Man is adjoin'd to Man by his Emanative portion,
> Who is Jerusalem in every individual Man.[39]

[38] *Vala*, IX, ll. 358–70.
[39] *Jerusalem*, p. 44, ll. 38–39.

In other words, the faculty which opens to man the possibilities of the universal brotherhood by which Blake set so much store is the imagination, for Jerusalem, which has several significances, being both city and woman,[40] sometimes veritably Blake's *civitas dei*, is the imaginative portion of the divine humanity, of the universal man. It is the imagination, then, that takes the center of the stage of Blake's psychology.

Man seems originally to have been in this state of imaginative perfection, for, according to the "Address to the Public" that opens *Jerusalem:* "The Primeval State of Man was Wisdom, Art, and Science."[41] From that happy state man fell. Blake has a great deal to say about that fall, but the precise details, in spite of the fact that Blake was apparently very clear on the whole matter himself, remain rather obscure. The fall seems to have been a disturbance of the primary balance of the four universes.

As we have seen in the story of Urizen, the fall resulted from the fact that Urizen (the reason, whose place is in the South) had usurped the place of Urthona (or inspiration, whose place is in the North). According to another account, the fall was the result of Luvah's (Luvah represents emotion) assuming the place of Urizen in the South, or Urizen's giving it to him, as Urizen tells Luvah at the end of the fifth "Night" of *Vala:*

> Because thou gavest Urizen the wine of the Almighty
> For steeds that they might run in the golden chariot of pride
> I gave to thee the steeds of light, I poured the stolen wine,
> And drunken with the immortal draught fell from my throne sublime.[42]

It seems that Urizen fell into the "sin by which the angels fell," and that when Luvah took his place dire confusion resulted:

> All fell towards the Center in dire ruin, sinking down.
> And in the South remains a burning fire: in the East, a void;
> In the West, a world of raging waters: in the North, a solid,
> Unfathomable, without end.[43]

In other words, all the powers of man were shaken from their places, and confusion filled the universe.

40 *Vala*, IX, l. 221.   42 *Vala*, V, ll. 234–37.
41 *Jerusalem*, p. 3, ll. 43, 44.   43 *Milton*, p. 17, ll. 21–24.

As has been noticed before, the fall was in no sense a definite historical event that had occurred at one definite time once and for all. Blake was not interested in time, but in eternity. For the fall was always happening, and man was always being redeemed. Nor was this agency in the disturbance of the balance of man's nature by any means limited to Urizen. As in the process of division to be described in a moment, each and all of the Four Zoas could and did rebel, with correspondingly disastrous consequences. Here as elsewhere Blake dwelt on the revolt of the reason because the rationalism, which he deemed the most pressing fault of his day and generation, made that seem to him the most significant.

But whether it be Urizen or Luvah who rebels, this usurpation of places that do not belong to them by rebellious parts of the human personality is usually followed by a process of division within the parts themselves, a process which plays quite as large a part in the central action of the "Prophetic Books" as the confusion of place or function described above. What happens is that the specter separates from the whole man and attempts to set up its independent rule. This process is defined in *Jerusalem:*

> The Spectre is the Reasoning Power in Man; & when separated
> From Imagination, and closing itself as in steel, in a Ratio
> Of the Things of Memory, It thence frames Laws & Moralities
> To destroy Imagination, the Divine Body, by Martyrdoms & Wars.[44]

Usually the tyranny of the specter drives away the Emanation, or the imaginative portion of man's nature, represented in the "Prophetic Books" often by a wandering female, and since "Man cannot unite with Man but by their Emanations,"[45] the individual man is then shut up within himself in fatal isolation. So he comes to know the desolation of the life that is shut out from vision as it is described by Albion, the "Universal Man," the "hero" of *Jerusalem:*

> Are you my Children, natives in the Grave to where I go?
> Or are you born to feed the hungry ravenings of Destruction,
> To be the sport of Accident! to waste in Wrath & Love, a weary
> Life, in brooding cares & anxious labours, that prove but chaff.
> O Jerusalem, Jerusalem, I have forsaken thy Courts,

[44] *Jerusalem,* p. 74, ll. 10–13. [45] *Ibid.,* p. 88, l. 10.

> Thy Pillars of ivory & gold: thy Curtains of silk & fine
> Linen: thy Pavements of precious stones: thy Walls of pearl
> And gold, thy Gates of Thanksgiving, thy Windows of Praise:
> Thy Clouds of Blessing, thy Cherubims of Tender-mercy
> Stretching their Wings sublime over the Little-ones of Albion!
> O Human Imagination, O Divine Body I have Crucified,
> I have turned my back upon thee into the Wastes of Moral Law:
> There Babylon is builded in the Waste, founded in Human desolation.[46]

In other words, when man falls, his intellect loses hold upon imagination, and he sinks into the life of the senses, not necessarily a life of sensual indulgence, but a life in which the wonders of the spiritual world are hidden from eyes that can behold only the material. So forsaken by the divine inspiration, man yields himself to the tyranny of the reason, which sets up the moral law.

This is the state of Ulro, the state in which man imputes "Sin & Righteousness to Individuals & not to States":[47]

> Such is the nature of Ulro: that whatever enters,
> Becomes Sexual, & is Created, and Vegetated, and Born.
> From Hyde Park spread their vegetating roots beneath Albion,
> In dreadful pain the Spectrous Uncircumcised Vegetation,
> Forming a Sexual Machine, an Aged Virgin Form,
> In Erin's Land toward the north, joint after joint & burning
> In love & jealousy immingled & calling it Religion.[48]

So the sexes, to which Blake owes much of his imagery, took their rise—symbols of division, but also potentialities of union. In this fallen state arose natural religions, religions depending not upon true inspiration, but upon the workings of the reason. Consequently, these religions became not only false and stultifying, but cruel, for they fettered the instincts and withered the soul of man by "Laws of Chastity & Abhorrence."[49]

Such is the way in which man came to his present state of spiritual deadness. It is primarily not an ethical, but an intellectual, fall, for the result, the state of Ulro, is primarily a state of closed vision. Therefore the problem of repairing that fall, of restoring man to his original sphere, is likewise more a problem of the mind

---

[46] *Jerusalem*, p. 24, ll. 13–25.   [48] *Ibid.*, p. 44, ll. 21–27.
[47] *Ibid.*, p. 25, ll. 15–16.   [49] *Ibid.*, p. 49, l. 26.

than of the will; it is the problem of opening man's spirit again to the world of vision.

It is at this point that most mystics and prophets invoke the help of their religious tradition, not for any cut-and-dried formula, but for the practical suggestion and help which a large body of experience, to say nothing of established truth, gives in any field. Blake considered himself a Christian, and a prophet of true Christianity. These are large and vague words, often used with a great many implications not apparent in the bare words; often used with very few. And opinion on these meanings is so vague and so varied that a study of Blake's Christianity had better be drawn from a study of his complete message than used as a means of defining that message. But with the conception of Christ the situation is simpler. Probably there is as much disagreement on this subject as on any, but the field is smaller and the main lines more discernible because most of our material is contained in a few definite sources. What Blake says of Christ, what he makes of Christ in the course of his "Prophetic Books" may therefore be taken as significant of his relation to the Christian tradition, even though the latter must be understood in a very general sense.

First of all, Christ is, for Blake, as for most traditional Christians, the Redeemer, as in *Jerusalem:*

> Jesus breaking thro' the Central Zones of Death & Hell
> Opens Eternity in Time & Space: triumphant in Mercy.[50]

Through him the mercy of God redeems the fallen man, and quite appropriately and traditionally, the heart of this Christ is forgiveness, but in Blake's conception Christ's forgiveness quite passes the conventional belief, for it dispenses with all conditions of repentance or amendment. It is simply the abundant overflowing of the humanity of Christ.

The second way in which Blake uses the name of Christ may be seen most plainly in the first "Night" of *Vala:*

> Then those in Great Eternity met in the councils of God
> As One Man, for, contracting their exalted senses
> They behold Multitude, or expanding they behold as one,
> As One Man all the Universal Family, and that One Man

[50] *Ibid.*, p. 75, ll. 21–22.

> They call Jesus the Christ, and they in him, and he in them,
> Live in perfect harmony, in Eden, the land of life,
> Consulting as one Man above Mount Gilead sublime.[51]

This use of the name of Christ, which may be paralleled in *Milton*, and, indeed, in all the "Prophetical Writings," particularly the greater ones, is very similar to Blake's employment of the terms, the "Human Form Divine," or the "Divine Humanity,"

> Who is the Only General and Universal Form,
> To which all Lineaments tend & seek with love & sympathy.[52]

It is not entirely clear how much more this means than the conventional "We are one in Christ." Very clearly, in some passages, like the passage from *Vala* just quoted, in which "those in Great Eternity" in all probability refers to the Four Zoas, Blake sees in Christ his complete, properly harmonized, man.

The third way in which Blake conceives of Christ takes its rise in a conception not very different from this of the perfect man, the way in which Christianity has always rejoiced to look upon Christ: as the pattern of perfection in human conduct. Except at its grimmest, traditional Christianity has dwelt on the love, the self-devotion, and the self-sacrifice, in short, the infinite tenderness of Christ. In his reiteration of this emphasis, therefore, Blake is following the tradition. But upon one aspect which has played an important rôle in much of Christian thinking, that which is suggested in the Bible saying, "I am not come to destroy [the law], but to fulfil," Blake broke with a large body of Christian tradition profoundly and essentially.

The clearest and most extended development of this aspect of Blake's Christianity is to be found in the *Everlasting Gospel*, a piecing together of fragments scattered through the "Manuscript Book." Mr. Sampson assigns these to a period certainly not earlier than 1810, and Dr. Keynes puts them about 1818. Therefore it seems sound to assume that the views here presented, although the fragments were never worked up into a finished whole, represent a fairly mature and well-considered view of Christian ethics. Par-

[51] *Vala* I, ll. 428–34. Cf. *Milton*, p. 19, l. 58.
[52] *Jerusalem*, p. 43, ll. 20–21.

ticularly does this conclusion seem reasonable when we discover throughout Blake's "Prophetical Writings" passages that repeat in detail aspects of these views, or that presuppose them as premises, or that are intelligible only on grounds such as these.

Blake's starting-point is fairly indicated in the opening lines:

> The Vision of Christ that thou dost see
> Is my vision's greatest enemy.
> Thine has a great hook nose like thine;
> Mine has a snub nose like to mine.
> Thine is the Friend of all Mankind;
> Mine speaks in parables to the blind.
> Thine loves the same world that mine hates;
> Thy heaven doors are my hell gates.
> Socrates taught what Meletus
> Loath'd as a nation's bitterest curse,
> And Caiaphas was in his own mind
> A benefactor to mankind.
> Both read the Bible day and night,
> But thou read'st black where I read white.[53]

The revolutionary note of this passage is the prelude to a series of refutations of what Blake believed to be the misconceptions of the Christianity of his day. To the theory of the meek and gentle Christ he opposes a series of episodes from the Gospel stories in which Christ displayed his powers of wrath. He then proceeds to the consideration of Christ's humility. He makes the conventional distinction between humility to God and humility to man, and then draws very interesting conclusions of his own:

> This is the race that Jesus ran:
> Humble to God, haughty to man,
> Cursing the Rulers before the people
> Even to the Temple's highest steeple,
> And when he humbled Himself to God
> Then descended the cruel rod.
> "If Thou humblest Thyself, Thou humblest Me.
> Thou also dwell'st in Eternity.
> Thou art a Man: God is no more:
> Thy own Humanity learn to adore,
> For that is My spirit of life."[54]

[53] Sampson, *op. cit.*, pp. 146 f.
[54] *Ibid.*, p. 151.

As for the other of the two virtues that have been so heavily emphasized by Christian writers, Blake frankly challenges the usual notion that Christ supported the ideal of chastity:

> Was Jesus chaste? or did He
> Give any lessons of chastity?
> The Morning blushèd fiery red:
> Mary was found in adulterous bed. . . . .[55]

Taken as a whole, the Christ of the *Everlasting Gospel*

> . . . . Scorn'd Earth's parents, scorn'd Earth's God,
> And mock'd the one and the other's rod;
> His seventy Disciples sent
> Against Religion and Government—
> They by the sword of Justice fell,
> And Him their cruel murderer tell.
> He left His father's trade to roam,
> A wand'ring vagrant without home;
> And thus He others' labour stole,
> That He might live above control.
> The publicans and harlots He
> Selected for His company,
> And from the adulteress turn'd away
> God's righteous law, that lost its prey.[56]

In brief, Blake's Christ was an antinomian, the pattern of the virtuous lawbreaker, of the boundless vitality that will not be fettered by any law.

Finally, there is much evidence, especially in *Jerusalem*, to show that just as Blake defined Christianity as "the liberty both of body & mind to exercise the Divine Arts of Imagination: Imagination, the real & eternal World of which this Vegetable Universe is but a faint shadow,"[57] so he identified Christ with the creative imagination which is the real redeemer in his system. For instance, when almost at the end of *Jerusalem*,

> Jesus appeared standing by Albion, as the Good Shepherd
> By the lost Sheep that he hath found, & Albion knew that it
> Was the Lord, the Universal Humanity, and Albion saw his Form
> A Man, & they conversed as Man with Man, in Ages of Eternity, ...

"the Divine Appearance was the likeness & similitude of Los."[58]

[55] Sampson, *op. cit.*, p. 155. [57] *Jerusalem*, p. 77, ll. 12–14.

[56] *Ibid.*, p. 154. [58] *Ibid.*, p. 96, ll. 3–7.

Albion did not seem in the least surprised at this resemblance of Jesus to the "Eternal Prophet," and no reader of Blake can be surprised either, for it is the logical consequence of the religion of the creative imagination to the exposition of which Blake devoted both *Milton* and *Jerusalem*.

His reinterpretation of the central figure of Christianity is of the utmost significance for the way in which Blake believed man's restoration to his proper world of vision was to be effected. Traditionally, the problem of redemption has presented itself to the Jewish prophet and the Christian mystic as the problem of sin, of warring against, of mastering man's lower nature, of purifying and strengthening his nobler nature by discipline. Now sin was not a problem that engaged Blake's interest. He felt that far too much stress had been already laid upon sin. Jerusalem's (Imagination) words to Vala (Nature) are significant of his general point of view:

> O Vala what is Sin? that thou shudderest and weepest
> At sight of thy once lov'd Jerusalem! What is Sin but a little
> Error & fault that is soon forgiven.[59]

In fact, sin makes a distinct contribution to the spiritual life, as Mary tells her husband, Joseph, in that remarkable scene in *Jerusalem* in which she defends the sin of adultery with which she has been charged:

> . . . . If I were pure, never could I taste the sweets
> Of the Forgiveness of Sins; if I were holy, I never could behold the tears
> Of love! of him who loves me in the midst of his anger in furnace of fire.[60]

Not sin, but the forgiveness of sins, was Blake's tenet. So with holiness, Blake departed from the usual Christian discrimination between the common and the holy. He sang no paeans of holiness, but rather devoted his energies to the propagation of his great insistence on the holiness of all life. The last line of the following passage is a refrain heard constantly through all he ever wrote:

> Arise, you little glancing wings and sing your infant joy,
> Arise and drink your bliss,
> For everything that lives is holy.[61]

[59] *Ibid.*, p. 20, ll. 22–24.
[60] *Ibid.*, p. 61, ll. 11–13.　　　　[61] *Vala*, II, ll. 356–58.

With the motive for the traditional discipline gone, it is not surprising that Blake rejected the discipline itself. Temperamentally he was more averse to discipline even than most artistic geniuses. His life and writings afford abundant evidence of his adherence to his own dictum in the "Proverbs of Hell" (*Marriage of Heaven and Hell*): "Improvement makes straight roads; but the crooked roads without improvement are roads of Genius." Always he hated anything that tended to interfere with his own course. There was doubtless much to be said against the schools of Blake's day, but it is the general character of the man, rather than any special critical consideration, that speaks in the lines:

> Thank God! I never was sent to school
> To be flogg'd into following the style of a fool.[62]

Moreover, most moral discipline sooner or later invokes moral precept or law in some fashion. And the very conception of general rule in this field was one bitterly repugnant to Blake's individualism. For it infringes on the freedom of the human being without any respect for individuals. "One law for the Lion and Ox is Oppression,"[63] is a line that occurs over and over again in his work of every period.

Furthermore, it must not be forgotten that the moral law is the work of Urizen-Jehovah, the Specter, that is "in every man, insane, brutish . . . . deformed."[64] It is inhuman, as Albion shows at the beginning of *Jerusalem* when he says:

> . . . . Here will I build my Laws of Moral Virtue :
> Humanity shall be no more : but war & princedom & victory.[65]

Its foundation is essentially loveless, as Vala tells Albion:

> All Love is lost, Terror succeeds, and hatred instead of love,
> And stern demands of Right and Duty, instead of Liberty.[66]

As for the elements of sheer restraint and repression that seemed to Blake inseparable from discipline, he anticipates some of

---

[62] "On Art and Artists," Sampson, *op. cit.*, p. 201.
[63] *The Marriage of Heaven and Hell*, Sampson, *op. cit.*, p. 260.
[64] *Vala*, VII, ll. 302–3.
[65] *Jerusalem*, p. 4, ll. 30–31.
[66] *Vala*, I, ll. 30–31. Cf. *Jerusalem*, p. 22, ll. 10–11.

the more radical of the psychologists of the present day in his objections, as in the following:

> I was angry with my friend:
> I told my wrath, my wrath did end.
> I was angry with my foe:
> I told it not, my wrath did grow.[67]

Likewise:

> Sooner murder an infant in its cradle than nurse unacted desires.[68]

It is the "Thou Shalt Not" of the moral law that blasts and
lays waste and sterile the fairest possibilities of the human spirit.
Here Blake joins issues squarely with the morality of his day on
what is still one of the burning problems of our day: sex. Not content with attacking his age for its hypocrisy and its timidity in fac-
ing that problem, he attacked even what the reasonable and the sin-
cere had been wont to cherish, the faith in chastity. For chastity,
he said, was sheer waste:

> Ah, Sun-flower! weary of time,
> Who countest the steps of the sun;
> Seeking after that sweet golden clime,
> Where the traveller's journey is done;
> Where the Youth pined away with desire,
> And the pale Virgin shrouded in snow,
> Arise from their graves, and aspire
> Where my Sun-flower wishes to go.[69]

Then too, chastity seemed to Blake a form of that ungenerous withdrawing into the self that he always held in abhorrence. And in that
form, instead of redeeming man's fall, it was often responsible for
its continuance, as is apparent in numberless passages on the cruelty
of woman's secrecy and reticence, of which one of the most striking
is Britannia's lament over Albion:

> O God, O God awake! I have slain,
> In Dreams of Chasti(ti)ty & Moral Law I have murdered Albion! Ah!
> In Stone-henge & on London Stone & in the Oak Groves of Malden

[67] "A Poison Tree," *Songs of Experience.*
[68] "Proverbs of Hell," *The Marriage of Heaven and Hell.*
[69] Sampson, *op. cit.*, p. 97.

I have Slain him in my Sleep with the Knife of Druid. O England,
O all ye Nations of the Earth behold ye the Jealous Wife!
The Eagle & the Wolf & Monkey & Owl & the King & Priest were there.[70]

There is an element of blasphemy, too, in chastity, in that it stands
in the way to union:

> But this, O Lord, this was my sin,
> When first I let these devils in,
> In dark pretense to chastity
> Blaspheming Love, blaspheming Thee.[71]

Here, on the ground where so many mystics had fought out the
battle of this world on its hardest terms, Blake refused to see any
need for battle, and took up his position firmly on the argument of
naturalism, which he puts into the mouth of Christ in *Jerusalem:*

> No individual can keep these Laws, for they are death
> To every energy of man, and forbid the springs of life.[72]

For those who appeared to succeed in the impossible, Blake had the
passionate man's contempt for the more even-tempered, as in that
sentence in the *Marriage of Heaven and Hell:* "Those who restrain
Desire, do so because theirs is weak enough to be retsrained; and
the restrainer or Reason usurps its place and governs the unwill-
ing." However William Blake might achieve his goal, it was not to
be by the paths of self-denial, self-discipline, or self-mastery. Nothing in his handling of the problem of redemption is more characteristic or more significant than this complete rejection, not only of
discipline, but even of the problem of discipline.

Moreover, Blake may very well be said to have taken the natural instincts, what the moralists have usually called the lower instincts, and out of them made his road to perfection; to have taken
the orthodox hell, as he implies in the *Marriage of Heaven and Hell,*
and out of it made his heaven. As he says in one of the "Gnomic
Verses":

> Abstinence sows sand all over
> The ruddy limbs and flaming hair,
> But Desire gratified
> Plants fruits of life and beauty there.

[70] *Jerusalem,* p. 94, ll. 22–27.
[71] "The Everlasting Gospel," Sampson, *op. cit.,* p. 157, ll. 69–72.
[72] *Jerusalem,* p. 35, ll. 11–12.

Here, in view of a great number of passages that imply a religious significance in sex, even on its most entirely physical terms, it is fair to take Desire as referring, as it usually does in a very particular sense, to sex. In "Europe," in his enumeration of the senses, Blake said of the fifth, Touch, or Sex, that through it man could

. . . . Pass out what time he please, but he will not;
For stolen joys are sweet and bread eaten in secret pleasant.[73]

And the same is implied in Los' praise of sex in *Jerusalem* (Los usually voices the author's own convictions) :

O holy Generation, Image of regeneration!
O point of mutual forgiveness between Enemies!
Birthplace of the Lamb of God incomprehensible!
The Dead [those shut out from vision] despise & scorn & cast thee out as accursed,
Seeing the Lamb of God in thy gardens & thy palaces
Where they desire to place the Abomination of Desolation.[74]

And in a hundred other places in Blake's works, explicit or implied, the same faith in the illuminating power of the free expression of sex energy may be found. Sex seems very definitely to have been one of the ways in which man might escape from the Ulro of materialism and rationalism into the life of vision.

This faith in the energy of sex extended to other forms of energy as well. Blake was, as the abundance of his work done under far from ideal conditions testifies, one of the most energetic of men. It is not surprising, therefore, that he always admired and trusted energy. "Energy is the only life, and is from the Body," said the "Voice of the Devil" in the *Marriage of Heaven and Hell,* a work which abounds in sayings of a congenial spirit: "The tigers of wrath are wiser than the horses of instruction"; "Expect poison from the standing water"; "Exuberance is Beauty."

The emotional source of this energy is, of course, the love and pity and sympathy that Blake believed should bind all men together in mutual serviceableness. Had his works attained to a wider appreciation and influence in his day, Blake might have been counted one of the leading figures in the modern humanitarian

[73] "Europe," Sampson, *op. cit.,* p. 303, ll. 5–6.
[74] *Jerusalem,* p. 7, ll. 65–70.

movement, for he preached with unremitting fervor the brotherhood of all men even in works so early as the *Songs of Innocence
and of Experience*. From the first he believed that the glow of
brotherly love would heal the sufferings of mankind and prevent
those misunderstandings that from time immemorial have so trag-
ically divided men. Above all, it would lead men to God and to the
life of vision from which their present state of suspicion and ani-
mosity and indifference excludes them. The conversation between
Albion and Jesus in *Jerusalem* is a good example of this insistence
of Blake's on the necessity of brotherhood:

> Albion reply'd. Cannot Man exist without Mysterious
> Offering of Self for Another: is this Friendship & Brotherhood?
> I see thee in the likeness & similitude of Los my Friend.
> Jesus said. Wouldest thou love one who never died
> For thee, or ever die for one who had not died for thee.
> And if God dieth not for Man & giveth not himself
> Eternally for Man, Man could not exist, for Man is Love,
> As God is Love: every kindness to another is a Little Death
> In the Divine Image, nor can Man exist but by Brotherhood.[75]

Energy, especially sex energy, is one key to the way in which
Blake hoped to restore fallen man to the life of vision. The other is
his faith in the power of what he calls the "creative imagination."
We have already seen that what Blake had set up as his goal was
vision, the ability to perceive the spiritual realities beyond this material world. Now "imagination" is, like "Christianity," a very
large and usually vague word. And sometimes Blake uses it in a
very special sense, as when, as he so often does, he makes it the
spiritual unity in which all things are comprehended. In other passages it is apparent that what he means by the imagination is the
artist's version of the spiritual life.

A great deal of light is thrown on this subject by Blake's letters. For instance, in a well-known letter to Dr. Trusler, Blake
quite explicitly obliterates the distinction between fancy and imagination that Coleridge's *Biographia Literaria* has made familiar to
us: "You certainly mistake, when you say that the visions of fancy
are not to be found in this world. To me this world is all one con-

[75] *Jerusalem*, p. 96, ll. 20–28.

tinued vision of fancy or imagination."[76] A little farther on in the same letter Blake defines the imagination as "spiritual sensation,"[77] and in a letter to his old friend, John Flaxman, he uses the word "spiritual" in a similar fashion: "Felpham is a sweet place for study, because it is more spiritual than London."[78] Still later, in some verses to another friend, Thomas Butts, Blake reveals the elements in which the spiritual superiority of Felpham lay:

> With happiness stretch'd across the hills,
> In a cloud that dewy sweetness distills,
> With a blue sky spread over with wings,
> And a mild sun that mounts & sings;
> With trees & fields, full of Fairy elves,
> And little devils who fight for themselves—
> .   .   .   .
> With Angels planted in Hawthorn bowers,
> And God Himself in the passing hours;
> With Silver Angels across my way,
> And Golden demons that none can stay;
> With my Father hovering upon the wind,
> And my Brother Robert just behind,
> And my Brother John, the evil one,
> In a black cloud making his mone;
> Tho' dead, they appear upon my path.[79]

And a few lines below Blake tells us the secret of his vision in that famous account of the thistle which has already been quoted. In a kindred spirit he defines poetry in another letter to Thomas Butts: "Allegory addressed to the intellectual powers, while it is altogether hidden from the corporeal understanding, is my definition of the most sublime poetry."[80] In all this one remembers John Varley's account of how he sat up with Blake far into the night, while Blake at his bidding summoned to his fancy Edward I, the man who built the Pyramids, and Lais the courtesan, and as each appeared, drew his or her likeness.

This suggests again that what Blake really meant when he used the term "creative imagination" was what we more normally call the creative fancy, a conclusion borne out by the impressions given

[76] *Letters*, p. 62.
[77] *Ibid.*, p. 63.
[78] *Ibid.*, p. 75.
[79] *Ibid.*, pp. 108–109.
[80] *Ibid.*, p. 121.

by certain types of his work as a pictorial artist. The suggestion of vast bleakness of a *Wuthering Heights* power in the tiny compass of the woodcut of the blasted tree drawn for Dr. Thornton's *Vergil;* the luminous delicacy of the tinted pages of the *Songs of Innocence and of Experience;* the rich beauty of the title-page to the *Marriage of Heaven and Hell;* the moving terror of that specter of the "Plague" striding over the doomed city; the fresh loveliness of Eve in the water-color of the "Temptation"; the airy swirl of the steps of "Jacob's Ladder"; the sublime daring of the "Ancient of Days"; the solid dignity of God the Father and the free-flung exaltation of the morning stars in the illustrations to the *Book of Job;* and the sensuous curves of the faintly penciled illustrations to *Vala*—all these confirm the testimony of the letters that the essence of Blake's mission in life was through the gifts of the fancy to reveal the form and movement of a world in many ways like this world, but in its fundamental spirit and feeling different.

The mystic way, then, which Blake proposes is not one of discipline, but of free expression and fulfilment of energy, notably sex energy, and of devotion to the exercise of the creative imagination, especially in his own field of seeing visions of the world of eternity, and of commemorating those visions in word and line and thus making them agencies of illumination for other men.

The most direct and intimate account that Blake has given of a personal experience of the life of vision that he sought in all his work is to be found in some verses that he inclosed in a letter to his friend and patron, Thomas Butts:[81]

> To my Friend Butts I write
> My first Vision of Light,
> On the yellow sands sitting.
> The Sun was Emitting

[81] The context of this letter is interesting because of the setting it affords for the verses: "Friend of Religion and Order,—I thank you for your very beautiful and encouraging verses, which I account a crown of laurels, and I also thank you for your reprehension of follies by me fostered. Your prediction will, I hope, be fulfilled in me, and in future I am the determined advocate of religion and humility—the two bands of society. Having been so full of the business of settling the sticks and feathers of my nest, I have not got any forwarder with 'The Three Maries' or with any other of your commissions; but hope, now I have commenced a new life of industry, to do credit to that new life by improved works. Receive from me a return of verses, such as Felpham produces by me, though not such as she produces by her eldest son [Hayley]. However, such as they are, I cannot resist the temptation to send them to you" (*Letters*, pp. 81–82).

His Glorious beams
From Heaven's high Streams.
Over Sea, over Land,
My Eyes did Expand
Into regions of air,
Away from all Care;
Into regions of fire,
Remote from Desire;
The Light of the Morning,
Heaven's Mountains adorning:
In particles bright,
The jewels of Light
Distinct shone & Clear.
Amaz'd, and in fear,
I each particle gazèd,
Astonish'd, Amazèd;
For each was a Man
Human-form'd. Swift I ran,
For they beckon'd to me
Remote by the Sea,
Saying: "Each grain of sand,
Every Stone on the Land,
Each rock & each hill,
Each fountain & rill,
Each herb & each tree,
Mountain, hill, earth, and sea,
Cloud, Meteor, and Star,
Are Men seen Afar."
I stood in the Streams
Of Heaven's bright beams,
And saw Felpham sweet
Beneath my bright feet,
In soft Female charms;
And in her fair arms
My Shadow I knew,
And my wife's Shadow too,
And My sister, & Friend.
We like Infants descend
In our Shadows on Earth,
Like a weak mortal birth.
My Eyes, more & more,
Like a Sea without shore,
Continue Expanding,
The Heavens commanding,

Till the Jewels of Light,
Heavenly Men beaming bright,
Appear'd as One Man,
Who complacent began
My limbs to infold
In his beams of bright gold;
Like dross purg'd away,
All my mire & my clay.
Soft consum'd in delight,
In his bosom Sun-bright
I remain'd. Soft he smil'd,
And I heard his voice Mild,
Saying: "This is my Fold,
O thou Ram, horn'd with gold,
Who awakest from Sleep
On the Sides of the Deep.
On the Mountains around
The roarings resound
Of the lion & wolf,
The loud Sea and deep gulf.
These are guards of my Fold,
O thou Ram horn'd with gold!"
And the voice faded mild,
I remain'd as a Child;
All I ever had known
Before me bright Shone!
I saw you & your wife
By the fountains of Life.
Such the Vision to me
Appear'd on the sea.

These verses were written at Felpham in 1800, when Blake was
about forty-three years old. They are very interesting for the student of Blake's mysticism because they set forth clearly and explicitly what is usually set forth impersonally and symbolically in the
"Prophetic Books." The position of this account in a letter might
seem to diminish its significance were it not Blake's habit in his
correspondence to speak of his visions with ingenuous frankness.
For him they were an everyday matter, a subject on which he could
converse even with the sceptical and obviously none too sympathetic Crabb Robinson. That everyday, normal, even matter-of-
fact way of referring to his visions is one of Blake's most striking

characteristics. In other ways, too, the verses quoted above are typical of Blake's handling of his mystical experiences. There is no suggestion of the ineffable in those lines. They are definite, clear, even concrete, at least as concrete as Blake ever was. They do not dwell on the subjective aspects of the experience, but simply report what was seen and heard. And finally, in the spirit and manner in which they make that report, they are, for all their complications, at bottom simple, in that they hardly pass the bounds of this life at its most definite and earth-keeping.

As to the achievement of the life of vision on universal lines probably the best picture Blake draws of it anywhere in the "Prophetical Writings" is to be found in the brilliant paean of joy that closes *Jerusalem:*

The Druid Spectre was Annihilate, loud thund'ring, rejoicing terrific, vanishing,
Fourfold Annihilation, & at the clangor of the Arrows of Intellect
The innumerable Chariots of the Almighty appear'd in Heaven,
And Bacon & Newton & Locke, & Milton & Shakespear & Chaucer.
A Sun of blood red wrath surrounding heaven on all sides around,
Glorious, incomprehensible by Mortal Man, & each Chariot was Sexual Twofold.

And every Man stood Fourfold, each Four Faces had, One to the West,
One toward the East, One to the South, One to the North, the Horses Fourfold.
And the dim Chaos brighten'd beneath, above, around! Eyed as the Peacock
According to the Human Nerves of Sensation, the Four Rivers of the Water of Life.
South stood the Nerves of the Eye, East in Rivers of bliss the Nerves of the
Expansive Nostrils, West flow'd the Parent Sense, the Tongue, North stood
The labyrinthine Ear: Circumscribing & Circumcising the excrementitious
Husk & Covering into Vacuum evaporating, revealing the lineaments of Man,
Driving outward the Body of Death in an Eternal Death & Resurrection,
Awaking it to Life among the Flowers of Beulah, rejoicing in Unity
In the Four Senses, in the Outline, the Circumference & Form, for ever
In Forgiveness of Sins which is Self Annihilation, it is the Covenant of Jehovah.
 .   .   .   .
And they conversed together in Visionary forms dramatic, which bright
Redounded from their Tongues in thunderous majesty, in Visions,
In new Expanses, creating exemplars of Memory and of Intellect:

Creating Space, Creating Time according to the wonders Divine
Of Human Imagination, throughout all the Three Regions immense
Of Childhood, Manhood & Old Age: & the all tremendous unfathomable
    Non Ens
Of Death was seen in regeneration terrific or complacent, varying
According to the subject of discourse, & every Word & every Character
Was Human according to the Expansion or Contraction, the Translucence or
Opakeness of Nervous fibres: such was the variation of Time & Space,
Which vary according as the Organs of Perception vary: & they walked
To & fro in Eternity as One Man, reflecting each in each & clearly seen
And seeing: according to fitness & order. And I heard Jehovah speak
Terrific from his Holy Place, & saw the Words of the Mutual Covenant
    Divine
On Chariots of gold & jewels with Living Creatures, starry & flaming
With every Colour. Lion, Tyger, Horse, Elephant, Eagle, Dove, Fly, Worm,
And the all wondrous Serpent clothed in gems & rich array, Humanize
In the Forgiveness of Sins according to thy Covenant, Jehovah!
. . . .
All Human Forms identified, even Tree, Metal, Earth & Stone, all
Human Forms identified, living going forth, & returning wearied
Into the Planetary lives of Years, Months, Days & Hours, reposing
And then Awaking into his Bosom in the Life of Immortality.
And I heard the Name of their Emanations: they are named Jerusalem.[82]

Such is the consummation of Blake's philosophy of the creative imagination. It is not the union with the ineffable in the spirit of the solitary worshiper. One does not think of the trance of St. Catherine or the Nirvana of the Buddha or the union with the Self of the Hindu when he reads that; one thinks rather of Botticelli's beautiful circle of shining ones in the garden of paradise. It is a social redemption, an intercourse of the awakened in visions of eternity. That is the clearest and the most express account Blake ever vouchsafed of the great regeneration.

[82] *Jerusalem*, p. 98, l. 6—p. 99, l. 5.

CHAPTER VII

THE VALUE OF BLAKE'S MYSTICISM

A discussion of the value of Blake's mysticism must take into account so many aspects of Blake's life and work that it is necessary to eliminate at the start certain very interesting questions that are either irrelevant or subordinate to the main issues of our inquiry. The first of these is Blake's pictorial art, a fascinating field in itself, but, except for incidental references, excluded by definition from a study of Blake's writings. The next is the historical interest of Blake's work, his pioneer achievements in the early days of the Romantic movement, his striking anticipation at many points of the findings of modern psychology, his less tangible, but even more striking, anticipation of certain contemporary tendencies in thought and feeling, as, for instance, his antinomianism and his celebration of the *élan vital*—these are all very remarkable phenomena from the historical point of view, but they have very little intrinsic importance for the question of value we are discussing unless we commit ourselves to a faith in the infallible and immediate validity of evolution that puts us forever at the mercy of the recent. So, of the interest of Blake's personality, his independence, his energy, his devotion, his originality—these things make him a very interesting and admirable human being, but they concern his mysticism only indirectly and incidentally. And finally, except at a couple of points which bear immediately upon the issues of mystical value, the early songs and lyrics will not come into this discussion.

When Blake's life and his message are set against the background of mysticism suggested in the third and fourth chapters of this discussion, and when the history of Blake criticism with the light it has thrown on the directions of Blake's influence is also taken into account, there emerge three categories according to which Blake's work may be critized. The first is that of the typical mystics. Is Blake one of these mystics in kind or in degree? If we must answer these questions in the negative, then there is the group of the prophets. Is Blake a prophet? Is he one of the major prophets of all time? Or is he one of the minor prophets? And finally, whatever the answer we return to these questions, the form in which he recorded his experience and set forth his message logically compels us to consider the visionary. Again, as in the fourth chapter, less time and space will be given to the second and third questions than to the first, since the discussion of the issues raised by the first will cover much of the ground of the other two.

As readily appears from the preponderance of faith over scepticism in the important studies of Blake's mysticism, Blake, on the surface, presents many of the familiar characteristics of the mystic. The sensitiveness bordering on emotional instability found in the sharp variations of mood noted sympathetically by Mr. Harold Bruce and not so sympathetically by Dr. Joseph Collins is a well-known element in the mystic temperament. The dissatisfaction with the ordinary confines of experience, the irrepressible urge to transcend them, is another. The positive belief that there is a world of supernal reality, under certain conditions and at certain points impinging upon our material world, is still another. The certainty that the properly enlightened human being can in some way pass the limits of the material world and put himself into some effective relation with that world above is, again, a familiar part of all mystic belief. The devotion of all the resources of the human spirit and of the human life to the compassing of that goal—this again is regarded as typically mystical. And finally, there are Blake's visions! In all these things, then, to some extent and defined in some way, Blake, on the surface of things, has been taken as a mystic. But while these things in themselves place him within the vast field of the mystical, they do not make him a mystic in the sense of the great mystics, or a prophet in the sense of the great prophets, or a visionary in the sense of the great visionaries. To answer the questions involved in these verdicts we must go into the problem much more deeply than these general surface descriptions imply.

To begin where the mystics began, then, with the belief in the existence of a world of what is usually called the spiritual in contradistinction to the purely natural and material, the word "spiritual" is used for such varying levels of phenomena that in itself it means little. For instance, the spiritual of the spiritualists is no more spiritual than the headless horseman who inspired Ichabod Crane's ride. And, on the other hand, there is even in man's shuddering at the vulgarest of attic-lurking, churchyard-haunting ghosts something of the immemorial human reaction to the spiritual.

There are, then, two elements to this of the spiritual: the conceptual and the emotional—what a man thinks the spiritual is, and how he reacts to it.

For the first, the most impressive thing about the spiritual of Blake's "Prophetic Writings" is its substantiality. It is of this world as much as is Milton's or Dante's *Hell*. It never leaves this world even imperfectly, as does the spiritual of Dante's *Paradise* or of the *Kath-Upanishad*. There is often beauty to it, but it is never ineffable. The following passage on the oneness of the universe, often cited as giving the heart of Blake's mystical view of the world, is, although more lucid and more glowingly imaginative than most of Blake's work, yet typical in its conception of what constitutes the spiritual:

I will tell thee what is done in the caverns of the grave.
The Lamb of God has rent the veil of mystery, soon to return
In clouds and fires around the rock, and thy mysterious tree.
And as the seed waits eagerly watching for its flower and fruit,
Anxious its little soul looks out into the clear expanse
To see if hungry winds are abroad with their invisible array.
So Man looks out in tree, and herb, and fish, and bird, and beast,
Collecting up the scattered portions of his immortal body
Into the elemental forms of everything that grows.
He tries the sullen north wind, riding on its angry furrows,
The sultry south when the sun rises, and the angry east
When the sun sets and the clods harden and the cattle stand
Drooping, and the birds hide in their silent nests. He stores his thoughts
As in store-houses in his memory. He regulates the forms
Of all beneath and all above, and in the gentle west
Reposes where the sun's heat dwells. He rises to the sun
And to the planets of the night, and to the stars that gild
The Zodiacs, and the stars that sullen stand to north and south
He touches the remotest pole, and in the centre weeps
That Man should labour and sorrow, and learn and forget and return
To the dark valley whence he came, and begin his labours anew.
In pain he sighs, in pain he labours, and his universe

Sorrowing in birds over the deep, or howling in the wolf
Over the slain, and moaning in the cattle, and in the winds,
And weeping over Orc and Urizen in clouds and dismal fires,
And in the cries of birth and in the groans of death his voice
Is heard throughout the universe. Wherever a grass grows
Or a leaf buds, the Eternal Man is seen, is heard, is felt,
And all his sorrows, till he re-assumes his ancient bliss.[1]

Usually only a portion of that passage is quoted, that which represents the fallen man as collecting his spiritual integrity from the scattered divinity of the world. In itself that suggests, as critics have already observed, the pantheism of some of the Upanishads, but it must be remembered that the more reflective of those teachers of the forests were careful to distinguish in their pantheism between the illusion and the reality, while the Christian mystics who have dwelt on the unity subsisting between the various orders of the universe have in general been very careful to define the sense in which they used the term and to discriminate within the bonds of union.

As a whole, Blake's visions are aggressively physical. This is no accident, for, as he himself insisted, his God was essentially solid and substantial, fully as sound and hard as material objects. Here Blake's early experience and life-long practice with the graver undoubtedly shaped his religious as well as his artistic views. Blake's God is man on an enlarged scale, and very little more. Consequently there is nothing surprising in the fundamental anthropomorphism of his Zoas, or the material definiteness with which their stories are told, both in line and in verse. Indeed, it may be wondered if Blake had any very precise notion of spirit in a sense different from that of matter. Certain it is that his conceptions of spirit are much closer to the experiences of the medium than to the ineffable visions of the neo-Platonist. The conception of spirit, not as a refined or subtilized form of matter, but as something essentially different from the material is probably the product of a greater degree of intellectual sophistication than Blake ever knew. Moreover, when the idea of spirit has been attained in any philosophy or religion (and it is essentially an attainment), it has been attained

[1] *Vala*, VIII, ll. 547-75.

not in the artistic or scientific fields, but in the ethical. Blake would never be guilty of the materialism of the conception of spirit betrayed in some discussions of ectoplasm, but he never came near the heights of a St. John or a Yagnavalkya. It may be seriously wondered if he ever could do so without that initial dualism between illusion and reality, matter and spirit, that has marked the thinking of the typical mystics.

As for the feeling of the spiritual, the response to what a recent German critic has called the "numinous" in human experience,[2] Blake's "spiritual" remains on a relatively low level. There is nothing of the mystery of life in Blake; very little of the tragic beauty of the inscrutableness of life. There is strangeness, there is terribleness, there is a sense of the preternatural. Some passages in the "Prophetic Writings" remind one of the winged lions of Assyrian sculpture, an expression of man's sense of the overhanging reality as something powerful, something "awful" in the literal sense. But one searches the pages of Blake in vain for the ineffable, for the beauty that passes understanding. In this sense, then, Blake's spiritual reality remains on a fairly primitive level.

This quality of Blake's "spiritual" is important not only for the understanding of his view of the world, but also for the understanding of the goal which he sought in his "mystical activity." The goal of the great mystics, it will be remembered, is a peculiarly intimate and profound union with God, or the Supreme Reality, in the soul of the mystic. It is a literal answer to that poignant prayer of St. Augustine: "Narrow is the Mansion of my soul; enlarge thou it that thou mayest enter in." The goal of Blake is, as we have seen in the sixth chapter, the entrance into the life of vision, into a life where the creative imagination of the individual artist compasses the strange riches of the world of the spirit. Superficially considered, the two goals might be deemed commensurate, two ways of viewing the same reality. But that apparent similarity vanishes when we consider the ground on which each conception is erected.

The fundamental issue is that of the relation of the individual will to the will of God. With the great mystics, faith or belief may be sufficient for salvation, but it is not adequate to the task of at-

[2] Rudolph Otto, *The Idea of the Holy*, translated by John W. Harvey (London, 1923).

taining their goal. Neither is mere following of their aspiration sufficient, for here, as elsewhere, only "the pure in heart . . . . shall see God." So all mystic effort, both eastern and western, requires not only strenuous discipline, but also a very real surrender of self. This latter is one of Blake's favorite teachings; in fact, he comes very near to making a goal of what is only a means. But his "self-annihilation" differs from that of the typical mystics in several very important respects. Blake's idea probably starts from the Swedenborgian self-annihilation which means very little more than the traditional putting off of the "old man" and putting on of the "new man." In Blake's hands the idea acquires an emotional coloring that makes of it something very different. Its motive force is essentially emotion, the emotion of love, one of the central tenets of Blake's teachings. But the "self-annihilation" of the mystics arises from the love of God that is not so much an emotional efflux as an integral act of the will. John Tauler's definition of the love of God will be remembered for its categorical identification of what has so often been regarded purely as an emotion with an act of the will, not merely a surging up of the human emotions, but a firm direction of the human will toward God. "Not my will, but Thy will," is the heart of the love of God defined in this way. The "most burning love" of God that warmed the aspiration of so many mystics is an addition to this central core, not a substitution.

Such a surrender of the personal will is very hard to conceive of in the case of a man in whose work one finds so much of a personal animus as one does in Blake's life and writings. Not only in private epigrams and letters does one discern a strong personal animus, but in at least one of the "Prophetical Books" Blake has used an episode of his own life, the sojourn at Felpham, with the famous irritation at Hayley's well-meaning but blind and philistine interference, as the foundation of the great religious action of *Milton*. It is, of course, difficult to separate the personal strand of vindicating a point of view and striking out the heat of a grievance from the perception in one's own personal experience of the great workings of the universal. But the spirit is very different, for that of the one consists in erecting the personal experience into the universal, and that of the other in viewing the personal through the eyes of the universal. Some of the symbolism of *Milton* suggests the first rather than the second. If "self-annihilation" means the freeing of the universal in one's soul from the stress of the individual and the narrowly personal, whether it be manifested or not in arrogance or pride, then Blake's "self-annihilation" is certainly very different from that of the typical mystics. For even the sacred region of the spirit was filled by his pride as he consoled himself for the neglect he suffered on earth with the reflection that in heaven his works were warmly acclaimed. To be sure, that is not so different from the consolation the devout Christian has been traditionally supposed to enjoy in his good works; yet in general good Christians have been far too conscious of the imperfection of their ways to flaunt it with such naïve defiance as did Blake.

It is because of this scorn of humility that one is not sure that Blake's faithful obedience to the direction of his spirits, his unflagging and wholly admirable loyalty to what he supposed he was by high heaven appointed to do, even in the teeth of financial and professional discouragement and bitter coldness where he had hoped for enthusiastic approval—that all this was due so much to a submission to heaven as to an extraordinary faith in himself and in the rightness of his inspiration. One remembers that passage in which he says that feeling a great power of wrath in himself he looked abroad to see if such an energy were not one of the characteristics of a great man. From even the most sympathetic point of view it is not at all certain that that is the best way for a man to arrive at a just notion of what the will of God is; and without that, all the zeal in the world to make the will of God prevail, to borrow Arnold's famous phrase, can hardly save a man from striving to make his own will prevail.

The consequences of Blake's denial of humility are obvious. Humility in the Christian sense means the bowing of the individual will before the infinite wisdom and nobleness of the will of God; it means the concentration of all the aspirant's energies upon the work of seeking to know and to do that will; it means indifference to all other considerations, and in that narrowing of the field of purpose, the widest possible expansion of interest and influence; it means the elimination of the personal and the biased from the individual's outlook upon life in great things and in small. In all these things humility is not a barren forswearing, but a conquest of positive advantage not only for goodness but for sheer intellectual clarity and, above all, for mystical insight.

Clearly then, Blake's goal belongs to an order different from that of the typical mystics. The degree of that difference will be more apparent upon closer scrutiny of his definition of his goal. That, it will be remembered, is the life of vision, of the free perception of the world of imaginative reality and of the unimpeded exercise of the powers of the creative imagination. And the great manifestation of this exercise of the creative imagination is the body of visions to which he devoted his life.

There is no doubt that Blake would unhesitatingly have placed his visions first from whatever angle his gifts or his works or his theories might be approached. They were the glory of his life, the distinctive mark of whatever authenticity he might claim, the goal of all his teaching and all his working. In the position he accords to them and in what he says of them may be found the heart of his philosophy. Consequently, it is in them more than in anything else that we shall discover the real meaning of points that his explicit teaching left puzzling or obscure. This means, of course, that Blake's estimate of the importance of visions for his goal is very different from that of the typical mystics.

Most of the great Christian mystics have seen visions, but in general they have looked upon their visions as preliminary steps which might or might not lead to complete union. Joan of Arc, for instance, saw visions in a sense that was perfectly intelligible and orthodox in the Middle Ages, but she was not a great mystic and has not in general been so regarded. In all this there is absolutely no question of ghost or apparition. By definition, this discussion is concerned, not with what appears to the eye of the body, but with what appears to the eye of the mind, or, as the mystics would say, to the eye of the soul. Even with that limitation the great mystics regard visions as preliminary challenges and graces in the vestibule of the heavenly kingdom. Hope and refreshment they do afford on the way of the mystic, but they certainly are in no sense his goal. To the great mystics Blake, no matter how authentic his visions, could never be more than one who had tarried on the way; one, it is true, to whom God had been abundant in his graces, but one who had never come into the fulness of the mystical experience.

For the main business of the mystic is not to voyage in strange lands of the imagination, but on the wings of the spirit to soar to God. Whatever halts him on that flight is an impediment and not an achievement. Were the vision of the celestial city—nay, even the beatific vision itself—to light up his imagination, still he would not have reached his goal, for he is striving to purify his spirit and widen the portals of his soul that God himself may enter in. *Domine, non sum dignus ut intres sub tectum meum* is the humble prayer of the liturgy, but that God should come into the soul was the aspiration of every Christian mystic. Never would he be content to rest in Blake's life of vision. For Blake's visions represent neither an intimate communion nor an intimate direction of conduct.

What they do represent is an elaborate series of myths with an elaborate dramatis personae and a series of complicated actions. The dramatis personae is remarkably catholic, for fairies as well as angels dictated his visions to him, and the thistle in his path turned into an old man gray, and the spirit of his brother, John the Evil One, followed behind in the wind. Christ, although a very different Christ from the Christ of the New Testament, yet still unmistakably God, finds a place in his supernaturalism, and God the Father in the guise of a very dignified old man slightly cramped in at the top of a plate figures in the illustrations to the *Book of Job*. In the *Marriage of Heaven and Hell* a devil chats affably with Blake, and in the sittings with Varley, king and warrior and courtesan come from the world of the beyond and, quite invisible to the sympathetic astrologer, Varley, sit for their portraits in what must have been a most notable midnight séance. But above all these in time and effort Blake's own world of Zoas and emanations and their children claimed his interest. Far more prominent than Christ or God in Blake's system is Urthona-Los, and the heavenly city of Christian longing becomes a half-human spirit Jerusalem, and its peaceful streets yield place to those storied halls of the city of Golgonooza on the lake of Udan-Adan.

That is the most important thing to take into account for the relation of Blake's supernaturalism to the question of whether or not he is a great mystic. The relation of Blake's visions to the tradition in which he professed to be working is no mere question of orthodoxy: it is a question of fundamental direction and massing of energy. The visions of the mystics have in general been a re-creation, a reinvesting with immediate vitality, of a vision of the world that has been something larger than the creation of one mind. They have been distinctly the fruit of religious activity, but Blake has devoted his powers to the invention of a new system, to the elaboration of what is in reality a new mythology. And that, however fresh or true or valuable, is something entirely different from the work of the typical mystics, something belonging to the field of religion only by virtue of its subject matter, in its method and its processes more akin to the achievements of the great romancers.

The mystic sought union with God. Blake sought a restoration of the soul to the life of vision. The mystic sought to experience God in his own soul. Blake sought to see the world of vision. The mystic found the realization of his goal in God alone, Blake found it in the heterogeneous and discursive visions to which he devoted the "Prophetical Writings." The objective of Blake's mystical effort was, then, so different from the goal of the great mystics in so fundamental a way as to make any identification of his activity with theirs impossible, and to make impossible the drawing of any real equivalence.

This conclusion finds striking confirmation when the problem is approached from what in a certain sense might be called the other side to the goal, the way in which Blake hopes to reach this goal. Moreover, since mysticism is essentially what Miss Underhill has called a life-process, its characteristic activity offers as helpful a way of defining its nature as either its fundamental point of view or its goal.

The first distinctive characteristic of Blake's effort to achieve his goal is his appeal from the jurisdiction of the reason to an independent insight. Here Blake is most certainly in accord with the typical mystics. For the supremacy of the human reason for the discovery and experience of spiritual reality is one thing that they have unremittingly challenged. Moreover, the century into which Blake was born was exactly the sort of time to send any mystic afield for himself, and Blake's opposition to the closed circle of his age was precisely what might be expected of any mystic. For the typical mystics would maintain with Blake that the human reason depends entirely on what the senses report to her of their environment. Her canons, so far as they grow out of individual experience (of course, here is where Blake's rejection of tradition led him to a narrower view of experience than the great mystic, or even the great poet, would admit), are limited by the senses, and the senses, by definition, can give no report of that world of the spirit that lies beyond their ken. In all this the mystics and Blake are at one. They are also agreed as to the perils of the rationalistic point of view, the danger of pride, of smugness, of cut-and-dried intolerance, even of cruelty; above all, of the starving of those imaginative and emotional elements that are indispensable to any really human living. So far Blake would seem to be in accord with the great tradition of mystical experience. And when he goes on to offer in place of this rationalism a view of life that provides for an insight beyond this restricted one, he again is at one with the masters of the spiritual life.

But at that point he diverges from the mystics in certain ways that very definitely distinguish his type of insight from theirs. In the first place, Blake insists throughout his work upon the effortlessness of his visions, pointing to the fact that the "Prophetic Books" were dictated to him without any effort of his, and that heavenly things were revealed to him without any solicitation on his part. And, in the second place, when Blake tries to lead other men into the life of vision he expressly rejects discipline and maintains that the life of vision is the spontaneous fruit of the release of man's energies, and that that release is to be effected, not by the traditional methods of ethical discipline, but by the cultivation of the creative imagination, especially as manifested in the powers of the artist—above all, the visionary artist.

Now, as we have seen, it is quite true that the supreme type of mystical achievement, like the supreme type of any human achievement, often comes, as it seems, quite from the outside, without any conscious effort on the part of the mystic or the artist. It seems as if reality suddenly poured in upon the spirit, as if a man spoke words not his own, as if for a brief moment the spirit were lifted above its ordinary pedestrian ways to fly on the wings of its dreams. But such experiences in no wise invalidate what the mystics have said as to the strenuous work by which they come to their goal, for they are very ephemeral, and they find their fitting context in the most strenuous endeavor of the artist or the mystic. Finally, they seldom come except after the most strenuous endeavor and after the most complete devotion of all the powers of a man's nature to the enterprise in hand. It is as if when the soul had spent all its resources—and often seemingly in vain—the price of its endeavor had suddenly been returned in a way undreamed of.

Consequently we must not confuse the way in which the experience of this type is arrived at with the character of the experience itself. They are two very different things. The first flash of insight that sends the mystic on his long quest, like the voice which St. Paul heard on the road to Damascus, is veritably a flash, coming seemingly without any effort or desert on the part of him who enjoys the illumination. But it is noteworthy that while it sometimes comes to the imperfect and the sinful and the unwise, even these are usually found to have cherished hidden and often unconscious aspirations toward higher things. St. Paul was certainly no Christian when he heard the voice, but he was, even from the very fact of his persecuting, a man who cared passionately for the truth and for good. So of the final insight. It is, however sudden or effortless or independent of conscious motivation, essentially the fruit of a strenuous discipline, in some part of an intellectual, but certainly for the greater part of an ethical, nature.

The intellectual discipline of the mystic has centred about the problem of the concentration of the attention. Many things may be done with a scattered and wandering attention, but not the work of the mystic. For that involves a mobilization of all the mind's powers and a focusing of those powers upon the goal to be won. That is the essential meaning of the term "concentration," which will occur frequently in this discussion. There is probably nothing in the world so unstable, so prone to disintegration, as the human attention, and those who, like the great philosophers or the great creative artists, have earned the right to speak whereof they know, testify that there is probably no human work so heroic as the fixing of that gipsy attention for long bouts of intellectual effort, for the bringing into order of that vagrant wilderness of the human mind. So whether it be the meditation of the Buddhist Bhikkhu, or the Christian mystic, the journey to that higher insight that is their goal takes its beginning in the strenuous intellectual labor of meditation. The reader who quietly and dispassionately peruses the pages of the *Manresa,* or the directions for meditation of the Buddhist sages is apt to be a little scornful at first of the importance attached to such very simple trains of thought as they describe. To anyone who has not attempted meditation it seems as if it would be very easy to hold one fairly simple idea before his mind until he has compelled even its most hidden recesses to yield their treasure of meaning and inspiration. But the train of reflection that appears so simple on the surface is in reality both complicated and profound, for it is from this sustained meditation that the mystic rises into the serene ecstasy of contemplation or union.

This intellectual discipline plays no part in Blake's mystical activity. What he stresses is the free expansion of the artist's imagination, sweeping heaven and earth with its creative fury, the surrender of the visionary's mind and will to the influx of vision. The secret is obvious. The object of Blake's mystical activity was so much more diffused and miscellaneous than the object of the mystic's activity that the character of the activity itself must inevitably be far less strenuous and concentrated even on the intellectual side.

As for the ethical side, Blake's rejection of discipline becomes one of the most important items of his mystical code. The key to this aspect of his thinking and his activity may be found in what he made of chastity. In the Christian tradition, as we have seen, chastity has played a very considerable rôle with very definite purposes and implications. At various times the word has been used in two different senses: sometimes as absolute celibacy, and again— and this for the majority of human beings—as moderation within definite religious sanctions. For nearly a thousand years the Catholic tradition has been one of celibacy for the "religious" and chastity in the second sense for the laity, while the Protestant tradition has upheld chastity in the second sense, of moderation, for both clergy and laity. As a result, the Catholic mystics have not unnaturally maintained the necessity of celibacy for the life of complete religious devotion. The reason for such a position is the belief that celibacy promotes the rigorous concentration of interest so essential to the mystic life. In spite of the fact that the celibate loses the discipline of the family life with all its attendant cares and responsibilities, they have felt that he gains in his freedom from the limitations and distractions of family interest. In this connection the conventual life to which so many of these mystics were devoted must not be overlooked, since it gave men social responsibilities and privileges while preserving them from more engrossing personal liens. To the Protestant mind, however, such freedom savors too much of the inhuman, both in the demand it puts upon natural instinct and in the deprivation that it involves of the humanizing influences of family life. From either point of view two things are certain: first, that the great mystic is an unusually concentrated human being; and second, that for the sake of this concentration he has made every sacrifice to insure that the passions of the body do not defeat the aspirations of the soul.

Blake attacked chastity because he believed that it fettered energy and fortified the selfish isolation of the spiritually incomplete individual. It sought to impose restraint in a field where he believed that absolute freedom was essential. This protest has been warmly applauded by some of Blake's critics who seem to forget that no amount of purely physical intensity of living can quite approximate high spiritual quality of living, that these two ideals belong to two distinct regions which, while not necessarily incompatible under ideal conditions, are certainly hostile to each other when the gates that bar the road to excess are broken down. In other words, Blake failed to see that the stress on chastity, like that on humility, had arisen, not from an arbitrary imposition of a moral tyranny, but from a faith in its potency as an intellectual and spiritual aid to the conquest of the heart's dearest choice.

The hatred of restriction, of interference with the free energy of human nature, which led Blake to reject chastity passionately also led him to reject the principle of discipline in any form. His fundamental objection to the moral law was not that it was carried to extremes, but that it was used to accomplish its fundamental purpose, to check the vagrant impulses of the individual. Even the Ten Commandments, for all their generality, he rejected as tyrannous. This impatience of the moral law is perhaps the best example that we have of Blake's intense hatred of discipline, a hatred that, however interesting it may be from the artistic point of view, is certainly, from the ethical or the religious point of view, one of the most consequential differences between Blake's mysticism and that of the typical mystics. For the typical mystic has generally found in the spirit of the moral law a necessary discipline for human life, one that in the restraint it imposes upon the growth of weeds in the human spirit gives the better chance for the flowers to bloom.

Likewise, Blake's arraignment of the reason, which he felt inspired and sustained the moral law, has made his revolt against rationalism a very different matter from that of the great mystics. The reason that proudly arrogates to itself the territory belonging to faith and to love the mystics have condemned quite as vigorously as Blake ever did. The Christian mystics who feared what they felt to be the palsy of the excessively rationalistic scholasticism of the fourteenth century, and who quietly and unacrimoniously parted ways with it, would be very sympathetic with Blake's indictment of the rationalism of the age of prose and reason, but when he came to flout the reason that holds in check the vagaries of impulse and instinct and subjects them to the criterion of the higher purpose, then they would, I think, have asked Carlyle's question: "True: from all men thou art free; but from Thyself and the Devil?" In other words, the great mystics have recognized that the fulfilment of any noble aspiration requires the subordination of all that would militate against it.

But Blake has not hesitated to intrust the achievement of his great purpose to the spontaneous energies of man's nature without question as to the ultimate worth of a particular outburst of passion or energy. Here he not only has parted company with the typical mystics, but he has taken up a method which may seriously be challenged even from the point of his own goal. It would seem as if only a very narrow or a very shallow personality could carry through such a program without expending most of its energy in a welter of turbulent and conflicting impulses. Only a colossal self-conceit would trust its dearest ends to the fickle mercy of spontaneity, and only a singularly phlegmatic temperament could give rein to all its impulses without eventually running into the wall of inner conflict. Here, like so many antinomians of our day, Blake seems to have taken for granted the fruits of a discipline which he repudiated.

Finally, Blake's reinterpretation of Christianity in terms of art involves certain conclusions for his mystical activity that cannot be disregarded. The core of this recension is the identification of Christ with the creative imagination, the most original feature of Blake's Christianity. This makes the creative imagination the agent of redemption, to translate Blake's ideas into the more conventional terms of theology. In other words, the exercise of an art is the way to achieve goodness. One is reminded of the medieval *laborare est orare*, but the old saying of the Benedictines never contemplated a replacement of prayer by work. Furthermore, when Blake said "art" he meant art in the very literal sense of the word. Whether he literally intended that all men should be artists is a question, but it is certain that the only mystic for whom Blake's teachings made any provision was the artist, the man in whom the powers of the creative imagination find expression in a very special form of talent. The mystic was therefore not to pray his way into heaven, or to meditate his way to the gates of contemplation, but to imagine his way into reality.

At that point the significance of Blake's rejection of the ethical discipline of the mystics for the more outgoing workings of love and energy becomes clear. Blake's way was not essentially ethical at all. He rejected discipline and substituted energy and intensity of emotion for the strife of the will because the region in which he was working was a very different one from that in which the will has been wont to operate. The mystical way of the typical mystics belongs to the ethical field, finding its great impulse in the will; the mystical way of Blake belongs to the imaginative field, finding its great impulse in the creative energies. What all this amounts to is Blake's famous identification of art and religion.

Any criticism of Blake's art-Christianity must begin with the time-honored question of the relations between art and religion. There are undoubtedly those who would not hesitate to maintain that a man without a sense of beauty could not be truly religious, and there are those who would declare that a man without religion could not be very much of an artist. But most of us would be quite willing to agree that a man without a sense of beauty would probably not be able to commend his religion to us, and that on the whole the work of an artist who comprehends in some fashion the elements of human experience that find expression in religion will probably have a deeper import than that of one who wants that understanding. At any rate, it is clear that religion and art have a common ground and that they can be of very real service to each other in the realization of their respective purposes, but it is also clear that in some very fundamental respects they are entirely different.

For each has its distinctive province. Religion aims to make men better, to purify their affections, to enlighten their judgments, to inspire their inclinations, to fortify their wills, and she does each of these things in the name of a higher will than man's, that, seeing more broadly and more profoundly and more timelessly, has conceived a nobler and a truer pattern of life than man could ever devise. And religion has assured man that whatever be the immediate consequences of his trying to follow her guidance, it will be better with him, and better for the whole of which he is a part, that he endeavor to serve this higher will. Religion calls in the arts that the words in which she speaks to man may be not only as just, but as moving as possible, for she knows that his feelings are a readier way to the warming of his will than is his understanding, but she keeps art in an ancillary rôle, however honorable; for again, she knows that to achieve her end she must go beyond both feelings and understanding. For no matter what she may do to make life more beautiful or more enjoyable, religion knows that her fundamental concern is with the sphere of conduct, to make man do better and be better ethically and spiritually.

Art, on the other hand, aims to give man beauty, for beauty, she knows, is the greatest gift which the world of sound and color and smell and form can give to man. The satisfaction she gives is a disinterested one that carries man beyond the narrow circle of himself into a world where the more limited instincts of material possession, of egotistical interest, of vanity, of inertia are swept away in a broader vision. Art does not ask man to be a better man, but she tries to make him prefer better things. If she be a good citizen in the universe—and the greatest art, of Raphael, of Dante, of Shakespeare, of Sophocles, of Michael-Angelo—has been that—she does not content herself with pleasing stupid men, and she does not try to please bad men, for she knows that a work of art is no greater than its subject. On the other hand, when she presents the conclusions of religion she does not present them as something men must believe, but she presents them as things that are true, and things that are beautiful, and if she makes ordinary men like great and high things, she knows that she has been the better art for it. But art, unless she be committed to the service of religion, is not trying to make men embrace any higher will than their own. When men have arisen from her she knows that they will remember her inspiration, and that the spirit which remembers will be a more gracious one than the spirit which forgets, but it is not her distinctive responsibility to follow and to direct their conduct. That is the function of religion. Then, too, art works in things, in sounds and in colors, and, by her handling of them appeals to man's spirit through his senses. But religion appeals directly to his will through his senses, it is true; but her handling of the material of sense, is entirely mediate and incidental. In other words, religion graves the commandments on tablets of stone that man may not forget the precepts he must keep, but art fashions the ark that shall hold them; art weaves the curtain and raises the pillar, but religion hallows the silence within and bows the worshiper's head.

So are religion and art at their best—they profit from each other's services, but they do not intrude into each other's purposes. For religion in particular is afraid that man may become so engrossed in the beautiful words of his prayer that he may forget that words alone will never open the gates of heaven to him, and that the chant of the *de Profundis* may be so impressive to his ears that he may forget that *he* is the sinner, and God may not hear the music of his voice in the distraction of his heart. On the other hand, no matter how noble or moving the aspiration, if it find no tongue or illumine no form, then art can have none of it. So they have both fared best when they have availed themselves each of the other's services and yet remembered the bounds of their own provinces.

That his confusion of these fundamental purposes of art and religion proved disastrous to Blake's art in the realm of poetry seems beyond question. For, however highly the ingenuity of the "Prophetical Writings" may be esteemed, there can be no question that as poetry and as art they are far from satisfactory. As has been suggested more than once, they are marvelously strange and powerful; but, except for passages of rare energy and magnificence, almost smothered in the obscurity and involution of their context, they are notably deficient in lucidity, in wholeness, in vitality, and in beauty—in all the essentials of great literature and of great art. The common opinion that their failure is due to their increasing subservience to Blake's visionary purposes is confirmed when we turn to works relatively free of the "system," to two such diverse achievements as the *Songs of Innocence and of Experience* and the illustrations to the *Book of Job*. The merits of the first have been so universally acclaimed that only the perfection of their simplicity and beauty need be mentioned here. They demonstrate beyond doubt the high order of Blake's original endowment. And the illustrations to the *Book of Job* are justly famous, for their majesty and beauty demonstrate what Blake can achieve in the way of mastering and transmuting material that has been given to him, in this case by the Bible, and so fashioning it that the observer can hardly miss the lucidity and luminous grace of the finished work. It would seem, then, that the same things that made Blake's visionary philosophy fall so far short of the goal of the mystics made him, so far as one can judge from the evidence, fall very far short of the artistic excellence promised in the early lyrics and, to a considerable extent, achieved toward the close of his life in the field of drawing. With the great mystics it has not generally been so. Their mystical efforts, their mystical experiences, have sent them back to the exercise of their peculiar abilities, to the fulfilment of their especial work, with added, not diminished or confused, power. The mystic achievement did not make Abbot Bernard the less moving preacher when he rose to admonish and to encourage his flock at Clairvaux; it did not weaken the magnetic powers of leadership of the Buddha when he drew to the austerity of his alms-bowl and yellow robe the pious from all India; it did not quench the stalwart eloquence or the shrewd sense of George Fox as he journeyed from one end of the United Kingdom to the other to strengthen the persecuted Quaker cause; nor did it impair the remarkable administrative ability and reforming ardor of St. Teresa when she set about to restore the Carmelites to their original spiritual fervor; nor did it in the least detract from the charm and the vitality of St. Augustine's rhetorical gifts when he sat down to tell the story of God's marvelous working with him.

"By their fruits shall ye know them." Again, when we penetrate below the categorical resemblances of the surface, we find that Blake's mysticism, in its fruit as in its essential nature and its characteristic working, is so different from the mysticism of the typical mystics as to necessitate our seeking some other category for it.

M. Berger has said that Blake "would have classed himself among the old Hebrew prophets, or the great poets of all time, compelled to proclaim to all men the way of escape from eternal death, and to open their eyes to the divine light, which, at the appointed hour, will reveal itself and shine forth in full splendour upon all."[3] To waive the quite incidental question of whether prophet and poet are interchangeable terms, Blake, as we have seen, did consider himself a prophet with a message to deliver upon the reception of which depended the salvation of his age. "Mark my words! They are of your Eternal Salvation" is a charge often repeated in the "Prophetic Books." And as we have seen, the content of that message bore very directly upon the age-old problem of how we shall live life. It contained a very definite criticism of the age in which he found himself, and a plan for escape from the limitations of that way of life. And it grounded both the criticism and the plan in a theory as to the fundamental nature of the world, and it claimed that this message had not been arrived at by the normal

[3] Berger, *op. cit.*, p. 59.

processes of the senses and the mind, but had, in a very special way, been revealed. In all this Blake belongs to the prophets, and for the so-called "Prophetic Writings" this is probably the most sympathetic and profitable approach.

But prophets are no more immune to the human liabilities of greater and lesser than any other race of men. And, as we have seen, the message of the prophet must, like every other mystical phenomenon, meet the test of what William James has called "confrontation with the total context of experience." That suggests what may roughly be gathered into three lines of inquiry: What, so far as we can deduce from what is actually given, is the source of this message? From what wells of verity, of this earth or beyond, has the prophet drawn the measure of his wisdom? And the second question may be put thus: What is the form in which this message comes? What marks of authenticity does it bear? What peculiar potency do we find in it? And the third question, which arises out of these two, is this: What of the message itself? Is its criticism, in the light of our answers to the foregoing, true? Is its suggestion of remedy practicable and helpful? Will it set right the situation revealed in the criticism?

The question of the sources of a prophetic message raises immediately one issue which a purely humanistic discussion must waive. That is, of course, the element of supernatural inspiration. There is no use in attempting to handle such a question, for this discussion is not, by definition, capable of answering it. That means that the problem of the source of the prophet's message will be treated like the problem of the sources of any man's ideas. The justification of this method is that historically what we should call the sources of a man's ideas appear to remain still the conditions of a man's ideas, even where supernatural inspiration is assumed.

The sources of any man's ideas, whether he be a prophet or whether or not they deserve the name of message, are to be found in these places: in his own character, in his personal experience, in that enlarged personal experience that comes from reading, from contact with friends, from a living appropriation of his traditions, from his own observation of other men's lives, from his study of other men's observations, from whatever gathers up human experience, as religion or science or philosophy. Two things seem to be especially important whatever the particular sources of his experience: the breadth of the field of experience upon which he draws, and the reality with which he views the field. Difficult as it is to insure, the meaning of the notion of breadth of experience is fairly self-evident; but the word "reality" used in this sense needs further definition. Reality of experience demands, first of all, objectiveness, so that, as Goethe says, the thing may be seen in itself, unobscured by personal prejudice or interest. Reality of experience demands also an adequate handling of the eternal problem of the idealist, the old problem of the many and the one, that in his eagerness to get at what is essential he disregard not the complexity of life, that, as in thinking he must be careful not to sacrifice principle to expediency, so in practice he must not, by oversimplifying, lose the many-sided life of the actual.

The narrowness of Blake's experience has already been pointed out in the chapter on his life. Not only was the physical sphere of his life limited, but, still more important, so was the intellectual. His education was meager; he was not by the nature of his work brought into many relations with men or affairs. His contacts with able men were few and not of sufficient intimacy or potency to enrich his own experience. His reading was limited. And he wanted even the broadening influences of a church tradition.

What is of still greater significance for a prophet, Blake's own temperament and fundamental cast of mind narrowed what experience he had. Prizing his own independence and originality as highly as he did, it is not surprising that he came to life in no teachable mood. He was sure that he knew, and being sure that he knew, he felt no need of extending his own personal experience with that of other men. The result was that his own moods, his own feelings, his own idiosyncrasies, tastes, and pursuits came to fill a larger place in his universe than they do for most men. He tended, then, to do what the egoist, however noble or generous, always does; he made the world in his own image and likeness. His own experiences, like the difficulty with Hayley or the quarrel with the drunken soldier, became not merely symbols of the universal course of things, but in themselves transactions of universal magnitude and significance.

It is true that he gained by this narrowing of his world. He gained in self-assurance—a matter of no mean moment to the prophet. He gained in a certain intense power, for all the energies of his nature, instead of being dissipated in the multiplicity of life, were concentrated in a few channels. He gained a sense of unity, for he was not distracted by the thousand conflicts of claim and of evidence that dilute the powers of most men. He gained, above all, a heightened sense of validity. What was, was for him a thousand fold more real than for men for whom more things are real. And this gives any man, especially the prophet, a dynamic which it is hard to obtain in any other way.

But he sacrificed in making these gains other values quite as essential if a man is to be a great prophet. Believing as he did that a firm persuasion that a thing is so makes it so, Blake put his truth in the keeping of his convictions. Even for a man of large experience this is a dangerous proceeding. For a man of limited experience it is fatal to genuine understanding. The very narrowness of his world, the very abstractness of a life undisturbed by external compulsions, gives to the mood of the moment, gives even to the fantasy of the moment a sharpness, an urgency, even a validity, not known when the mind is moving in a larger current of life. When to this is added a strong faculty of visualization, a power of seeing substantially what for most men remains an imageless concept, the personal and fortuitous are suddenly invested with a preternatural significance with which nothing in the everyday world outside the darkened room can compete. Moreover, the way is cleared for the endless multiplication and persistence of auto-suggestion. The texts which haunted John Bunyan with a conviction not only of sin but of eternal damnation offer a very suggestive parallel[4] for Blake's visions. The power of the texts seems to have arisen in Bunyan's case from a state of nervous excitement in which whatever by chance of association presented itself to his insulated consciousness seized upon it with the immediacy and the tenacity of obsession. Something of the same sort of thing seems to have happened to Blake. Only in his case the obsession was usually not a matter of sound, but of visualizations. One cannot say that any of

---

[4] Josiah Royce, "The Case of John Bunyan," *Psychological Review*, I (1894), 136.

Blake's terrifics are meaningless, but there is a tone about some passages that in its violence rather exceeds the significance of the content, in a fashion strongly reminiscent of Ossian. The following description of the unilluminated man is a very typical example of this quality:

Albion cold lays on his Rock: storms & snows beat round him,
Beneath the Furnaces & the starry Wheels & the Immortal Tomb.
Howling winds cover him: roaring seas dash furious against him:
In the deep darkness broad lightnings glare, long thunders roll.
The weeds of Death inwrap his hands & feet, blown incessant
And wash'd incessant by the for-ever restless sea-waves, foaming abroad
Upon the white Rock. England, a Female Shadow, as deadly damps
Of the Mines of Cornwall & Derbyshire lays upon his bosom heavy,
Moved by the wind in volumes of thick cloud, returning, folding round
His loins & bosom, unremovable by swelling storms & loud rending
Of enraged thunders.[5]

Especially is this true of certain incidental descriptive passages in which phrases of scant meaning and impressive volume of sound are retailed with an air of preternatural significance that clearly suggests the obsession.

Finally, Blake's rejection of tradition in any form and his inaccessibility to outside criticism left him peculiarly at the mercy of these impulses of his own fancy. For in religion as in other fields of human activity, it is precisely where a man contemns and forsakes the ways of his fellows and sets out on the trail of his own inspiration that he most needs criticism. The great artist and the great prophet can perhaps afford to proceed without the safeguard of criticism, but they are not the ones to attempt it. In general the great prophet, like the great mystic, has availed himself of the tested experience that he found to his hand in the tradition within which he arose. When St. Paul forsook the old law that for centuries had been the glory of his people, it was because he had found the finer breath and spirit of that tradition in the new, whose Master had laid down the work of the mystic in that famous sentence: "I am not come to destroy [the Law], but to fulfil." This does not mean that all the great prophets and mystics have been endowed

[5] *Jerusalem*, p. 94, ll. 1-11.

with the critical power of a St.Paul or a Buddha, nor that they have possessed the ability to weigh themselves that is the accolade of the spiritual leader, but, working in a mature religious tradition, they have found in the resources of experience that constitute the value of such a tradition the criticism they needed to winnow the genuine from the spurious in a region peculiarly exposed to the corruption of misunderstanding and self-deception.

For the form in which these visions came to Blake and in which he expressed his prophetic message, it will be remembered that symbolism played a very large part in the religious writings to which he was indebted. Boehme, Swedenborg, Paracelsus, Ezekiel, and the author of the Revelation had all communicated their message in varying degrees through symbols. The use of symbol had seemed to Blake not just a means of communicating truth, but a means of insuring that the knowledge of the truth should not fall into unworthy hands, but should be preserved for those who were fit to understand. With such a point of view it is not surprising that Blake came to regard obscurity as an essential mark of truth; that here, as elsewhere, he mistook what might be called the accidental—at most the incidental—for the essential and ultimate. It is difficult to determine precisely to what extent his symbolism came to him and to what extent he invented it. Probably the larger part of the process was unconsciousness, but it seems impossible that his faith in obscurity should not have fostered it. Here, probably, more than anywhere else, Blake's deficiencies in education and experience become apparent, for the faith in magniloquent obscurity is one of the characteristics of the uneducated mind.

The most serious consequence of this faith in obscurity was that it led Blake to misapprehend the entire problem of symbolism. A magazine article of the late Mr. Clutton-Brock puts the case, not only of Blake but of many of his disciples, very succinctly in the following words:

> Unfortunately many writers and readers now seem to be weary of the great ways of literature and to hope that in byways they may find some secrets unknown to the great masters of sense and language. There are no such secrets. It is not symbols or catchwords but the noble use of words that

gives to them a sense beyond their plain meaning. That noble use is a sign of the effort to express great things; whereas symbols and catchwords are a sign that the effort is declined.[6]

The greatest symbolism, like that of the Four Horsemen or the Scarlet Woman or the Heavenly Jerusalem of the Apocalypse has been revealing and illuminating because it expresses the experience, as well as the idea, of the prophet as literal language never could. But it has observed the laws of all figurative language in clearness, simplicity, suggestiveness, dramatic quality, beauty, and, usually, wealth of association. In approaching symbolism as a problem of wrappings rather than of revelation, Blake incurred difficulties enough. But when he proceeded to elaborate a fresh symbolism of his own, the difficulties were doubled. For what he was trying to do was in itself an artificial thing. To take a very simple example, the place names of ancient Palestine have come, through centuries of association, to mean much more than the literal places, which in so many instances have ceased to exist. Sodom, the Dead Sea, Mount Sinai, Tophet—one might extend the list almost without end—have come to mean far more than the historical place to which the name once referred. Blake made use of the same device of using place names for symbols, and with a zeal for the contemporary and the native he took up the names of places around London and made them the vesture of his meanings. But in so doing he overlooked several elements essential to all mythology. In the first place, the old Hebrew names had come to mean what they did not because someone had decided to use them as symbols, but because certain transactions and certain personalities had become so indelibly associated with those localities in a perfectly natural and incidental fashion that the localities were made memorable by that very fact. And because of that natural association the bare names of those places came to suggest what had taken place there and the people who had been connected therewith and the whole body of significance that had inevitably made the expressive symbol. And the second important point is that this was in no sense an individual or a deliberate effort made at any one time. Usually the process begun

---

[6] A. Clutton-Brock, "The Poetry of William Blake," *The Living Age*, CCLI (December 29, 1906), 809–13.

in the memorableness of dramatic fitness was one of unconscious ac-
cretion, extending over a considerable number of years and involving a large number of people. Such a symbol was essentially a
racial product.

Blake disregarded both of these factors. He tried to invent at
once a whole body of symbolism. He took suburbs of London suggestive of little more than comfortable shopkeepers and pleasant
week-end outings and tried suddenly to invest them with universal
spiritual significance, and then proceeded to refer to them as if
they possessed the meaning he assumed. The result, for even the
illuminated, is little better than a glorified cross-word puzzle. For
the uninitiated it is a dreary blank. It is the fundamental problem
of language over again. Anybody can invent a language of his own,
and even persuade a few lovers of puzzles to learn it, but no one
person can, even in a lifetime, make a living language. That is the
inescapable problem of Blake's literary symbolism. Here again
comparison of Blake's poetry with his art is illuminating, for it
shows how much more effective Blake's visions were when expressed
in the common language of line and color in his drawings and paintings than in the individual language of his poems. The story of
Blake's pictorial art, from "Joseph of Arimathea among the Rocks
of Albion" to the great illustrations to the *Book of Job*, is a story of
growth in expressiveness and beauty, while the story of Blake's
poetry from the *Songs* to *Jerusalem* is a story of deepening obscurity.

The prophetic message of William Blake likewise bears upon
its forehead the mark of imperfect experience. It shows amazing
energy. It possesses the intensity of the radical theorist who con-
centrates all his powers upon the black-and-white outlines of the
problem without pursuing it into the confusing and blurring complexities of life. Characteristically, it is stronger in indictment than
in constructive suggestion, for constructive suggestion demands
that one go humbly and open-mindedly to school to the facts. And
such schooling is usually cramping to revolutionary style. Moreover, no paper scheme of life can possess the robustness and color
and vitality of life itself until it has left the world of vision and
met the inexorable demands of reality. It will emerge from the

process crumpled and dusty, but it will possess the truth that only the transmutation of fact by vision can give.

Blake's indictment of his age may be summed up, as we have seen, in what he said about rationalism. Man habitually oscillates between an extravagant faith in the reason which gives him the sense of mastery over his universe and a horror of its unfeeling and self-sustaining rigor. Here, as in so many cases, the desirable lies between the two, or, what is probably closer to the truth, gathers up the two in a higher synthesis. But no alchemy has ever been discovered so subtle as to be able to commend either the *via media* or the higher synthesis to the fundamental instincts of humanity. And the extremist is probably in essence a purer expression of some, at least, of the fundamental instincts of man than the supposedly average human being. What this amounts to is that Blake, for all he said about the relativity of moral states and "Everything that lives is holy," was essentially in temper and in quality of mind a black-and-white man. It is true that he insisted on reversing some of the prevailing judgments of his time as to which was which, but after all, reading white where the rest of the world reads black, to use his own striking figure, does not disturb the fundamental state of the universe or betray any habit of mind different from that of the old dichotomy.

Nowhere is this fundamentally unrealistic habit of mind better shown than in Blake's incessant arraignment of rationalism. There is no question that for all that England had gained from eighteenth-century rationalism she had paid dearly, and paid dearly in those directions which Blake most prized. The rationalistic point of view always tends in its moments of ascendency to underprize faith and spontaneity and energy and feeling and imagination. And as Blake pointed out in his epigram on Voltaire, to undervalue these things is veritably to throw sand against the wind, which will inevitably blow it back again. And if we take up the specific accounts of Blake's indictment we shall find again a very sound grasp upon principles not so well understood among so many people then as now. Blake pointed out the dangers of repression in very simple, black-and-white terms, when, for instance, he told of how repressed wrath against an enemy became murderous, or of how suppressed instincts poisoned the whole spirit. On the purely diagnostic side, modern psychology of even the most advanced schools has probably added very little to the theory which Blake expounded over a century ago.

So, too, Blake insisted that the qualities of imagination and spiritual energy had been discouraged in art by an age which gave its patronage to the "tame perpetuators of paltry blots," by an age which tended to prefer elegant and finished ineptitude and triviality to crude and imperfect inspiration. While Blake's criticism in this field cannot, in view of his own bitter experience of public indifference, be called disinterested, still it presented truth at a time when most people were blind and indifferent to the problem. Here again Blake was ahead of his time with a very much-needed criticism.

The same is true of his special defense of energy in the field of sex. The problem of sex the eighteenth century on the whole left either to the circumscribed and not always sympathetic handling of morality or to the flippancy and lack of frankness and directness of social convention. Again there seems to be no question of the need of criticism, of a fresh and free opening of a subject that had been approached timidly and conventionally by people unaware of, or afraid of, the deeps of human nature. At its lowest levels the eighteenth century had either regarded sex as unclean or made it so. At its highest it had in most cases put too much faith in a type of morality at its best adequate but rare, and for its average, conventional and by no means clear-eyed, and in its practice it had left far too much to sentimentalism and romance. What was needed was a recognition of the inherent cleanness and importance of the subject, and a full and human handling of what is, in a very full sense, a human problem. The recognition Blake gave brilliantly and enthusiastically. But when it came to the human handling of the human problem, Blake's lack of a wide and rich grasp upon experience, and the prevailingly theoretic cast of his mind, led to defects of reality and humanity that are characteristic of all the constructive side of his message. It is not only that the positive suggestions, or, since Blake was a prophet, the prescriptions, of his message, were impracticable. They were, fundamentally, not only out of contact with, but even oblivious of, reality. He wrote out of his own personal experience and more in the interest of a theory than in recognition of the facts.

The most remarkable thing about Blake's handling of sex from this point of view is its almost incredible bareness. It is not only bare of any suggestion of detail, but it is singularly bare of all human feeling or significance. It is partly a matter of abstractness. As one reads of the relations of Oothoon, Bromion, and Theotormon he feels as if he were reading of the loves of the algebraic symbols A and B. It is not reticence or purity that inspires this bleakness of suggestion; it is a singular literalness of dwelling upon the abstract idea. The following passage represents not even the average, but the most glowing and concrete handling of the subject to be found in all Blake's work (it is Oothoon speaking in the *Visions of the Daughters of Albion*):

"I cry: Love! Love! Love! happy happy Love! free as the mountain wind!
Can that be Love, that drinks another as a sponge drinks water,
That clouds with jealousy his nights, with weepings all the day,
To spin a web of age around him, grey and hoary, dark;
Till his eyes sicken at the fruit that hangs before his sight?
Such is self-love that envies all, a creeping skeleton,
With lamplike eyes watching around the frozen marriage bed!

But silken nets and traps of adamant will Oothoon spread,
And catch for thee girls of mild silver, or of precious gold.
I'll lie beside thee on a bank, and view their wanton play
In lovely copulation, bliss on bliss, with Theotormon:
Red as the rosy morning, lustful as the first-born beam,
Oothoon shall view his dear delight; nor e'er with jealous cloud
Come in the heaven of generous love, nor selfish blightings bring."[8]

As this passage shows, the subtler transformations for which art and literature have so long and so enthusiastically wrought play very little part in Blake's work. It is not that Blake's treatment of this important factor in man's life fails in elevation; it is that it fails, first of all and primarily, in humanity. Consequently, unlike the Sufis and other poets for whom sex loomed very large in the arena of life, Blake does not wrest either beauty or depth of passion

[8] "Visions of the Daughters of Albion," Sampson, *op. cit.*, pp. 291–92.

from it. In a curious abstractness that at once isolates and intensi-
fies the nakedness of his use, Blake's references to sex are appall-
ingly untransmuted. While there is absolutely no evidence that can
be relied on, in the reports either of Blake's life or of his sayings
(the speculations of some critics are built on the most insubstantial
fabrics of rumor), to contradict the tradition of the felicity of his
marriage and his loyalty to it, and while all available testimony is
unanimous as to the general sobriety of his way of living, still there
is much in all his work to suggest that he had never either fully
realized or defined the rôle of sex in human life.

It is not surprising, therefore, that in his eagerness to free sex
and to make use of it for the realization of his spiritual purposes
Blake should not have taken into account some of the most obvious
facts of general human experience, like, for instance, the peculiarly
absorbing nature of the passion, or the difficulty for many people
of making its energy available for anything but its own purposes.
Nor has he taken into account the amazing paradoxes of sex in
which the less enlightened and less aspiring elements of passion
jostle the noblest and most generous. Consequently, he has no way
of forecasting the possibilities of confusion, of self-deception, which
attend any effort to make sex the paramount end in life. In other
words, if the problem were as simple and as theoretic as Blake sees
it, his suggestions would do very well. But the complexity of the
problem is an inevitable part of its nature, and must be fully taken
account of for any fruitful solution.

The same difficulty besets the gospel of love, which plays so
large a part in Blake's message. There is probably no term in the
world that has more meanings than the word, "love"; consequently,
to be sure of what it stands for at any one time, it is necessary to
examine its premises and its context, for it varies with both. As a
Christian ideal, to take the example best known to most of us,
"love" may be used in two ways: first, for the love of God; and
second, for the love of one's neighbor. The first does undoubtedly
entail a very glowing personal emotion on the part of the genuinely
religious, but the emotion is not its essential or distinguishing quality. That is, to repeat a very important point already made in our
discussion of the mystics, the whole-hearted, utterly disinterested

surrender of the individual will to God. That is the first and essential element in *caritas*. And upon that is grounded the love of our neighbor. Recent times have seen various efforts to establish a code of love of neighbor that has not been grounded in the love of God, and we have seen the sentimentalism and the extravagances in which they have too often resulted. The shallowness and the sentimentality of such attempts should not, however, be suffered to stigmatize all effort to make man his brother's keeper. But they should make clear the truth that love of one's neighbor, to be fruitful, must have a deeper root than a general enthusiasm or an outgoing benevolence. Such a root the love of God affords in that it offers a higher and more steadying purpose and an independent and objective standard to carry on through the vicissitudes of emotion. Love of neighbor in that sense is patient and long-suffering, but not blind; it desires, not the prosperity of imperfection, but the perfecting of what may, with help, become better. It does not seek the emotional satisfaction of generosity or the subtle incense to vanity that rises from the subjection or gratitude of those whom one fancies inferior. It does not spend its force in wasteful or indiscriminate expression of charitable impulses. In other words, for the love of God it works that one's neighbor may draw nearer to God and be enabled to do the will of God more joyously and more fully than he otherwise could. It is a defense and a propagation of goodness in itself. In other words, love that is fruitful and lasting and ennobling can be fostered only under the aegis of standards.

And it may be added that not all can so love. The high love of mankind seems feasible only to those who are themselves disciplined and self-mastered. For the sound and fruitful love of one's neighbor often exacts that one restrain his outgoing ardor to do tangible and immediate good that some further and more lasting benefit be assured to the object of his good will. Furthermore, our daily experience teaches how suddenly and easily the fickle wind of emotion may veer from love to hate. For even the most exuberant of good wills must run the gamut of heat and cold and disappointment and impatience and irritation of the common day. Verily, it needs stout hearts and "the armor of the invincible knights of old" to compass such an undertaking as this, and human nature needs to fortify its frailty and inform its instability with the highest allegiance before it undertakes it.

What it all amounts to ultimately is that there are no sure ways, no panaceas, no infallible programs for the life of the human spirit. There is no wind of the spirit to which one can surrender himself and be sure that it will blow him safely into the port of heaven. Blake saw clearly the imperfections, the inadequacies, the perversions of the idol in which the rationalists had put their trust. What he did not see was that his idol of energy was, although not liable to those defects, still exposed to weaknesses of quite as serious a nature at the other extreme. "Life," said Epictetus, "is a soldier's service." Man yearns for a holiday, but sex offers no more of a moral vacation than religion. Like religion, sex has its various levels. Like religion, it has its inherent problems, its practical difficulties. Like religion, it must be constantly criticized, constantly referred to the whole circle of man's experience. And when man has done all he can in the way of perfecting his ideal and has realized that it is, to borrow again from Matthew Arnold, not a having and a resting, but a doing and a becoming, he still faces the problem of unremitting effort to make only the best of that ideal prevail, to keep it fresh and living by ceaseless striving with the incessant demands of reality. It is at this point that, largely because of the narrowness of his experience and the bias of his mind toward abstract theorizing, Blake's prophetic message fails to achieve the scope and reality of that of the great prophets.

In the course of these discussions of Blake as a mystic and a prophet so much has been said of his visions that little remains for our discussion of Blake the visionary but to gather up the conclusions suggested or implied in these last two chapters. Blake's visions represent, as has been pointed out before, an elaborate series of myths with an elaborate dramatis personae and a series of complicated relations and a very elaborate system of transactions. The word "elaborate" is used advisedly here, for the complexity of the result, which is one of the things that make the "Prophetic Books" such difficult reading, arises not from the complexity of the fundamental conceptions, but from the complexity of the relations. They present, as we have seen, an original mythology, the mastery of which requires so much logical concentration that the effect upon the reader's mind is akin to that of solving a puzzle, rather than an experience of beauty or a spiritual illumination. This effect is enhanced by the striking lack of emotional or imaginative reality in the presentation of these protagonists. While they are definite enough in limb and movement both in the verses and in the illustrations, they remain curiously abstract and, for all their tremendous agonies and perturbations, cold to the sympathies and imagination of the reader. But this abstraction is not due to vagueness; they are not, as has been erroneously suggested, great shadowy forms. They are rather huge, sharply cut, outlines that are capable of much variety of shape and movement, but which, for lack of light and shadow, have not yet assumed human proportions. The reason for this deficiency in spiritual richness and vitality is probably the secret of Blake's myth-making—it is not transcendent, but symbolical. That is, these great figures are not so much transcendent powers as psychological diagrams. It is one of the most remarkable qualities of Blake's work that with all the stress he lays upon the imagination, these figures remain intellectual aggregations rather than living beings.

A great many passages in the "Prophetic Books," viewed purely as visions, make one think of the type of dream that, without leaving the sinister apprehensions of the nightmare, yet partakes of its peculiar intensity and even violence. In these passages from the "Prophetic Books," Urizen and Los and Enitharmon and all the host of major and minor personages come before the reader with the kaleidoscopic swiftness of the dream, with the same immediacy, the same preternatural sharpness of impression, the same aura of significance. It is no wonder, if these beings actually came into Blake's consciousness, that he thought they must mean something quite beyond all earthly significance, for at moments the reader himself feels the aura of their presence. But with all this distinctness, even sharpness, the sequence has no imaginative or emotional continuity. Its coherence, especially in the longer poems, is purely logical and systematic. So far as any fulness of personality is concerned, these figures come like dreams, and like dreams they pass. The reader knows that that was Tharmas, but although there is

no question as to his logical identity, there is no lingering sense of
personality.   It is this which makes it possible for one person to
have very different and even conflicting relations, like Orc, and for
two characters to mingle and to separate until one is not sure which
one is involved, as in the case of Satan and Palamabron in *Milton*.
It is no longer wise for a layman to prate of the subconscious, or
we should be tempted to say that the source of Blake's visions is
his own subconscious. But even a layman may talk of states of
mind. And there is much in the character of these visions to suggest that they come from a very passive state of mind when the
grip of the attention on the consciousness has been relaxed, as in
those border states between sleeping and waking familiar to all but
the most business-like of sleepers.

Blake believed, as we have seen, that all this was the work of
the creative imagination. But there is much in the foregoing to
raise some doubt of the accuracy of that description. The autom-
atism, the vagrancy, the confusion, even the waywardness of these
visions do not sound like the imagination. Neither does the extraordinary lack of anything like architectonics, especially in the longer
works. The fact that Blake never settled in his own mind the final
order of some of the pages of *Milton,* for instance, that the order of
Vala is by no means clear, and that in large sections of *Jerusalem*
there is no particular reason why one episode should precede another betrays a fundamental lack of the organic quality that is one
of the most essential marks of the work of the imagination. For
Blake's "creative imagination," even when dealing with what he
believed universals in human experience, tends to move outward in
its general progress rather than inward. It tends to go on discur-
sively from detail to detail rather than to sweep together and to
organize all details so as to arrive at a unifying solution of their
complexity. It puts more stress on force and intensity of expression than on formative shaping of its material. In other words, the
working of Blake's "creative imagination" savors more of the discursive fecundity of the fancy than of the shaping power of the imagination. Indeed, the most significant quality of Blake's imagination, in theory and in practice, is just this fact: that it is not so
much imagination as fancy, not so much the large centralizing of

the world of human experience as the supplementary creation of a world like yet alien.

This world of Blake's fancy is like our world in its substantiality, in the conception of its form and its movement. But it is very unlike our world in two important respects that have very much impressed students of Blake. The first is a matter of approach, of point of view, of way of looking at things, that has usually been somewhat roughly, but adequately enough, summed up in the word "wonder." And Blake's wonder has been distinguished from that of other men by the fact that Blake, in a large part of his work, and that the best known and most loved part, has dwelt upon the wonder of very little, and usually very commonplace, things that we pass by every day without any appreciation of how extraordinary they are. He once said to his friend and disciple, Richmond: "I can look at a knot in a piece of wood till I am frightened at it,"[9] and his latter-day disciples have rung all the possible changes on that sentence without saying very much about what it means. The looking at a piece of wood is of no intrinsic account, for obviously its meaning is entirely vicarious in that it is merely a step in the train of meditation or reverie that ensues. The Christian enthusiast like Richard Rolle of Hampole also could look at a piece of wood until his normal equilibrium was profoundly disturbed. But the piece of wood on which he gazed had been fashioned into a cross; consequently the ecstatic devotee brought to its contemplation a rich treasury of reflection and association, the story of the events that had led the centuries to invest two crossed sticks with so much meaning, the many-sided human personality of Him who to the devout fancy still hung there, the place which that scene that the wood could not fail to conjure up held in the Christian's view of the universe, and finally, its tremendous emotional and ethical implications for the life of the aspirant himself. In other words, as in the question of the ethical power of nature, the bare object, the rapt attention, are not sufficient. It is what the contemplative brings, and not the mere contemplation or the knot in the piece of wood in itself, that counts for meaning. Here, as in

[9] Quoted, Symons, *op. cit.*, p. 233.

the old Spanish proverb, "He that would bring home the wealth of the Indies must carry out the wealth of the Indies."

There is also another side to this famous power of Blake to find wonder in the common things of life. In some cases, as in the above, the wonder comes from an importation of meaning. But the same result may be obtained from the reverse process. We understand the world around us in our ordinary sense of knowing enough about it to use it for everyday practical purposes because we have unconsciously built up around the simplest object a body of associations which tell us what we may expect of that object and what its relations to the rest of the world are for our ordinary purposes. Usually these associations become so firmly entangled about the object that we never see the latter for itself. Our immediate impression, and this seems to become increasingly true as we grow older and the ruts of habit are worn deeper, comes to consist entirely of just these associations. It is not surprising, therefore, that when in some way the old association-incrusted object is suddenly divested of its well-known meanings it becomes at once an object of wonder, something new and startling which teases us by its unwonted detachment from the context of our ordinary expectations. Especially is this true of the wonder of the child's vision, of which we have been hearing so much for the last century. Blake lamented that man as he grew up ceased to be able to see everything as when a child. It is a favorite lament of the victims of infantile nostalgia. But the trouble is not that the man sees less than the child, but that he sees so much more.

And therein lies the charm of the thing. For the child's vision is simpler, clearer, less complicated by the thousand and one impingements of larger areas of experience that forever perplex the grown-up's enjoyment of the world as it is. And the more harassed the grown-up, the wearier he be of the multitudinous claims of mature reality, the more grateful he will be for the relief and the consequent refreshment of the child's vision. That is not the whole story of the popularity which Blake's *Songs of Innocence and of Experience* have enjoyed, but it is certainly the major part of it. And there is no reason why we should not so solace and refresh ourselves when this vision is presented by such a master in this field as Blake.

But we must remember that we are committed to meanings by long habit, and that we are apt to satisfy the stimulus of our wonder by meanings which may or may not be relevant. Again, there is no reason why we should not; but we must not lose sight of the fact that it is not the presence of subtler and profounder meanings that is stimulating us, but their absence; that wonder such as this is perfectly adequate to give us the delight of a holiday and a fresh glimpse of a simpler world in which we, too, once sojourned, but that it has nothing to do with meaning, especially in any meaning-laden undertaking like the "Prophetic Books."

The second way in which the world of Blake's fancy is unlike our world is in the aura that invests it, an aura not to be defined in terms of meaning, hardly in terms of feeling. It is best studied in some of Blake's drawings and paintings, perhaps best of all in a woodcut which Blake made to illustrate Dr. Thornton's edition of Vergil's *Pastorals*. It is a tiny thing representing a single blasted tree on a desolate heath, but it suggests amazingly size and power, with an intensity that comes from the very cramped meagerness of space with which it secures its effect. Much the same thing is true of the famous watercolor of the "Plague," in which the plague is represented by a gigantic green monster striding through the darkness of a stricken city with dusty hands that one feels instinctively must be scattering death on the fetid air; this is a good example of a large part of Blake's work that is apt to draw from the unreflecting observer some reaction like: "What a supernatural thing it is!" Probably this type of effect is more easily secured in drawing or painting than in poetry. But something is due to the matter of technique. This does not by any means require perfection of technique, but it does require clarity, simplicity, and compression if the peculiar sense of intense and strange power is to be communicated. Blake gets it in some of his simpler earlier poems, as in that famous quatrain from the "Auguries of Innocence" which everyone knows:

> To see a World in a grain of sand,
> And a Heaven in a wild flower,
> Hold Infinity in the palm of your hand,
> And Eternity in an hour.

But it is very difficult to get such an effect as this in long poems so deficient in lucidity, in wholeness, in vitality, and in beauty—in all the essentials of great literature and great art—as the "Prophetic Books." It is only in passages of rare energy and magnificence that one there finds this characteristic quality of Blake's fancy, and then it is almost lost in the obscurity and involution of the context. Emphatically, the "Prophetic Books" are not the place to seek Blake's visionary qualities at their best and most artistically effective.

After all, much as we want a prophet for this modern world of ours, both to help us in our need and to send us forward in our strength, to gather up what we have discovered and to carry it forward into the Promised Land which we believe we are working toward, we must admit that William Blake is not the man. It is hard to reject a prophet who comes in so many ways in such a congenial guise—poor, hard-working, a fresh and original genius, a rebel against a time which we, too, until quite recently, have disliked, a forerunner of some of our choicest intellectual developments, and the author of a series of works in both literature and painting, the very deficiencies of which are not unpleasing to our predilections. But he is not a great mystic in any sense that means anything; he is a prophet, interesting and suggestive, but very imperfect and incomplete. And as a visionary his real power is not to be sought in the works by which he himself set most store, but in the lyrics of his early manhood and in his pictorial art.

Here the instinct of the intelligent and discriminating general reader is sounder than that of the specialist. The consolation that the specialist may take in labors arduous and obscure is that, though so far as the great prophet of our modern age is concerned, "we look for another," yet when that other comes, if he have the curiosity and the passion for learning that seem to mark the great teachers of men, he will find abundant lessoning in the incomplete prophecies and the imperfect vision of William Blake.

BIBLIOGRAPHY

BLAKE'S WORK

The Works of William Blake, Poetic, Symbolic, and Critical. Edited, with lithographs of the illustrated "Prophetic Books" and a memoir and interpretation, by Edwin J. Ellis and William Butler Yeats. 3 vols., London, 1893.
The Writings of William Blake. Edited by Geoffrey Keynes. 3 vols., London, 1925.
Poetical Works of William Blake. Edited, with an introduction and textual notes, by John Sampson. London, etc., 1914.
Jerusalem. Edited by E. R. D. Maclagan and A. G. B. Russell. London, 1904.
Milton. Edited by E. R. D. Maclagan and A. G. B. Russell. London, 1907.
Vala. Edited by Ellis and Yeats, *op. cit.*, Vol. III.
The Paintings of William Blake. Darrell Figgis. New York, 1925.
The Letters of William Blake. Edited by A. G. B. Russell. London, 1906.

BOOKS ON BLAKE

BABBITT, IRVING. *Rousseau and Romanticism.* Boston and New York, 1919.
BABENROTH, A. CHARLES. "William Blake," *English Childhood* (New York, 1922), pp. 262–98.
BASSALIK-DE VRIES, J. C. E. *William Blake in His Relation to Dante Gabriel Rossetti.* Basel, 1911.
BEECHING, H. C. "Blake's Religious Lyrics," in *Essays and Studies by members of the English Association,* III (Oxford, 1912), 136–52.
BÉNOIT, FRANÇOIS. *Un maître de l'art, Blake, le visionnaire.* Lille et Paris, 1907.
BENSON, ARTHUR CHRISTOPHER. "William Blake," *Essays* (New York, 1896), pp. 147–79.

246

BERGER, PAUL. *William Blake, Poet and Mystic*. Translated from the French by Daniel H. Conner. London, 1914.

BINYON, LAURENCE. *Introduction to Illustrations of the Book of Job*. London, 1906.

BRUCE, HAROLD. *William Blake in this World*. New York, 1925.

BUTTERWORTH, ADELINE. *William Blake, Mystic*. Liverpool and London, 1911.

CHESTERTON, G. K. *William Blake*. London, 1910.

COX, KENYON. *Old Masters and New*. New York, 1905.

DAMON, S. FOSTER. *William Blake: His Philosophy and Symbols*. Boston and New York, 1924.

DE SÉLINCOURT, BASIL. *William Blake*. London and New York, 1911.

ELLIS, EDWIN J. *The Real Blake*. London, 1907.

ELLIS, EDWIN J., and YEATS, WILLIAM BUTLER. *The Works of William Blake, Poetic, Symbolic, and Critical*. 3 vols., London, 1893.

FIGGIS, DARRELL. *The Paintings of William Blake*. New York, 1925.

GARDNER, CHARLES. *Vision and Vesture: A Study of William Blake in Modern Thought*. London, 1916.

GARDNER, CHARLES. *William Blake the Man*. London, 1919.

GARNETT, RICHARD. *William Blake: Painter and Poet*. London, 1895.

GILCHRIST, ALEXANDER. *Life of William Blake, "pictor ignotus."* 2 vols., London and Cambridge, 1863.

GOSSE, EDMUND. "Blake and Gray," *More Books on the Table* (New York, 1923), pp. 341–50.

GRIERSON, H. C. *Introduction to William Blake's Designs for Gray's Poems*. London, 1922.

HOUSMAN, LAURENCE. *Introductory Essay to Selections from the Writings of William Blake*. London, 1893.

HUNEKER, JAMES G. *Egoists: A Book of Supermen* (New York, 1909), pp. 277–90.

IRELAND, WILLIAM W. *Through the Ivory Gate* (Edinburgh, etc., 1889), pp. 130–34.

KRANS, HORATIO S. *William Butler Yeats and the Irish Literary Revival* (New York, 1904), pp. 175–83.

LAMB, CHARLES, and MARY. "Letters," *Works*, edited by E. V. Lucas (New York and London, 1905), VII, 642.

LANGRIDGE, IRENE. *William Blake: A Study of His Life and Art Work*. London, 1904.

MALKIN, BENJAMIN HEATH. *A Father's Memoirs of His Child* (London, 1806), pp. xviii–xl.

MILSAND, JOSEPH. *Littérature anglaise et philosophie* (Dijon, 1893), pp. 305–46.

MOORE, T. STURGE. *Art and Life*. London, 1915.

MORE, PAUL ELMER. *Shelburne Essays* (4th Series; New York and London, 1906), pp. 212–38.

MORRIS, H. N. *Flaxman, Blake, Coleridge, and Other Men of Genius Influenced by Swedenborg* (London, 1915), pp. 75–104.

NEWTON, A. EDWARD. *A Magnificent Farce and Other Diversions of a Book Collector* (Boston, 1921), pp. 196–221.

NICOLL, ALLARDYCE. *William Blake and His Poetry*. London, 1922.

POWYS, JOHN COWPER. *Suspended Judgments* (New York, 1916), pp. 257–75.

RALEIGH, WALTER. *Introduction to the Lyrical Poems of William Blake*. Text by John Sampson. Oxford, 1905.

RICHTER, HELENE. *William Blake*. Strassburg, 1906.

ROBINSON, HENRY CRABB. *Blake, Coleridge, Wordsworth, Lamb, etc.: Being Selections from the Remains of H. C. R.*, edited by Edith J. Morley. Manchester, etc., 1922.

ROSSETTI, WILLIAM MICHAEL. *Prefatory Memoir to the Poetical Works of William Blake, Lyrical and Miscellaneous*. London, 1874.

RUSSELL, ARCHIBALD G. B. *Introduction to the Letters of William Blake*. London, 1906.

RUSSELL, ARCHIBALD G. B. *The Engravings of William Blake*. London, 1912.

SAINTSBURY, GEORGE E. B. *History of Criticism*. 3 vols. (Edinburgh and London, 1900–1904), III, 266–69.

SAURAT, DENIS. *Blake and Milton*. Bordeaux, 1920.

SECCOMBE, THOMAS. *Preface to "Songs of Innocence."* London, 1911.

SHEPERD, R. A. *Introduction to the Poems of William Blake.* London, 1874.

SKIPSEY, JOSEPH. *Prefatory Notice, Biographical and Critical, to the Poems of William Blake.* London, 1885.

SMETHAM, JAMES. *Literary Works,* edited by William Davies (London and New York, 1893), pp. 98–194.

STOKES, FRANCIS GRIFFIN. *Introduction to the "Marriage of Heaven and Hell" and "A Song of Liberty."* London and New York, 1911.

STORY, ALFRED T. *William Blake: His Life, Character and Genius.* London, 1893.

STRACHEY, LYTTON. *Books and Characters, French and English* (New York, 1922), pp. 219–33.

SWINBURNE, ALGERNON CHARLES. *William Blake: A Critical Essay.* London, 1868.

SYMONS, ARTHUR. *William Blake.* New York, 1907.

TATHAM, FREDERICK. *The Life of William Blake.* Printed with *Letters of William Blake,* edited by Archibald G. B. Russell. London, 1906.

THOMSON, JAMES. *Biographical and Critical Studies* (London, 1896), pp. 240–69.

TIMBS, JOHN. *English Eccentrics and Eccentricities* (London, 1877), pp. 338–50.

VON TAUBE, OTTO. *William Blake, der Ethick der Fruchtbarkeit. Zusammengestellt aus seinem Werke und Aufzeichungen übersetzt und eingeleitet.* Jena, 1907.

WALLIS, J. P. R. "Blake," *The Cambridge History of English Literature* (New York and Cambridge, England, 1914), XI, 200–223.

WICKSTEED, JOSEPH H. *Blake's Vision of the Book of Job.* London and New York, 1910.

WILKINSON, GARTH. *Introduction to "Songs of Innocence" and "Experience."* London, 1839.

YEATS, WILLIAM. BUTLER. *Ideas of Good and Evil* (New York, 1903), pp. 168–225.

PERIODICALS (SIGNED ARTICLES)

BINYON, LAURENCE. "The Art of Blake," *Living Age,* CCXLI (May, 1904), 487–92.

BINYON, LAURENCE. "Blake's Work as a Painter," *Putnam's Monthly,* III (January, 1908), 410–17.

BINYON, LAURENCE. "Blake and Van Gogh," *London Times Literary Supplement,* No. 1091 (December 14, 1922), 829–30.

BROWN, A. R. "Letter on Blake Plates," *Literary Review,* III (July, 1923), 822.

BRUCE, HAROLD. "William Blake and His Companions from 1818 to 1827," *Publications of the Modern Language Association,* XXXIX (June, 1924), 358–67.

CARR, J. COMYNS. "William Blake," *Living Age,* CXXVI (July, 1875), 67–77.

CARR, J. COMYNS. "William Blake," *Belgravia,* XXIX (May, 1876), 366–79.

CARY, E. L. "William Blake as an Illustrator," *Critic,* XLVI (March, 1905), 214–16.

CHASE, LEWIS NATHANIEL. "The Fame of William Blake," *South Atlantic Quarterly,* VII (January, 1908), 93–99.

CLARK, THOMAS M. "William Blake, Painter and Poet," *Old and New,* VII (January, 1873), 67–82.

CLUTTON-BROCK, A. "The Poetry of William Blake," *Living Age,* CCLI (December, 1906), 809–13.

COLLINS, JOSEPH. "Sanity of William Blake," *Bookman,* LXI (July, 1925), 553–55.

CONWAY, MONCURE D. "Critical Notice of Swinburne's *William Blake,*" *Fortnightly Review,* IX (February, 1868), 216–20.

COX, K. "Review of Story's *William Blake,*" *Nation,* LVII (November, 1893), 376.

DAMON, S. FOSTER. "William Blake," *The Freeman,* VI (January, 1923), 491–92.

DE SÉLINCOURT, BASIL. "Parallelism of Religion and Art: A Comment on William Blake," *Hibbert Journal*, V (January, 1907), 397–406.

DODGE, MARY ABIGAIL. "Pictor ignotus," *Atlantic Monthly*, XIII (April, 1864), 433–47.

DOIN, JEANNE. "William Blake," *Gazette des Beaux Arts*, Ser. 4, VII (1912), 113–30.

EGLINTON, GUY C. "Blake Illustrates Gray," *International Studio*, LXXIX (April, 1924), 39–47.

EGLINTON, GUY C. "Dante Alighieri and Blake," *International Studio*, XXC (December, 1924), 239–48.

EVANS, E. P. "William Blake, Poet and Painter," *Hours at Home*, I (May, 1870), 55–65.

FEHR, B. "William Blake und die Kabbala," *Englische Studien*, LIV (1920), 139–48.

FICKE, ARTHUR DAVISON. "A Divine Visionary," *Dial*, LIX (October, 1915), 323–25.

FLETCHER, JOHN GOULD. "Yale Discovers Blake," *Poetry*, IX (March, 1917), 315–20.

FLETCHER, J. G. "William Blake," *North American*, CCXVIII (October, 1923), 518–28.

GILLET, L. "Le cas de William Blake," *Revue des Deux Mondes*, Ser. 7, XVI (July, 1923), 195–206.

GOOKIN, FREDERICK W. "The New Books on William Blake," *Dial*, XLV (July, 1908), 34–36.

GUTHRIE, WILLIAM NORMAN. "William Blake: Mystic," *Sewanee Review*, V (January, 1897), 328–48.

GUTHRIE, W. N. "William Blake: Poet and Artist," *Sewanee Review*, V (October, 1897), 438–47.

HARPER, GEORGE MCLEAN. "Review of Professor Pierce's *Selections from the Symbolical Poems of William Blake*," *Yale Review*, New Series, V (April, 1916), 633–35.

HEWLETT, HENRY G. "Imperfect Genius: William Blake," Part I, *Contemporary Review*, XXVIII (October, 1876), 756–84.

HEWLETT, HENRY G. "Imperfect Genius: William Blake," Part II, *Contemporary Review*, XXIX (January, 1877), 207–28.

HOOD, THURMAN LOS. "An Allusion to Blake," *Nation*, XCIII (September, 1911), 240.

Housman, Laurence. "Blake as an impressionist," *Universal Review*, VI (1890), 209.

Ives, Herbert. "William Blake as a Teacher," *Fortnightly Review*, XCIII (March, 1910), 569–74.

Ives, Herbert. "Trial of William Blake for High Treason," *Nineteenth Century and After*, LXVII (May, 1910), 849–61.

Ivins, William M. "The Blake Exhibition at the Grolier Club," *Arts and Decorations*, XII (January, 1920), 183.

Jenkins, Herbert. "The Grave of William Blake," *Nineteenth Century and After*, LXX (July, 1911), 163–69.

Johnson, Lionel. "Blake's Works," *Academy*, XLIV (August, 1893), 163–65.

Keeble, S. E. "Imagination and William Blake," *London Quarterly Review*, CCXXVII (April, 1917), 215–27.

Lehr, Marie C. "Notice of Blake Exhibition," *International Studio*, LXIX (December, 1919), 2–4.

Moore, T. Sturge. "William Blake: Poet and Painter," *Quarterly Review*, CCVIII (January, 1908), 24–53.

Morris, Lloyd R. "William Blake, the First of the Moderns," *Forum*, LI (June, 1914), 932–39.

Mullin, Glen H. "Blake and the Poet, Gray," *Literary Review of the New York Evening Post*, III (September 16, 1922), 22.

Norton, E. E. "Blake's Songs and Poetical Sketches," *North American Review*, CVIII (April, 1869), 641–46.

Nutt, T. "Lord Crewe's Blake Collection," *Critic*, XLII (May, 1903), 463–64.

Paton, Lucy Allen. "Romanticism of William Blake," *Poet Lore*, V (October, 1893), 481–88.

Pierce, F. E. "Blake and Seventeenth-Century Authors," *Modern Language Notes*, XXXIX (March, 1924), 150–53.

Rae, W. F. "The Life and Works of William Blake," *Fine Arts Quarterly Review*, III (October, 1864), 56–79.

Roberts, Richard. "The Ethics of William Blake," *Hibbert Journal*, XVII (April, 1919), 660–71.

Scott, William B. "A Varley-and-Blake Sketchbook," *Portfolio*, II (1871), 103.

SCUDDER, H. E. "The Genius of William Blake," *North American Review*, XCIX (October, 1864), 465–82.

SHERWOOD, MARGARET. "William Blake and Catharine," *North American Review*, CCII (October, 1915), 576–91.

SMETHAM, JAMES. "The Life of William Blake," *London Quarterly Review*, XXXI (January, 1869), 265–311.

SMITH, HENRY JUSTIN. "The Poetry of William Blake," *Century Magazine*, XXXVIII (June, 1900), 284–91.

SPURGEON, CAROLINE F. E. "Mysticism in English Poetry," *Quarterly Review*, CCVII (October, 1907), 427–59.

STANDING, PERCY CROSS. "Was Blake a Poet?," *Catholic World*, XXCI (July, 1905), 445–50.

STATHAM, H. H. "The Blake Drawings at the Burlington Fine Arts Club," *MacMillan's Magazine*, XXXIV (May, 1876), 55–68.

STEDMAN, EDMUND C. "William Blake: Poet and Painter," *Critic*, I (January, 1881), 3.

VAN RENSSELAER, M. G. "The Works of William Blake," *American Architect and Building News*, VIII (October, 1880), 215.

WEDMORE, FREDERICK. "William Blake," *Living Age*, CXLIX (May, 1881), 557–63.

YEATS, WILLIAM BUTLER. "William Blake and His Illustrations to the *Divine Comedy*," *Savoy*, III (July, 1896), 41.

PERIODICALS (UNSIGNED ARTICLES)

Academy, LXI (July, 1901), 15–16. "The Poetry of William Blake."

Athenaeum, II (July, 1904), 102–3. Review of Maclagan and Russell's edition of *Jerusalem*.

Blackwood's Edinburgh Magazine, XCVII (March, 1865), 291–307. "William Blake."

Contemporary Review, Literary Supplement, CV (May, 1914), 745–50. "The Poems of William Blake."

Current Literature, XXXII (January, 1902), 111. "The Poetry of William Blake."

Current Literature, XLII (February, 1907), 169–73. "The Simple and Fantastic Genius of Blake."

Current Literature, XLIII (December, 1907), 646–47. "William Blake as the Pontiff of a New Spiritual Dispensation."

Current Literature, XLIX (September, 1910), 325–29. "The Vital Import of Aesthetics as Illustrated by Flaubert and Blake."

Current Literature, LXVIII (February, 1920), 227–28. "The Ethics of William Blake Applied to Our Own Time."

Current Opinion, LXXVII (September, 1924), 350–51. "Ranking Blake with Shakespeare."

Eclectic and Congregational Review, CXIX (April, 1864), 373–91. "William Blake."

Eclectic Magazine, XXCIV (March, 1875), 372–76. "William Blake's Poems."

Edinburgh Review, CCIII (January, 1906), 171–79. "The Visionary Art of William Blake."

Gentleman's Magazine, New Series, LII (April, 1894), 429. Article on Blake.

Literary Digest, LVI (January 12, 1913), 25–26. Article on Blake's Art.

Literary Digest, XXCII (August 2, 1924), 31–32. "England's Glory in Blake."

Living Age, LXXVII (December, 1863), 579–83. "William Blake, the Painter."

Living Age, CCCXII (January, 1922), 102–6. "Poetry of William Blake."

London Quarterly, III (1868), 265–311. Article on Blake.

Nation, LXXV (November, 1902), 427. Notice of facsimile copy of Blake's illustrations of the *Book of Job*.

Nation, XXCV (September, 1907), 286–87. Review of Symons' *William Blake*.

Nation, XXCV (October, 1907), 401. Review of E. J. Ellis's *The Real Blake*.

Le Navire d'Argent, Numéro consacré à William Blake (Septembre, 1925).

Outlook, XXCVII (October, 1907), 307–8. Review of Symons' *William Blake*.

Penn Monthly, VII (November, 1876), 843–52. "The Poetry of the *pictor ignotus*."

Quarterly Review, CXVII (January, 1865), 1–27. Review of Gilchrist's *Life of Blake.*

Quarterly Review, CCXI (October, 1909), 415–17. "The Earliest English Illustrations of Dante."

Saturday Review, LXXV (February, 1893), 126–27. Review of Ellis and Yeats' *Works of William Blake.*

Scribner's Monthly, XX (June, 1880), 225–40. Article on Blake's Art.

Spectator, LV (October, 1882), 1351–52. Review of new edition of Gilchrist's *Life of Blake.*

Spectator, CXI (November, 1913), 715–16. "Notice of Blake Exhibition at Royal Academy."

Spectator, CXII (April, 1914), 567. "The Poetry of Blake."

Spectator, CXIV (April, 1915), 566–67. Review of Berger's *William Blake.*

Spectator, CXVI (May, 1916), 571. "William Blake's Homes in Lambeth and Sussex."

Temple Bar, XVII (July, 1866), 95–105. "William Blake: Seer and Painter."

Times Literary Supplement (London), No. 1037 (December 1, 1921), pp. 777–78. "The Poetry of Blake."

Times Literary Supplement (London), No. 1050 (March 2, 1922), p. 138. Review of Geoffrey Keynes' *Bibliography of William Blake.*

Times Literary Supplement (London), No. 1053 (March 23, 1922), p. 195. "Letter from John Sampson on a Manuscript Poem Attributed to Blake."

Times Literary Supplement (London), No. 1072 (August 3, 1922), p. 510. Review of Allardyce Nicoll's *William Blake and His Poetry.*

Times Literary Supplement (London), No. 1237 (October 3, 1925), pp. 645–66. "The Complete Blake."

MYSTICISM, GENERAL DISCUSSION

BENNETT, CHARLES. *A Philosophical Study of Mysticism.* New Haven, 1923.

BESANT, ANNIE. *Mysticism*. London, 1914.

BURR, ANNA ROBESON. *Religious Confessions and Confessants*. Boston and New York, 1914.

DAWKINS, MURIEL BACHELER. "Mysticism: An Epistemological Problem" (Dissertation Yale University).

GORDON, RUTH M. "Has Mysticism a Moral Value?" *International Journal of Ethics*, XXI (October, 1920), 66–83.

HODGSON, GERALDINE E. *English Mystics*. London, 1922.

INGE, WILLIAM RALPH. *Christian Mysticism*. London, 1899.

JAMES, WILLIAM. *The Varieties of Religious Experience: A Study in Human Nature*. London, 1903.

JONES, RUFUS M. "The Mystic's Experience of God," *Atlantic Monthly*, CXXVIII (November, 1921), 637–45.

JONES, RUFUS M. *Studies in Mystical Religion*. London, 1909.

KAPLAN, JACOB A. *A Study of the Prophetic Mind as Manifested by the Ancient Hebrew Prophets*. Philadelphia, 1909.

LEUBA, JAMES H. *The Psychology of Religious Mysticism*. New York, 1925.

MILLER, H. CRICHTON. *The New Psychology and the Preacher*. New York, 1924.

NORDAU, MAX. "Mysticism," *Degeneration* (New York, 1896), pp. 44–240.

OTTO, RUDOLF. *The Idea of the Holy*. Translated by John W. Harvey. London, 1923.

ROYCE, JOSIAH. *The World and the Individual*. New York, 1920.

SHARPE, A. B. *Mysticism: Its True Nature and Value*. London, 1910.

SILBERER, HERBERT. *Problems of Mysticism and Its Symbolism*. Translated by Smith Ely Jelliffe. New York, 1917.

UNDERHILL, EVELYN. *The Essentials of Mysticism and Other Essays*. London and Toronto, 1920.

UNDERHILL, EVELYN. *Mysticism—A Study in the Nature and Development of Man's Spiritual Consciousness*. London, 1912.

UNDERHILL, EVELYN. *The Mystic Way*. London, 1913.

MYSTICS AND MYSTICAL WORKS
ORIENTAL—PRIMARY

Bhagavad-Gita. Translated by Charles Johnston. Flushing, New York, 1908.

Buddhism in Translations. Henry Clarke Warren ("Harvard Oriental Series," Vol. III). Cambridge, 1896.

Céna Upanishad. Translated by Rammohun Roy. Calcutta, 1816.

Dhammapada. Translated by F. Max Müller ("Sacred Books of the East," Vol. X). Oxford, 1881.

From the Upanishads. Charles Johnston. Portland, Maine, 1899.

Kuth-Oopunishud. Translated by Rammohun Roy. Undated.

Sutta-Nipata. Translated by V. Fausböli ("Sacred Books of the East," Vol. X). Oxford, 1881.

Texts of Taoism. Translated by James Legge ("Sacred Books of the East," Vol. XXXIX). Oxford, 1891.

Upanishads. Translated by F. Max Müller ("Sacred Books of the East," Vol. I). Oxford, 1879.

Upanishads. Translated by F. Max Müller ("Sacred Books of the East," Vol. XV). Oxford, 1884.

Vedantasara: A Manual of Hindu Pantheism. Translated by G. A. Jacob. Boston, 1881.

Vedanta-Sutras, with Sankara's Commentary. Translated by George Thibaut ("Sacred Books of the East," Vol. XXXIV). Oxford, 1890.

ORIENTAL—SECONDARY

DAVIDS, W. RHYS. "Nirvana," *Contemporary Review*, XXIX (January, 1877), 248–70.

DEUSSEN, PAUL. *Outlines of Indian Philosophy*. Berlin, 1907.

DEUSSEN, PAUL. *Religion and Philosophy of India—The Philosophy of the Upanishads*. Translated by A. S. Geden. Edinburgh, 1906.

DEUSSEN, PAUL. *Outline of the Vedanta System of Philosophy according to Shankara*. Translated by J. H. Woods and C. B. Runkle. Cambridge, Mass., and New York, 1906.

DUTT, ROMESH CHUNDER. *A History of Civilization in Ancient India*. London, 1893.

MORE, PAUL ELMER. "The Forest Philosophy of India" and "The Bhagavad-Gita," Studies of Religious Dualism ("Shelburne Essays," 6th Series). New York and London, 1909.

MÜLLER, F. MAX. Lecture on "Buddhist Nihilism," Lectures on the Science of Religion. New York, 1874.

MÜLLER, F. MAX. Three Lectures on Vendanta Philosophy. London, 1904.

ROLLAND, ROMAIN. Mahatma Gandhi. Translated by Catherine D. Groth. New York, 1924.

SWÂMI VIVEKÂNANDA. Lectures Delivered in New York, Winter of 1895–96, on Râja Yoga, with Patanjali's Yoga Aphorisms. London, 1897.

JEWISH

Bible (Ezekiel, Hosea, Isaiah, Song of Solomon).

JOACHIM, HAROLD H. A Study of the Ethics of Spinoza. Oxford, 1901.

Kabbala Denudata. Translated by S. L. MacGregor Mathers. London, 1887.

SPINOZA. "De intellectus emendatione—ethica," The Chief Works, translated by R. H. M. Elwes. (London, 1891), Vol. II.

The Sword of Moses: An Ancient Book of Magic. Translated by M. Gaster. London, 1896.

GREEK—PRIMARY

Hermetica: The Ancient Greek and Latin Writings which Contain Religious or Philosophic Teachings Ascribed to Hermes Trismegistus. Translated by Walter Scott. Oxford, 1924.

PHILO JUDAEUS. Works. Translated by C. D. Yonge. (London, 1855), Vol. IV.

PLATO. Dialogues. Translated by B. Jowett. 5 vols. Oxford, 1892.

PLOTINOS. Complete Works. Translated by Kenneth Sylvan Guthrie. 4 vols. London, 1918.

GREEK—SECONDARY

GARDNER, PERCY. A Manual of Greek Antiquities. London, 1895.

INGE, WILLIAM RALPH. The Philosophy of Plotinus. London, 1918.

MORE, PAUL ELMER. Platonism. Princeton, 1917.

PERSIAN—PRIMARY

AL-GHAZZALI. *Confessions.* Translated by Claud Field. London, 1909.

HAFIZ OF SHIRAZ. Selections from his *Poems.* Translated by Herman Bicknell. London, 1875.

HAFIZ. *The Rubaiyat.* Translated by Syed Abdul Majid; rendered into English verse by L. Cranmer-Byng. London, 1912.

HAFIZ, Versions from, by Walter Leaf. London, 1898.

Jalalu'd-Din-Rumi. Translated by T. Hadland Davis ("The Persian Mystics," Vol. I). London, 1912.

Jami. Translated by F. Hadland Davis ("The Persian Mystics," Vol. II). London, 1908.

SADI. *The Bustan.* Translated by A. Hart Edwards. London, 1911.

SADI. *The Gulistan, or Rose Garden.* Translated by Edward B. Eastwick. London, 1880.

SADI. *Scroll of Wisdom.* Translated by Arthur N. Wollaston. London, 1906.

CHRISTIAN—PRIMARY

ANGELUS SILESIUS. *A Selection from the Rhymes of a German Mystic.* Translated by Paul Carus. Chicago, 1909.

ST. AUGUSTINE. *The City of God.* Translated by John Healey. London, 1903.

ST. AUGUSTINE. *Confessions.* Translated by William Watts (1631). 2 vols. London, 1912.

BEHMEN, JACOB. *Works.* Translated by William Law. 4 vols., London, 1764.

ST. BERNARD (OF CLAIRVAUX). *Life and Works.* Edited by Dom. John Mabillon; translated and edited by Samuel J. Eales. 4 vols. London, 1896.

Bible (the Fourth Gospel, the Epistles of St. Paul, Revelation).

ST. BONAVENTURA. *The Goad of Divine Love.* Translated by B. Lewis Augustine, 1642. London, 1906.

ST. BONAVENTURA. *Bonaventura. Itinerarium mentis in deum.* Operum tomus septimus. Lugduni, 1668.

ST. BONAVENTURA. *Bonaventura. De septem itineribus aeternitatis.* Operum tomus septimus. Lugduni, 1668.

ST. BONAVENTURA. *Bonaventura. Meditations on the Supper of Our Lord, and the Hours of the Passion.* Drawn into English verse, Robert Manning of Brunne, London, 1875.

BUNYAN, JOHN. *The Pilgrim's Progress; Grace Abounding,* etc. Oxford, 1879.

ST. CATHERINE OF SIENA. *As Seen in Her Letters.* Translated and edited by Vida D. Scudder. London, 1905.

CATHERINE OF SIENNA. *Dialogue, Dictated by Her While in a State of Ecstasy, to Her Secretaries.* Translated by Algar Thorold. London, 1907.

DANTE ALIGHIERI. *The Divine Comedy; Paradise.* Translated by Charles Eliot Norton. Cambridge, 1902.

DIONYSIUS THE AREOPAGITE. *The Mystical Theology,* and the *Letters to Caius and Dorotheus.* Translated by A. B. Sharpe (*Mysticism: Its True Nature and Value*). London, 1910.

MEISTER ECKHART. *Mystische Schriften.* Übertragen von Gustav Landauer. Berlin, 1903.

ECKARTSHAUSEN. *Mistische Nächte.* München, 1791.

ERIGENA, JOHANNES SCOTUS. *Über die Eintheilung der Natur.* Übersetzt von Ludwig Noack. Berlin, 1870.

FOX, GEORGE. *Journal.* Philadelphia, no date.

GERSON, JOHN. *Opera omnia,* tom. III, pars II, "opera mystica et pia." Antwerpiae, 1706.

GUYON, MADAME. *Les Opuscules Spirituels,* tom. I. Paris, 1790.

GUYON, JEANNE MARIE BOUVIERES DE LA MOTHE. *La vie, écrite par elle-même.* 3 vols. Paris, 1791.

HUGO PARISIENSIS (DE SANCTO VICTORE). *De modo diciendi et meditandi* (Martine et Durand: *Thesaurus Novus Anecdotorum,* Vol. V). Lutetiae Parisiorium, 1717.

ST. IGNATIUS LOYOLA. *Manresa, or the Spiritual Exercises.* New York and Cincinnati, 1914.

ST. JOHN OF THE CROSS. *Complete Works.* Translated by David Lewis. 2 vols. London, 1864.

JULIAN OF NORWICH. *Revelations of Divine Love* (1373). Edited by Grace Warrack. London, 1901.

THOMAS À KEMPIS. *The Imitation of Christ.* Translated by William Benham ("The Harvard Classics," Vol. VII). New York, 1909.

LAW, WILLIAM. "The Grounds and Reasons of Christian Regeneration," *Works* (London, 1778), Vol. V.

LAW, WILLIAM. "The Spirit of Prayer," *Works* (London, 1778), Vol. VII; Part I, 1762; Part II, 1777.

LAW, WILLIAM. "The Way to Divine Knowledge," *Works* (London, 1778), Vol. VII.

S. MECHTHILDIS. *Revelationes selectae,* ("Bibliotheca mystica et ascetica, Vol. X). Coloniae, 1854.

MOLINOS, MICHAEL DE. *The Spiritual Guide.* Translated from Italian copy, Venice, 1685. London, 1688.

MORE, HENRY. *Divine Dialogues.* 2 vols. London, 1668.

MORE, HENRY. *A Brief Discourse of the True Grounds of the Certainty of Faith in Points of Religion.* London, 1713.

MORE, HENRY. *Complete Poems.* Edited by Alexander B. Grosart. Edinburgh University Press, 1878.

PARACELSUS. *The Hermetic and Alchemical Writings,* edited by Arthur Edward Waite. 2 vols. London, 1894.

PARACELSUS. "Liber paramirum," *Oeuvres complètes,* translated by Grillot de Givry (Paris, 1913), Vol. I.

PARACELSUS. *Of the supreme mysteries of nature, etc.* Translated by R. Turner. London, 1655.

PORDAGE, JOHN. *Theologia mystica, or The Mystic Divinitie of the Aeternal Invisibles.* London, 1683.

PORDAGE, JOHN. *A Treatise of Eternal Nature with Her Seven Essential Forms.* London, 1681.

RICHARD ROLLE OF HAMPOLE. *An English Father of the Church and His Followers.* Edited by C. Horstman. 2 vols. London, 1895.

RICARDUS SANCTI VICTORIS. *Omnia opera.* Lugduni, 1534.

RUYSBROECK, JOHN OF. *The Adornment of the Spiritual Marriage, The Sparkling Stone, The Book of Supreme Truth.* Translated by Dom. C. A. Wynschenk. London, 1916.

Suso, Henri. *Oeuvres*. Translated by M. E. Cartier. Paris, 1852.

Swedenborg, Emanuel. *Arcana Coelestia (The Heavenly Arcana Contained in the Holy Scriptures or Word of the Lord Unfolded)*. New York, 1870.

Swedenborg, Emanuel. *Conjugal Love and Its Chaste Delights; also Adulterous Love and Its Sinful Pleasures*. New York, 1871.

Swedenborg, Emanuel. *Heaven and Its Wonders, the World of Spirits and Hell: From Things Heard and Seen*. Translated by Samuel Noble. New York, 1872.

Swedenborg, Emanuel. *Of the New Jerusalem and Its Heavenly Doctrine, as Revealed from Heaven*. Boston, 1829.

Swedenborg, Emanuel. *The True Christian Religion, containing The Universal Theology of the New Church, Foretold by the Lord*. New York, 1912.

Swedenborg, Emanuel. *New Jerusalem Tracts—Selections from the Writings of Swedenborg* (Boston, 1830), Vol. I.

Tauler, John. *History and Life with Twenty-five of His Sermons*. Translated by Susanna Winkworth. London, 1857.

St. Teresa. *The Interior Castle or the Mansions*. Translated by the Benedictines of Stanbrook. London, 1912.

Woolman, John. *Journal*. Philadelphia, no date.

CHRISTIAN—SECONDARY

Bailey, Margaret L. *Milton and Jakob Boehme*. New York, 1914.

Campagnac, E. T. *Introduction to the Cambridge Platonists*. Oxford, 1901.

Cheever, Henry T. *Correspondencies of Faith and Views of Madame Guyon*. London, 1887.

Delaporte, Le P. A. *Étude sur l'itineraire de l'ame à Dieu de Saint Bonaventure*. Paris, 1863.

Fournier, Paul. *Études sur Joachim de Flore et ses doctrines*. Paris, 1909.

Gardner, Alice. *Studies in John the Scot (Erigena)*. London, 1900.

HARTMANN, FRANZ. *The Life and the Doctrines of Phillipus Theophrastus, Bombast of Hohenheim . . . . Extracted and Translated from His Rare and Extensive Works.* London, 1910.

HOBART, NATHANIEL. *Life of Swedenborg, with Some Account of His Writings.* Boston, 1845.

HODGSON, GERALDINE E. *English Mystics.* London, 1922.

JONES, RUFUS M. "Jacob Boehme: His Life and Spirit," *Spiritual Reformers in the Sixteenth and Seventeenth Centuries* (London, 1914), chap. ix.

LEA, HENRY CHARLES. "On the Brethren of the Free Spirit," *History of the Inquisition of the Middle Ages* (New York, 1888), II, 350–77.

MOSHEIM, JOHN LAWRENCE. *An Ecclesiastical History.* Translated by Archibald Maclaine. Berwick, 1809.

ROYCE, JOSIAH. "The Case of John Bunyan," *The Psychological Review,* I (1894), 22–33; 135–51; 230–40.

STEELE, FRANCESCA MARIA. *The Life and Visions of Saint Hildegarde.* London, 1914.

STEINER, RUDOLF. *Mystics of the Renaissance.* London, 1911.

STILLMAN, JOHN MAXSON. *Paracelsus, His Personality and Influence as Physician, Chemist, and Reformer.* Chicago, 1920.

STODDART, ANNA M. *The Life of Paracelsus.* London, 1911.

THOMPSON, ELBERT N. S. "Mysticism in Seventeenth-Century English Literature," *Studies in Philology* (University of North Carolina), XVIII (April, 1921), No. 2, 170–231.

THOROLD, ALGAR. *An Essay in Aid of the Better Appreciation of Catholic Mysticism, Illustrated from the Writings of the Blessed Angela of Foligno.* London, 1900.

TULLOCK, JOHN. "Henry More—Christian Theosophy and Mysticism," *Rational Theology and Christian Philosophy in England in the Seventeenth Century* (London, 1872), II, 303–409.

WAITE, ARTHUR E. *The Life of Louis Claude de Saint-Martin, the Unknown Philosopher, and the Substance of His Transcendental Doctrine.* London, 1901.

CONTEMPORARY PHILOSOPHY

BERGSON, HENRI. *Creative Evolution.* Translated by Arthur Mitchell. New York, 1911.

BRADLEY, FRANCES HERBERT. *Appearance and Reality.* London, 1893.

HOCKING, WILLIAM ERNEST. *The Meaning of God in Human Experience.* New Haven, 1923.

ROYCE, JOSIAH. *The World and the Individual.* New York, 1920.

INDEX

INDEX

267

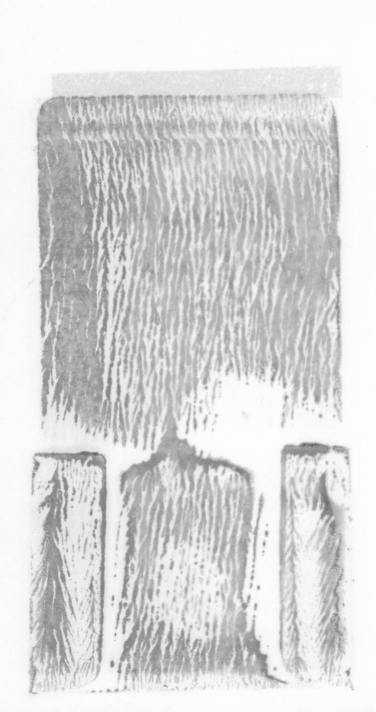